Walking London's
Circle Line

Walking London's Circle Line

A Pedestrian Guide to Central London

Fredric Schwarzbach

HAMILTON BOOKS
AN IMPRINT OF
ROWMAN & LITTLEFIELD
Lanham • Boulder • New York • London

Published by Hamilton Books
An imprint of The Rowman & Littlefield Publishing Group, Inc.
4501 Forbes Boulevard, Suite 200, Lanham, Maryland 20706
www.rowman.com

86-90 Paul Street, London EC2A 4NE, United Kingdom

British Library Cataloguing in Publication Information Available

Library of Congress Cataloging-in-Publication Data

Names: Schwarzbach, F. S. (Fredric S.), 1949- author.
Title: Walking London's Circle Line : a pedestrian guide to central London / Fredric Schwarzbach.
Other titles: Pedestrian guide to central London
Description: Lanham : Hamilton Books, an imprint of Rowman & Littlefield, [2023] | Includes index. | Summary: "Walking London's Circle Line: A Pedestrian Guide To Central London is a series of fifteen guided walks that focus on the history, architecture, and curiosities of central London. Each walk begins and ends at a station on the London Underground Circle Line"—Provided by publisher.
Identifiers: LCCN 2023002253 (print) | LCCN 2023002254 (ebook) | ISBN 9780761873747 (paperback) | ISBN 9780761873754 (epub)
Subjects: LCSH: Walking—England—London—Tours. | London (England)—Tours. | London Underground Limited. Circle Line—Tours. | London (England)—Description and travel.
Classification: LCC DA679 .S38 2023 (print) | LCC DA679 (ebook) | DDC 914.2104—dc23/eng/20230124
LC record available at https://lccn.loc.gov/2023002253
LC ebook record available at https://lccn.loc.gov/2023002254

Contents

Acknowledgments

A number of people have wittingly and unwittingly contributed to my life-long obsession with the Great Smoke, too many to name here. But I owe a particularly great debt to Professor Emeritus John Sutherland, who gave me encouragement early on in the project, and to Professor Emerita Rosemary Ashton and Professor Emeritus Michael Slater, both of whom read and commented incredibly helpfully on portions of the text. I am also grateful to the Liberal Studies Program of New York University for assistance—and the gift of time—that proved essential to research and writing.

My greatest debt is to my wife and perambulatory partner, Michele Krause Schwarzbach, whose love for London equals my own. She has not only shared with me many places and arcana in the city that I would otherwise have never found out, but whenever my own commitment lagged, she prodded me to complete this book.

A Note on Sources

Over the years, I have read countless books about London and London history, and as I began this project, I read many more. I've borrowed shamelessly from many, but a few have been invariable guides and companions, and I sometimes mention them in the text. First, I owe a great debt to Ian Nairn and the first London guidebook I owned, his classic *Nairn's London* (1966); his gift for responding to the built environment was both inspiring and a constant reminder of my own amateur standing. Other works that I must acknowledge are the very first London guide, John Stow's *A Survey of London* (1598, revised 1603), as well as Thomas Pennant, *Some Account of London* (1790), and Charles Dickens, Junior's *Dickens's Dictionary of London* (1879). There are two other sources that must get special mention. One is A.D. Mills's invaluable *A Dictionary of London Place Names* (2001, revised 2010), which manages to tease out the origin of the name of just about every metropolitan place you will ever visit while also providing a riveting history of the city and its dominant languages. Another is Christopher Hibbert *et al., The Encyclopedia of London* (2010). However, I have relied most heavily on my own perambulations of London stretching back some fifty years. Hence any errors or lapses you may discover are entirely my own.

Introduction

When my daughter was quite young—some thirty years ago—we visited the London Transport Museum. This was to be her first *bona fide* museum experience, one that she would enjoy on her own, and not merely one that she tolerated passively, waiting only for her parents to leave so she would be rewarded with whatever bribe we'd promised her for good behavior. And enjoy this museum she did, as we were encouraged to climb all over old buses, trains, and carriages, and to poke and prod all sorts of interactive exhibits. But what drew us back time and time again—aside from my own endless fascination with all things bus- and train-related—was one particular exhibit. It comprised the front end, the driver's compartment, of an actual tube train that a child (and her parent) could enter, play with actual driver's controls, and look out on a video screen displaying on an endless loop a driver's view of a journey around the Circle Line. Betsy and I both loved that experience, and we shamelessly monopolised it every time we were there, which for quite a few years was very often indeed. I couldn't say which of us enjoyed it more.

But in truth I have always had a special relationship to the Circle Line. My first visit to London was in 1972, and when, the following year, I became a postgraduate student at a London college, I developed a particular work routine: I worked like a demon for the first four days of the week and that left Friday free for me to explore a different London neighbourhood. I told myself that this was also research related to my doctoral dissertation about Charles Dickens and the city, and I was endlessly fascinated by how much of Dickens's London was still there to be seen.

On those jaunts, I particularly looked forward to any journey on the Circle Line, and for several reasons. One was that it might involve a ride on what I knew was the route of the original underground railway, the section running from Paddington to Farringdon. And unlike the "deep" tubes, the Circle Line carriages in essence were capacious full-size railway cars. Best of all, the journey might involve running over an open section of track, where one could see London life from an entirely different, almost secret, perspective, as if the back ends of adjacent houses had been cut away—which often was actually the case. To this day, I have a very positive visceral reaction to seeing the Circle Line's signature yellow color on Harry Beck's classic tube map.

Little did I know then that my time in London would inspire a five decade long love affair with the city. I still can imagine no better way to spend a day than to take the tube to a new area of the city, or an old favorite neighbourhood, and to explore it on foot. And over the years, as a faculty member and academic administrator at a U.S. university with a strong presence in London, I often led groups of students, parents, alumni, and colleagues on informal walking tours of central London, drawing on a lifetime accumulation of arcane knowledge of metropolitan history and life.

Many times, after such a tour, I would be asked if I had ever thought of writing down my commentary—it would make a great book, I was often told. Fortunately, a few years ago, when I stepped down from my administrative role, I was granted a year of study leave, which I used to complete the first draft of that very book—the book that you now hold in your hands.

What follows here is a series of guided walks around Central London organised as a clockwise journey around the Circle Line. Why the Circle Line, you may well ask, other than that I've always been fascinated by it? There are in fact several good reasons why this Underground line is a useful key to unlocking central London's secrets.

For one thing, the Circle Line is itself a bit of living history—very appropriate for a book that explores London's topography as the intersection of the past and the present. To ride any section of Circle Line track and to visit its stations is in many ways an opportunity to travel back in time on a railway built fully a century and a half ago, when Victoria sat on the throne, and that has changed remarkably little since. Yes, the rails have been replaced many times, the signals have been upgraded and automated, the trains are powered by electricity and not steam, most of the station buildings above ground have been demolished, and there is now only one class of service (where at first there were three!)—but taking a journey today on the Circle Line is very much to experience what those Underground passengers experienced when the Inner Circuit (as it then was known) first opened in 1884.

The Inner Circuit (it became the Circle Line only in 1949) had its origins in the world's first urban underground rail line, the Metropolitan Railway, which opened its four-mile section of track from Paddington to Farringdon in 1863. It was designed to move passengers between the several main line rail stations spread across the northern edge of the city—Paddington, Euston, King's Cross, and Farringdon—and it was a phenomenal success, despite passengers braving the hazards of smoke and soot produced by the coal-burning locomotives. Even before the Met (its popular nickname) opened, there were schemes afoot to create an underground railway circular route that would connect the other main line rail stations, and before long the Metropolitan and a new partner, the Metropolitan District Railway (known just as the District) both were authorised to move eastward and to link up at Tower Hill. This took much longer to accomplish than at first anyone expected, in part because the two railways, meant to collaborate, instead became bitter rivals, and in part because construction of the last sections was through the eastern end of the city, the most densely populated and expensive real estate in London. But the Met and the District eventually did meet at Tower Hill and on 6 October 1884 a circular service of sorts finally went into operation—with each company running trains in one direction only.

It is an interesting coincidence that almost at the very moment that the underground railway circular service was inaugurated, the scattered entities that made up London at long last were being transformed into a unitary city under a single government authority. Indeed, throughout the most of the Nineteenth Century, London was not legally a city at all. It was infamously ungovernable, with authority for what we would now regard as essential civic services divided, and in some cases completely dispersed, among different and very independent bodies that spanned arbitrary and often archaic geographical boundaries. London as a legal entity was solely the ancient "square mile," the city corporation at the center of the metropolis—but its powers extended no further than its boundaries. Traditionally, the parish vestries and the counties over which London had grown were the seats of what little local government there was, but there were no formal structures or even informal practices to encourage coordination or communication among them. The result was a hotchpotch of competing special interests, none of which had any real interest in change.

Public safety was the first government function in London to be partly centralised with the formation of the Thames River Police (properly the Marine Police Force) in 1798 to secure the docks; the Metropolitan Police came into being in 1829, with authority over the whole built-up area except for the City itself (which has a separate police force to this day). For decades afterward, the only other civic governmental authority with a city-wide remit was the Metropolitan Board of Works, created in 1855, in the wake of several devastating cholera epidemics; it was given responsibility for the construction of all *new* sewers, roads, bridges, and parks (but, perversely, not existing ones). Whilst its early accomplishments (including the Thames embankments) were heroic, it still was an appointed body, with all of the vices appointed bodies are heir to; by the 1880s, with corruption rampant, it had become known as the Metropolitan Board of Perks. Finally, Parliament could avoid action no longer and passed the Local Government Act of 1888, creating the London County Council, whose jurisdiction embraced almost all of the metropolitan area, creating with it the city's (but not the City Corporation's) first elected government.

So, in a very real sense, the Circle Line and the city are siblings, having come into being only a few years apart, and born of the same efforts to make a "real" city of the inchoate mass that was London. But it is the way in which the line was built—the "cut and cover" method—that also makes it so suitable for our purposes. The name says it all: a trench was dug, tracks were laid in it, a platform was built over it, and then it was covered over, though some sections intentionally were left open to ensure proper ventilation of the steam engines. For the first section of the Underground, the rights of way had to be purchased, but as the lines penetrated into the commercial heart of the City the costs of doing so escalated dramatically. The Corporation decided to resolve this by giving away the rights of way under public thoroughfares, and so the Circle Line runs under some of the oldest and most storied streets in London. What better places could there be, then, to start a walking tour.

Finally, I would argue further that there is no better guide to exploring central London than the Circle Line because its opening also helped define and even create what we regard as "central" London. There are no convenient topographical features—save the river—that delineate what parts of the metropolis comprise central London, nor did the ancient city walls last long enough to be converted into boundary highways, as they were in Paris and Vienna. But in their absence, the route of the Circle Line has come to serve that function. So, almost by default, the circular line has helped to shape what now think of as the heart of the city—what is within the Circle Line is central London; what lies outside is not. (Perhaps it is also no coincidence that Google's N-gram chart [denoting frequency of occurrence in the corpus of Google Books] for the phrase "Central London" shows a spike in the 1880s just as the Inner Circuit was completed.)

So, then, we are about to embark on a series of walks around central London that start and end on Underground stations on the Circle Line. As we walk, I shall be guided by what I see and what strikes me as of interest, but despite a certain degree of randomness, four distinct themes will emerge from our observations.

Firstly, there is the living legacy of the past visible everywhere in the present. However ordinary a street may look now, one has only to scratch the surface, literally and figuratively, to discover its rich and enduring history. Everywhere in the city there are places where past and present rub close against each other. Indeed, all of central London is like this—layer after layer of its history barely hidden away, waiting to be uncovered, each level of the city built upon all of those past, stretching back at least as far as Roman times. Indeed, London's history is still very much with us, in many ways quite visible (in its place names and its not so deeply buried ruins), and that past still very much shapes both our experience and our conception of the city.

Secondly, even in central London, we see that the city also has always been a nexus of immigration, its history largely a narrative of successive waves of new residents. It has benefited over the centuries and continues today to benefit from its ability to draw together millions of the world's most talented and interesting people. Some of the earliest waves of immigrants now are long assimilated—French Huguenots, Irish Catholics, Eastern European Jews—but Twenty-First Century London continues to embrace large and vibrant Polish, French, Somali, Bengali, Jamaican, and Nigerian immigrant communities—a list far from complete. Each group has stamped a part of London with its own identity and at the same time they have all become Londoners, an identity that complements and transcends local differences. London for hundreds of years was the centre of an empire; ironically, with its empire gone, London has become the quintessential global city.

Moreover, London is very much a city of diverse and distinct neighbour-hoods. Even in the very centre, despite market forces that enforce uniformity, many of London's former villages—like Chelsea, Westminster, Kensington, Bayswater—retain their long-standing identities, or, in some instances, develop new ones. And even when districts are in close proximity, somehow their distinctive characteristics persist: Sloane Square is still surrounded by leafy gardens and quiet mews; next door, South Kensington still is the museum quarter; and just a couple of tube stops away, Kensington High Street remains a centre for shopping. The same generalisations might have been made at any time in the last century, and likely may still be made one hundred years hence.

Finally, there is London's dynamism. For more than two thousand years London has been a place of continual movement, change, and growth—and in the Twenty-First Century it continues to grow, to change, to adapt, and most of all to innovate. Standing at the foot of a Roman city wall in the midst of the beating heart of the world's financial system—as you shall do presently on the Barbican walk—demonstrates powerfully that the city has had many identities over the millennia. But age notwithstanding, the growth and inno-vation continue: even after Brexit and Covid-19, London still stakes its claim to be one of the leading high tech centres in Europe and the world. And—for better or for worse—as it enters a new millennium, London provides a model for successful community in our increasingly globalised and urbanised world.

This, then, is what I will explore in these guided walks through Central London—the richness of the city's present, the indelible imprint of its past, and the ceaseless growth and change that make it one of the most exciting cities on the planet. Fortunately, despite its size, London remains a very walk-able city—as long as the walks are divided into manageable pieces. Each tour is designed to take about two to four hours, depending on how quickly you walk and how easily you are distracted and led astray. And by design I have provided no maps: Instead, I advise readers to use Google Maps and a smart phone. A great advantage of the map software is that it always knows where you are and consequently it is nearly impossible to get lost.

Our first tour takes as its starting point Paddington Station. It is an apt beginning because it was the first station on the original Metropolitan Railway, but our choice is somewhat constrained by an unfortunate event that took place in 2009. In that year, the Circle Line became what is in effect a branch of the Hammersmith and City Underground Line and its route was changed so that, despite its name, it is no longer circular. The line now begins out in Hammersmith and it terminates at Edgware Road, resembling nothing so much as a spiral snail shell or the email "@" sign. The reason for the change, I must admit, was a good one. From its opening, the line had been plagued by delays, and whenever a train was late for whatever reason, there was no place to wait to move on but on the line itself, generating cascading delays for itself and for the other services that shared the tracks, currently the Hammersmith and City, the Metropolitan, and the District Lines. The new configuration in effect created on the section from Paddington to Hammersmith a holding pen for delayed trains.

Alas, a perhaps unanticipated result of the change, violating all common sense, is that it is actually no longer possible to complete a circular journey on the Circle Line, except by boarding an eastbound train at either Paddington or Edgware Road and then getting off at the same station. Well, almost the same station—as we shall see presently there are in fact two Paddington Underground stations and no way to communicate between them without surfacing to the street.

Nevertheless, to Paddington we shall go to begin our own circular journey. We will begin with this station in recognition of its distinguished history as the very first station on the very first underground railway. We will follow that original line eastward into the City, stopping at about half the stations; then, after rounding the eastern end of the line, we travel westward and close the circle at the "other" Paddington station. The rambling walk that starts at each station is also far from systematic, following my own interests in London's long history, observing its present social diversity, and ranging across whatever else catches my fancy—and I hope yours as well.

Cordially,
Fred Schwarzbach

P.S. If you are interested in the history of the Circle Line itself, I suggest you first read the appendix, which gives a summary of its origins and development. It is a fascinating tale.

Chapter 1

Paddington

Paddington is where it all started—as the westernmost station of the Metropolitan Railway when it opened in 1863. From 1857, Paddington had served as the London terminus of Isambard Kingdom Brunel's Great Western Railway, linking Bristol and the South West to London with its distinctive oversize rolling stock on broad gauge tracks. But even after the coming of the railway, Paddington in the 1860s was not yet completely built up, and some of its open leafy spaces remained undeveloped. Many London neighbourhoods grew from ancient villages, but Paddington was very much a blank space with no real center and no settled identity—neither town nor country—and it has continued to exhibit that "betwixt and between" ambience ever since.

The new underground Metropolitan Railway, as we have noted, was built to link Paddington to the other main line rail stations on the northern edge of the city. The Underground station opened with the name Paddington (Bishop's Road); but a second Paddington station (Praed Street, now also serving the Bakerloo Line) opened in 1868 as part of the District's push outward from Kensington. The two Underground stations remain physically separate to this day, and while interchange is free, it requires passengers to exit and to walk through the main line station concourse, now all too predictably a generic shopping arcade. The original Underground station buildings are gone, Praed street replaced by a later nondescript box covered in striking white ceramic tiles. In both stations, the original elegantly functional arched retaining walls of tan brick that parallel the tracks are easily seen from the platforms.

Alas, with the recent reorganization of tube lines, the Metropolitan now turns north at Baker Street and no longer serves its first station, and the Circle Line, as it travels west, no longer curves southward but instead meanders to Hammersmith. Travel between the two Paddington Stations on a Circle Line train thus requires a trip all the way around the loop, a distance of about 13 miles. Perhaps by way of recompense, TfL allows you to walk from Paddington Underground Station and to reenter at no additional charge either at the nearby Marylebone Station for the Bakerloo Line or the Lancaster Gate Station for the Central Line.

The origin of the name is probably Saxon—"Padda's tun" or Padda's Farm. And as I've remarked, even in the mid-Nineteenth Century, the area was surprisingly rural. Development came late, the first wave in the 1790s after the opening of the Paddington branch of the Grand Junction Canal and a second wave after the arrival of the Great Western in the late 1830s. The southern half of district was owned by the Bishop of London and plans were hatched in the 1820s to create from his estate an elegant residential neighbourhood –renaming it Tyburnia, a *sobriquet* that never really caught fire, reminiscent of other attempts by estate agents to use a catchy name to put lipstick on the proverbial property pig. For a very brief time, it was reckoned to be one of the most socially exclusive neighbourhoods in London. Yet as early as 1879, Charley Dickens (the novelist's eldest son) was referring to it in his encyclopedic London guidebook as "not, strictly speaking, a fashionable quarter."

The stuccoed terraces here that were the first attempts at fashionability look very much like those of Belgravia or Pimlico. But the district had far other popular associations that it never quite shook loose. The Tyburn was a stream, one of London's several principal watercourses back in the day, and a tiny village of the same name was located very near today's Marble Arch. Tyburn, however, was most famous as the site of the Tyburn Tree, where gallows stood that were London's principal place of execution from the Twelfth to the late Eighteenth Century—even for estate agents a challenge to wipe the neighbourhood slate clean of that association. In the Eighteenth Century, executions often became macabre popular spectacles, attended by tens of thousands—Hogarth's print "The Idle Prentice Executed at Tyburn" in his series, *Industry and Idleness*, gives a good idea of the size and disposition of the crowd on a hanging day

The main line station is actually named London Paddington, though no one ever calls it that. (All the main line stations in fact are named in the same manner, but the "London" has become silent for all except London Bridge.) The present main line terminus building, completed in January 1854, was also designed by Brunel, the guiding genius of the entire Great Western project. Much of the original fabric of the huge building remains. Perhaps drawing on the design of the Crystal Palace, Brunel built a vast train shed roofed in glass and supported by cast iron, its three spans stretching 699 feet in length, and unusual in that it also has an arch-roofed transept, making the whole structure resemble a cast-iron cathedral. Platforms 1 to 8 are under that original shed; they are best viewed from the elevated walkway that spans the north end of the platforms.

Every main line terminus needed a hotel, and six months after it opened, Paddington added the Great Western, still there today as the Hilton London

Paddington. Most international visitors today know the station as the London terminus of the Heathrow Express, said to be the most expensive railway in the world mile for mile (at about £1.50 per). It is also an Elizabeth Line station now that service has begun.

And perhaps you already know the most famous passenger to pass through Paddington Station—a bear of the same name, who was purchased in a station shop in 1956 and first appeared in print two years later. (He would have landed at Bristol via steamer from South America and then taken the train up to town.) He now has a shop devoted entirely to him in the shopping arcade, should you be in need of a suitable souvenir.

By the 1980s, the streets fronting the station had become rundown and shabby, and the area developed a reputation for petty crime, especially prostitution. Behind the station to the north, the once-thriving canal had fallen into disuse, and the canalside warehouses were abandoned and derelict. The neighbourhood was further riven—literally—by the construction of the Westway, an elevated highway that was one of the few parts ever built of a planned inner ring road. (It is supposedly the largest concrete structure in Britain.) Completed in 1970, it sliced the station and surroundings off from the (mainly) working class residential districts to the north. Since 1998, when the Paddington Partnership was formed, the area around the canal has seen massive redevelopment, the changes very similar to those experienced more recently at King's Cross (which we will visit in a future walk). Still more development is planned on a site adjoining the main line station, to be called Paddington Quarter.

The main line station arcade leads directly to Praed Street, which retains something of the shabbiness of a generation back, though incipient gentrification is under way. One street further south is Sussex Gardens, a broad avenue flanked by garden strips, home to many small, inexpensive hotels (well, relatively inexpensive, bearing in mind that this *is* London), many of which once upon a time rented by the hour, but nowadays, they are mostly smartened up and cater to the international tourist trade. The little streets beyond form a triangular residential island bounded by Sussex Gardens, the Edgware Road, and Hyde Park; it is an interesting mix of large and rather bland housing estates, some exclusive and some not, and Victorian brick and stucco terraces. There are two grand Victorian churches, St John and St Michael, as well, hard to miss as their steeples can be seen from almost anywhere hereabouts, both impressively large, and both good examples of brick-and-stone Gothic revival ecclesiastical architecture.

The streets south of Sussex Square are pretty enough, and this small enclave of residential calm terminates at the Bayswater Road. Ahead is Hyde Park (of which more later), and off to the east, Marble Arch, the result of an exercise in one-upmanship in competition with Paris. Now stranded on an island at the top of Park Lane, it is best be admired from afar. It was in its first life London's answer to Napoleon's *Arc de Triomphe*. That monument to French military prowess had revived the ancient Roman practice of erecting grand arches to celebrate great victories. Ironically, London's grand arch, the work of John Nash (who, as we shall see presently, also designed Regent's Park and Regent Street) celebrates Nelson's victories over the French. (Napoleon's arch also contained the first monument to an unknown soldier; London waited another hundred years for one of its own.) The arch was meant to be the ceremonial entrance to the newly expanded Buckingham Palace, but further work to extend the front of the palace and to create the balcony from which successive generations of royals have waved to crowds necessitated its relegation to the present site. Here it serves as the ceremonial entrance to the park and, rather oddly, for many years it also was a fully functional police station. The traffic island around the arch was created when Park Lane was widened in the 1960s; the police station seems to have disappeared at around the same time.

Let us now retrace our steps and turn back toward Sussex Gardens, continuing in the direction of Paddington Station via London Street to Norfolk Square. This square is pretty enough, with three of its original sides still there in all their stuccoed glory. The square proper is a pleasant little park with some very fine flower beds, a nice spot for a picnic lunch or just to sit and enjoy a quiet moment.

Sitting here, it is well to reflect on the importance of London's garden squares, generously sprinkled throughout the West End. They were extolled by Steen Eiler Rasmussen in his pioneering study of English urban architecture, *London, the Unique City*, which remains an indispensable guide not only to English domestic buildings but to the life lived within and around them. A handful of accidental square-like spaces (including Moor Fields and Lincoln's Inn Fields) date from the early Seventeenth Century, but the first purpose-built square was Covent Garden, laid out by Inigo Jones for the Duke of Bedford and completed in 1631. Its success guaranteed that it would serve as the model for further development on the Bedford Estate and many others. On the Bedford Estate alone, there are Bedford, Bloomsbury, Gordon, Russell, and Woburn Squares, to name only the best known. Many of these spaces were private at first, but over time, most have become public, though to this day a select few allow keyed access only for local residents. The first legislation to protect these open spaces was passed in 1906, but it covered only 64 of the hundreds of garden squares; a Royal Commission in 1927 to address the continuing loss of these precious open spaces led to the London Squares Preservation Act of 1931, which protected over 400 listed squares.

Walking east along either long side of this square (both sides lead to narrow pedestrian alleys), turn left along Norfolk Place back to Praed Street, and just across the road is St Mary's Hospital. Founded in 1845, and opened in 1851, it probably is best known as the lying-in hospital of choice of the Princess of Wales (the Prince having paved the way for his children by being born there himself in 1982). But it has also been the site of an important medical school, now merged into Imperial College. Two world-changing pharmaceuticals emerged from its precincts: the very first synthetic opioid, diamorphine, in 1874, and in 1928, the first effective broad-spectrum antibiotic, penicillin. Alexander Fleming's laboratory, where he discovered penicillin quite by accident, is now a museum, open mornings, Monday to Thursday, or by appointment; it is well worth a half hour's visit, although what I am struck by most is how primitive were the conditions in which medical research was conducted a century ago. Most elementary school science labs today are far better equipped.

Our destination now is the appealing but not terribly accurately named neighbourhood called Little Venice. It is situated around the junction of the Grand Union Canal and Paddington Basin, just a stone's throw north of Paddington, but thanks to the Westway almost impossible to reach on foot from the station except via the canal towpath. The best way to walk there is a pathway that begins just east of the hospital entrance, near the Tesco at the junction of Praed Street and South Wharf Road. Behind the Tesco and accessible by a footpath just to the west is a bridge across Paddington Basin, leading directly to Merchant Square. The bridge doesn't look particularly interesting, but if you are lucky enough to see it open, you will appreciate why its informal name is the fan bridge; it is made of five parallel sections that pivot upward to open and when they do, it looks very much like a Japanese fan.

Turn west on this side of the canal, and you can take in the stark post-modernist architecture and cityscape of Merchant Square. The area is busy enough at certain times of the day—the morning and evening commutes and the lunch hour—yet it has a certain air of sterility, especially in contrast to the hustle and bustle of Praed Street. Before long, you cross another little bridge, this one equally famous, the work of superstar designer Thomas Heatherwick, a rolling structure that curls up like a giant worm. Not far off is a more traditional bridge that will take you back across the canal; the canal towpath itself (passing close to the tube station where we began our walk), lately home to a number of busy restaurants and cafes, now leads us on to Little Venice.

The name Little Venice is a relatively recent coinage. The canal dates from the early Nineteenth Century—part of a network of internal waterways that revolutionized freight transport a half century before the railways—but the name came much later. Both Byron and Browning are credited with comparing the developments that sprung up here to Venice; the diminutive "Little" first appeared as recently as the 1950s. Little it certainly is, extending only a few streets in any direction from the canal junction, but the only similarity to Venice is the presence of water. All the same, it is a pleasant enough neighbourhood of Georgian, Regency, and Victorian villas and cottages, many stuccoed and brightly painted; there are several pleasant waterside cafes and restaurants to visit as well.

The towpath has plenty of signs displaying maps of the whole district, but the best way to explore it is just to climb up from the towpath to the street and wander a bit. You'll get lost no matter what your plan is, so I suggest having no plan, but do include a saunter eastward along Blomfield Road facing the canal. On a warm, sunny, summer day there's nothing that London can offer finer than this—tree lined streets, elegant houses, smartly painted canal barges, and a peaceful body of water mirroring it all upside down.

The canal barges, most of which are private residences, are a distinctive feature of London's waterways. There are about fifteen hundred on the various metropolitan canals (we will see some of them again at King's Cross) and several thousand diverse house boats on the Thames. They are surprisingly affordable—a basic narrow boat may be as cheap as £10,000, and a rather posh one £100,000—quite attractive pricing in a city where the average property is well over half a million. The catch is the mooring, whose numbers are limited and which turn over for almost as much as an average narrow boat on its own. There are permits not tied to a particular mooring that require the boat to be moved every 14 days, which seems like a very perilous form of peripatetic life that most certainly would drive me mad though evidently a few hardy souls embrace it. Still, on a bright sunny day the usually brightly colored boats are easy on the eye, and I'm happy to admire them and to imagine what life on the water would be like without feeling the need to experience it first hand.

Blomfield Road terminates at the Edgware Road. Turn around and walk back on the other side of the canal on Maida Avenue, which calls up a vision of the genteel residential district to the north, Maida Vale. The name Maida is another tribute to British arms—it is a place in southern Italy that saw a yet another victory over the French during the Napoleonic wars. We will turn south instead on Park Place Villas which in a few minutes takes us to Paddington Green. This is a fairly unremarkable, small green space, but it is the oldest surviving part of "old" Paddington. The church on the green, St Mary's, dates from the 1790s, and the graveyard (partly lost to the Westway) has monuments to Sarah Siddons, the famous Georgian actress, and Peter Mark Roget, he of thesaurus fame.

The simplest and easiest way back to the Underground station is to retrace our steps via the towpath, thus again avoiding the tangle of elevated roadways that block nearly all pedestrian traffic. And so back into the tube at Bishop's Road—our next stop Baker Street, our journey 'round the Circle Line well and truly begun.

Chapter 2

Baker Street

Baker Street Station, opened on 10 January 1863, is another of the original stations on the Metropolitan Railway. It is the first footfall in Central London for innumerable first-time visitors by virtue of its proximity to two major tourist attractions, Madame Tussaud's waxwork exhibition and the putative abode of Sherlock Holmes. The street itself is one of the few in London named for a builder, one William Baker, who in the second half of the Eighteenth Century developed the district on land leased from the Portman estate. That estate still is one of the largest—and certainly among the most valuable—in Central London, comprising over 100 acres that cover much of Marylebone, including 68 streets, 650 buildings, and four garden squares.

The Portman Estate is one of a small number of privately held property empires in Central London, some family-owned for many hundreds of years, and several of those linked to the massive transfers of land that followed the Dissolution of the Monasteries in the 1530s. The Grosvenor Estate (owned by the Duke of Westminster), the Cadogan Estate (Earl Cadogan), the Bedford Estate (the Duke of Bedford and the Russell family), the Howard de Walden Estate (Baroness Howard de Walden), as well as the Crown Estate, all have shrunk somewhat over the years as bits have been sold off here and there—often to pay inheritance tax—but collectively they still own vast swaths of Central London and thus they retain hugely disproportionate influence on what gets built and what doesn't. Other large institutional landholders include the Wellcome Trust (of which more in due course), the Church of England, and several "Oxbridge" colleges. It is worth noting, however, that by most measures the largest landowner in London at present is the government of Qatar, which among its many holdings owns the land under the old U.S. Embassy in Grosvenor Square and much of Canary Wharf. A few large landlords are of more recent vintage, including the Raymond Estate, a huge chunk of Soho assembled over the years by Paul Raymond, best known as the entrepreneur who managed to evade the Lord Chamberlain's censorship to operate a commercially successful strip club; he funneled much of his profits from soft core porn into what then was relatively cheap Central London real estate—a shrewd move indeed.

The Baker Street Underground station building itself has been much altered over time as additional services joined the Metropolitan—the Hammersmith and City, Bakerloo, and Jubilee Lines—but the platforms serving the Circle Line, numbers Five and Six, are more or less as they were when the first Metropolitan railway train rumbled through in 1863. They are most definitely still the same length, shorter than the current Circle Line trains, so be warned—some doors at the rear of the train don't open when it stops here. (Ironically, the Metropolitan Line itself no longer serves points west of Baker Street, though the Circle Line still uses the original Met tracks.)

Baker Street Station's greatest fame, needless to say, is as the closest tube station to 221B Baker Street, the "real" home and headquarters of the not-so-real sleuth, Sherlock Holmes. It is also the nearest tube to Madame Tussaud's, back in 1863 already a famous magnet for tourists. Every year some two and half million people, roughly the population of Chicago or Rome, visit the waxworks display. I must admit that I have never been inside, having absolutely no interest in simulacra of famous people, living or dead, whether made of wax or not—but clearly I am in a very small minority on this point.

We will walk north on Baker Street, away from the queue waiting to enter Madame Tussaud's, and pull up at 221B, actually a street number that did not exist at the time that Arthur Conan Doyle identified it as the lodgings of Sherlock Holmes. The house that bears the number is now the Sherlock Holmes Museum, although it ought to be and for many year was number 239—the Royal Mail in 2005 having sanctioned the non-sequential renumbering for obvious reasons. You can't miss it—standing outside during opening hours is a faux Victorian police constable beckoning you to enter. I must confess that this is another leading tourist site I have never actually visited, but the reviews on various web sites suggest that while clearly still a "must see" for devoted Holmesians, it is not a hugely edifying experience for the rest of us. (Another famous occupant of 221B is Danger Mouse, the 1980s cartoon rodent superspy, who lives in a red pillar mailbox just outside the front door.) The house itself apparently is now owned by the president of Kazakhstan.

Baker Street ends a short distance to the north of the Underground station exit, but a little spur road off to the east leads immediately to the Outer Circle of Regent's Park. The park's 410 acres comprise one of the most diverse and fascinating of all London green spaces. Originally a parcel of land owned by Barking Abbey, it was one of the few properties of the many seized by Henry VIII at the Dissolution that the king didn't sell off. First used by Henry as a hunting preserve, during the Commonwealth era it was leased out as small farms. When in 1811 the agricultural leases finally expired, the Prince Regent charged John Nash with creating a master plan for its development. Nash proposed building a new royal palace, a few elegant villas, and, around the perimeter, grand stuccoed terraces. The palace was never built (the money instead was spent to upgrade Buckingham House into a royal residence), but a few of the planned villas and the terraces were (mostly to designs by Decimus Burton). And what a grand sight they are on a sunny day when London looks as clean, fresh, elegant, and inviting as ever it does.

The park would be impressive enough simply for its setting, but it also contains diverse riches aplenty—a boating lake, a huge rose garden, an open-air theatre, a bandstand, a section of the Grand Union Canal, the London Zoo, and the Central London Mosque, as well as Winfield House, the official residence of the American ambassador, to name but the highlights. One could do worse than to spend a full day exploring Regent's Park.

This is as good a moment as any to reflect on how fortunate London is in its complement of parks, and how little Londoners seem to appreciate their extraordinary luck. Very few Londoners live more than a ten-minute walk or a short bus ride to the nearest open green space, which adds immeasurably to the overall quality of life in the metropolis. (A recent study found a strong correlation between overall public health in cities and the provision of accessible green space.) In part, this is historical accident: so much of central London was in the possession of the Crown, and so much of it stayed in royal hands for so long, that large centrally located parcels were preserved in a park-like state, most of them opened to public use fairly early on. In addition to Regent's Park, the central core today includes Kensington Gardens, Hyde Park, Green Park, and St James's Park. Moreover, fairly early on in the Nineteenth Century the practice was established of preserving and if needed creating open green spaces in new quarters of the city as they were developed, including Victoria Park, Brockwell Park, and Battersea Park, among others. The conversion of urban graveyards to parks added to the green inventory as well.

We will cross the Outer Circle (the circular road that girdles the park) to enter the park at the boating lake. This is one of the more pleasant places in Central London where one may rent a small rowboat or a pedalo, and despite its location, the lake rarely seems crowded. The lake is Y-shaped, and while one can saunter around it either way, we shall veer off to the right (or east) where the lake's long tail curves gently as it narrows, leading us to a footbridge that will take us toward Queen Mary's Garden.

Just over the bridge, on our left, is Regent's University, one of the handful private institutions of higher learning in the U.K. (Literally a handful, as currently there are five.) It occupies the site that formerly was home to Bedford College, Britain's first women's college, founded in 1849, and from

1900 a constituent college of the University of London. The college moved to Regent's Park in 1913, but, having first gone co-ed in the Sixties, sadly it lost its independent status when it was merged with Royal Holloway College (also at first a women's college) in 1985. (The amalgamation was in response to Thatcher-era cuts to government funding.) While the name of the successor institution officially is Royal Holloway and Bedford New College, it is now generally known simply as Royal Holloway, and its distinguished origins are in danger of fading from memory. (I have one particularly fond memory of Bedford College—the *in viva* [oral] examination of my doctoral dissertation was held on its premises; for the record, I passed.)

Before us now lies the magnificent rose garden. When the park was first laid out, this land was leased to the Royal Botanic Society at its founding in 1839. When the long lease at last expired in 1932, the decision was made to turn it into a public rose garden in honor of Queen Mary. (Queen Mary's other claim to fame is that she was said to be something of a kleptomaniac; when she visited other people's houses, she had the habit of expecting to be given the things she admired, and if she wasn't, supposedly she pocketed them herself.) Opened in 1934, this is one of the largest collections of roses in the world, with over 12,000 specimens of 85 varieties, many of which are strongly scented. It is spectacular, even to one who knows nothing about roses (that would be me). The Royal Parks advise visiting in early June for peak blooms, but in this era of climate change, I have found it ablaze with color as early as mid-May and as late as mid-November. There's not much to be said in favor of global warming, but it does seem to make English roses very happy indeed. (By the bye, the Royal Parks web site has an interactive tree map of the park, which contains a fascinating variety of native and other species, as well as a mysterious cluster of fossil tree trunks hidden away in the Rose Garden.)

Exit the garden to the east, and just ahead, running north-south, you will see the splendid Avenue Gardens, yet another stunning display of British horticultural art. I can think of no better place to sit and relax, surrounded by elaborate and colorful floral displays in which to delight. After a good long sit, and possibly a snack from the two nearby cafés (one very small and the other quite large)), wander north along a broad avenue called, appropriately enough, the Broad Walk, enjoying the shade of the grand trees, and eventually you will come upon a rather large and impressive (though dry) stone fountain that marks the southern tip of the Zoo.

This is the Readymoney Fountain, erected in 1896 by Sir Cowasji Jehangir Readymoney, a successful Parsee (Zoroastrian) businessman from Bombay, as a gesture of gratitude for British protection of the Parsee minority of India. Three of the sides feature portraits of Victoria, Albert, and Readymoney him-self; the fourth hosts a clock. We will bear left along the Zoo's southern edge toward the main gate. The choice before you now is to enter the Zoo or not, but bear in mind that a proper visit will take several hours, especially if you are accompanied by young children. For now, let's assume you will carry on walking, saving the zoo visit for another day. Past the Zoo, cross the road (part of the Outer Circle again), and you are soon crossing a bridge over the Regent's Canal.

This is another section of the Grand Union Canal, formed in 1929 as the successor to and amalgamator of several canal projects dating from the 1790s to the 1820s and that together linked London's port to the Midlands. (We have already touched upon another part of the canal further to the west, Little Venice; we will encounter another section when we explore the area around Kings Cross.) Nash was one of the directors of the company that was empowered to build the canal, and so it was possible for him engage in a bit of landscaping legerdemain by incorporating this section of the canal into the design of the park, whose graceful, curved northern border it forms. Commercial traffic on the canal dried up for good in the Seventies, but the waterway has taken on new life in recreational use, with pleasure boats on the water as well as pedestrians and cyclists on the towpath. (For some cyclists, however, it functions as a speedway, so walkers beware.)

Our goal now is Primrose Hill, a green space that lies ahead of us just past Prince Albert Road. This too was part of the abbey lands seized by Henry VIII, but eventually it became part of the endowment of Eton College, from whom the Crown repurchased it in 1841, only one year later designating it as a public park. It is, as well you might expect given its name, a hill, some 213 feet in height, from which there is a spectacular view of the city to the south. Charley Dickens remarks that "It is very popular with holiday makers who are unable to get out of town, although . . . there is nothing to contribute to the public amusement"—nothing that is save the view itself.

Before entering the park, turn to the left (west) along Prince Albert Road and take the steps down, following the tow path west to the Macclesfield Bridge over the canal. The unofficial name—Blow-Up Bridge—is a clue to what made it famous. At around 5 a.m. on October 2, 1874, the Tilbury, one of a tow of five barges headed to the Midlands, exploded. Its cargo included six barrels of petroleum and five tons of gunpowder, and the blast (possibly set off by a crewmember lighting a pipe) destroyed the barge and the bridge and damaged buildings as far as a mile away. (A few animals in the zoo escaped when their cages were blasted open.) Remarkably, the cast iron support columns of the bridge survived, and they were used again when the bridge was rebuilt. Note, however, that the columns were turned 180 degrees—the short horizontal slash marks running up and down them are where the canal boat tow ropes had cut into the iron before the blast. The heads of the columns bear very prominent castings of the name of the maker, COALBROOKDALE, the same foundry that manufactured the iconic Iron Bridge in the village of that name in the North of England—remarkably, the foundry closed as recently as 2017 after more than 300 years of continuous production.

Retrace your steps and then cross the road to enter the Primrose Hill park, taking the steepest upward path. As I've already remarked, Primrose Hill is all about the view—and once you crest the rise, what a view it is, embracing most of London's signature buildings and structures. Easily spotted off to the east are Canary Wharf and the Shard, and center-west, the Post Office Tower and the London Eye. (Of course, I call them by the names in common use, but the Eye now is officially the Coca Cola London Eye and the P.O. Tower is officially the BT Tower.) The Eye Ferris wheel was intended to be a temporary attraction for the Millennium celebrations, but its popularity has endured, justifying a longer (and now indefinite) lease on life. The BT Tower was designed as a key part of the U.K. microwave communications network, and from 1965 to 1980 it was also the tallest building in the city. Both have profiles so distinctive that they have joined the select group of structures (with St Paul's Cathedral and the tower housing Big Ben) that are instantly recognizable as synecdoches for London itself.

There is one interesting landmark in the park, though its specific location seems to be in question. Somewhere near the top of the hill is the second Shakespeare oak tree. The first Shakespeare memorial tree was planted on April 23, 1864, to mark the tercentenary of his birth. The event was a genuinely democratic response to what was regarded as the government's failure to give the occasion its proper due: 100,000 ordinary Londoners turned up for the planting ceremony. It was very much a political gesture, aimed to reclaim Shakespeare as part of the common culture even as he was being appropriated by the rich and powerful. Alas, the tree eventually died, and in 1964 Dame Edith Evans presided over the planting of a replacement. The tree was marked with a plaque that was stolen soon after and never replaced, leading to the present uncertainty as to which of the half-century old oak trees is *the* tree.

Having savored the extraordinary view for a few minutes, retrace your steps down the hill and back into Regent's Park, and once in the park, walk due south, continuing all the way to the park's southern border. Exiting the park by the York Bridge and York Gate, we come upon first the Edwardian brick and stone main building of the Royal Academy of Music. Founded in 1822, it is Britain's oldest conservatory school. It nearly went bust in the 1860s, but now it is formally a another of the constituent colleges of London University. Before us, across the busy road, is the imposing classical façade of the Church of St Marylebone, built 1813–17, and the fourth church erected on this site. Those of a literary bent may recall that Elizabeth Barrett and Robert Browning were married in secret here in 1846 before decamping to Italy; the church also features in Dickens's *Dombey and Son*, though not in a very good way, as the frozen venue where little Paul Dombey is baptized. Crossing the road (traffic zooms by at great speed so wait for the lights!), we will walk off to the left (or east) a short distance to the top end of Marylebone High Street.

This gently meandering street has been the center of life for the village of the same name since 1400, or thereabouts. A popular spurious etymology derives the name from "Mary la bonne" but in fact it is a corruption of "Marybourne"—bourne is an archaic synonym for "brook"; the waterway in question was the Tyburn, a minor tributary of the Thames (now mostly underground). The "le" is what linguists call intrusive and it first appeared as early as the Seventeenth Century; but though intrusive it has stuck, both in spelling and pronunciation. In any event, the grand name notwithstanding, for most of the Twentieth Century this was something of a shabby backwater in an otherwise posh corner of London. I knew it in the Seventies as the site of a shop that specialized in brightly colored and quite inexpensive Italian dinnerware with which my wife and I furnished our first English flat. (The shop survived many years and later moved to Knightsbridge, where it is still in business on Brompton Road.) Property values here lately have soared—where in Central London have they not?—but I can remember frequenting a number of charity shops here as recently as the early Nineties. (As I write, one thrift shop, a branch of Oxfam, is still there.)

There are some local businesses here still, but on the whole the street has succumbed to the same up-market forces that have run unchecked in most of the rest of London; you'll find all of the usual posh chain shops as well as a few ridiculously expensive and very fashionable restaurants. There are even a few night clubs. All the same, it is a pleasant enough stroll from one end to the other, and one still has a great choice of tempting places to stop for refreshment. (I recommend the local branch of Patisserie Paul, the Parisian bakery chain that miraculously preserves its quality even as the number of locations has burgeoned.)

Our goal now, however, is the Wallace Collection, on Manchester Square, just off to the west via Hinde Street. The Wallace is housed in Hertford House, the London home of the Marquesses of Hertford, bequeathed by the fourth Marquess to his illegitimate (and only) son, Richard Wallace, along with most of his estates all over the U.K. and Ireland. (The Marquess never married and had no legitimate heir.) Wallace, an inveterate collector, built on the treasures previously acquired by the third Marquess, his grandfather, and his father, collectively specializing in French art and decorative objects of the Eighteenth Century. Wallace the heir spent his childhood in Paris, and he became in time a great philanthropist, donating vast sums to charities in France, most notably during the siege of Paris by the Germans in 1870. He was created a baronet in 1871 and in 1897 his widow left some 5,500 works of art to the nation; the nation reciprocated by buying Hertford House from her to serve as the museum in which they would be displayed. The house dates from the Eighteenth Century but it was extensively renovated by Wallace in the 1870s and the interior is a fine exemplar of what Victorian opulence and wealth could achieve.

The museum inside contains one of the best collections of French *ancien regime* painting, furniture, porcelain, and *objets de vertu*, as well as a considerable haul of assorted other old masters, including works by Titian, Van Dyck, Rembrandt, Hals, Velázquez, Gainsborough and Delacroix. It also has an extensive collection of European arms and armor. As for the seemingly countless Bouchers, Fragonards, and their ilk—well, if you like that sort of thing, you will be overwhelmed by riches. If you don't warm to it (and I must confess that I do not), you'll feel as if you've entered the museum of chocolate box illustration. A renovation completed in 2000 enclosed the inner courtyard with a glass roof, and it now is home to a marvelous eatery, the Café Bagatelle, named after the Chateau de Bagatelle in the Bois de Boulogne, once owned by Wallace (and now a museum owned and operated by the city of Paris).

Leave the Wallace and cross to the south side of Manchester Square. If shopping is of great interest to you, you perhaps will already have realized that a little further south at the bottom of Duke Street is Selfridges and beyond it Oxford Street, once one of the great shopping streets of Europe, although falling now on hard times. Selfridges was founded by the American Harry Gordon Selfridge in 1908; he opened this grand edifice a year later. It was from the first a shrine to the world of things, raising marketing to a level that had yet to be experienced in Britain, and a great success it was, ushering in the golden age of department stores, which proliferated across Central London and throughout the realm. Oxford Street before the pandemic still seemed as crowded as ever, but with most shops catering to the fickle foreign tourist rather than the English native, it is difficult to predict what will come next. (At the moment it is quite shabby and many shop premises are vacant.) The department store as an institution clearly has lost its lustre, and several of those that have graced Oxford Street for decades now are gone; the grand emporium's role as the place where one could buy anything and everything has been supplanted by the internet retail giant whose name I need not mention. Selfridges so far seems to be able to draw in the crowds and, even better, actual paying customers, but whether it can tilt at the internet windmill successfully for much longer remains to be seen. If you are tempted to enter Selfridges (and maybe you should before it moves from the endangered species list to the extinct one), my recommendation is to start with the food hall, a cornucopia of endless culinary delights, though at far from affordable prices.

The west side of Selfridges fronts Orchard Street, and walking north on it we come to Portman Square, a 2.5 acre private garden, once one of the poshest residential addresses in the West End. The square leads directly to Baker Street, taking us back to the Underground for our next journey.

Chapter 3

Kings Cross

King's Cross is another of the original main line stations served by the underground railway when it opened in 1863. It is now the busiest underground station in the system—before the pandemic used by some 100,000,000 passengers a year. It was not always thus: in the Seventies, the neighbourhood surrounding the station had become notorious for flagrant prostitution and drug trafficking. In that decade, I lived just across the road (in Judd Street) for about a year, and even in daylight I generally would avoid using the Kings Cross Underground station, though it was the closest to home. As it transpired, the greatest danger in the station was not crime but the dilapidated state of the London Underground infrastructure.

On 18 November 1987, a cigarette butt tossed by a passenger astride one of the ancient wooden escalators started a catastrophic fire that caused 31 deaths and destroyed most of the station. The fire rightly became a symbol of the decline of the Underground network after decades of neglect. The station eventually was completely rebuilt and the Underground renovations were coordinated with the transformation of the main line St. Pancras Station into the terminus for the rail link to the Continent via the Chunnel. The project was completed in 2012 in time for the summer Olympics, and it has triggered massive changes to the entire neighbourhood, changes still very much in process.

The transformation of Kings Cross has been much remarked in the press and it is often represented as test case for gentrification. What has happened is viewed either as the remarkably successful revitalisation of a forlorn district or as the cleansing dismemberment of an established low-income community to create an upper-middle class playground. It is in fact something of both: it is now an attractive, safe, and vibrant neighborhood, but most of those who once lived nearby have been pushed out—and if not pushed then priced out. Even were those original residents still in the neighbourhood, and for the most part they aren't, they probably couldn't afford a £3 cup of coffee in one of the swish new independent cafes here (and that have sprouted like weeds on every busy Central London street). Clearly, this is a scenario being enacted not only in London (where we have already remarked the similar rebirth of Paddington) but also in virtually every large city around the globe.

Plus ca change: ironically, the very name King's Cross reflects the gentrification project of an earlier age. The district was at first called Battle Bridge, the bridge in question a crossing over the Fleet as it turned South into the City. The battle in question (which almost certainly never took place) supposedly was in AD 60 between the Romans and rebellious Celts led by Boudicca. As we all know, the Romans won that particular war, if not this particular imaginary battle, ending Boudicca's revolt and her life. If you credit the tale, she is buried somewhere nearby and her ghost haunts the railway station platforms. (However, if imaginary celebrities are your cup of tea, head inside the main line station to visit Platform 9 3/4 of Harry Potter fame.)

In the early Nineteenth Century, this area was the site of one of London's largest and most notorious dust mounds—supposedly the model for those at the center of the inheritance plot of Dickens's *Our Mutual Friend*. "Dust" is a Victorian euphemism for trash, garbage, rubbish, or waste (whichever term you may prefer), and once upon a time these dust mounds and others scattered around the outskirts of the city were quite profitable to their owners, principally as a source of the coal ash used in the manufacture of bricks, critical to London's rapid growth, but also yielding scrap metal, cloth, and bones, among other saleable goods. (It seems that the recycling of household waste is not a new phenomenon.) In 1830, in an effort to dignify the neighbourhood, a 60' column topped by a statue of King George IV was erected here and the intersection given the name King's Cross. The column lasted only 15 years, not much longer than the hugely unpopular (and hugely overweight) King himself, but the name has proved durable. (The mounds themselves lasted only a bit longer than the column, removed in 1848 and supposedly shipped to Russia to be made into bricks in St. Petersburg.)

The Great Northern Railway, running along the East Coast as far north as Scotland, arrived here in 1850 and the present main line station opened in 1852. It was in its day the largest railway station in Europe. Train sheds were miracles of engineering in their day, elegant structures that spanned great distances without intervening posts or pillars. These glass-paneled cast iron arches over the platforms are quite impressive still in their vast height and breadth. The station building fronting the shed is of tan brick and its facade has a simple functional design that was dictated by frugality but anticipates the geometric, undecorated vernacular of Twentieth-Century modernist architecture. The recent extension of the station building has preserved the old exterior and added a shopping and dining plaza; the new and monumentally vast roof is supported by fans radiating out like the vaults of a Gothic cathedral. The marriage of early Victorian and post-modernist architecture is striking; whether it is successful is arguable.

The same disjunction (or, if you like it, happy marriage) of styles is evident throughout the new, redeveloped district to the north of the terminus in what once were the station goods yards. To those of us who are old enough to remember the vast desert of tracks that once were there, this change is nothing less than alchemy—the real estate equivalent of making gold from dross. King's Cross Central (as the new district is called) is home to Google UK and one of the campuses of the University of the Arts London. The new district spans the once hidden Regent's Canal, a mélange of old warehouses repurposed and sympathetic new construction laid out around two newly hatched "squares"—an attempt inspired by London's most distinctive and most successful urban spaces. (One of the refurbished warehouses is home to the small but interesting London Canal Museum, difficult to find but definitely worth a visit.)

King's Cross Central is also a vital link in the chain of new enterprises that will thrive in post-Brexit Britain. London's bankers, who had rather hoped for special treatment in whatever deal emerged but were disappointed, prudently are establishing beachheads on the Continent, mostly in Frankfurt (affectionately known in the industry as Bankfurt). The presently unanswered and unanswerable question that will in any case be answered in a few years' time is, how many London financial services jobs ultimately will be lost? 5,000 is the low end estimate, a number everyone agrees is not very worrisome; there really is no high end figure other than "a lot more" and everyone agrees that is worrisome. So, and now I get to the point, a key question is, will high tech become the new hot industry and job creator for London? The phoenix-like rebirth of Kings Cross may be critical to answering that question.

Is Kings Cross Central a success? Time will tell, but the augurs are trending positive—thanks to the presence of Google, Kings Cross may well become the new center of "silicon" London. (The "old" center is in fact on Old Street in the City at what is sometimes called the Silicon Roundabout.) If another measure of success is that people actually use the spaces around King's Cross, then it does indeed seem to be working: thanks to the students at UAL, the "streets" (mostly vehicle-free) are fairly busy during the working day, and as the pandemic has receded at weekends as well. And the laid-back corporate culture of Google and the other tech firms it has attracted apparently allows employees to take long breaks to source caffeine outside the office at any and all times of the day. The retail mix and the bars and restaurants are decidedly up market—even the huge Waitrose supermarket here has a wine bar and its own cooking school.

The severe, functional lines of the Kings Cross Station suffer by their proximity and inevitable comparison to the rather grander St Pancras terminus and hotel of the Midland Railway, the hotel built in 1868 to the designs of George Gilbert Scott (the first of the three generations of similarly named Scott architects) and one of the most striking Victorian buildings in London. The station itself, largely invisible, is the work of the nearly forgotten William Henry Barlow. It is remarkable in that the main line tracks entered the station at a height that would allow them to pass over and well above the Regent's Canal; thus the station entrance is some four to six meters above the adjacent street level. (The space below the tracks rather ingeniously was used for freight storage.)

Many know the hotel-station from John O'Connor's famous 1884 painting that depicts it towering above surrounding buildings against a luminous late evening sky, and amazingly enough it still looks much as it did then. It is a wonderful amalgam of Victorian design elements that recalls the pseudo-medieval Houses of Parliament but made of red brick instead of Portland stone. Grand as it is, British Rail thought it superfluous in the Sixties and, with few trains routed there and the hotel long abandoned, it was threatened with demolition. (BR even tried to sell the tower clock but apparently it broke as it was taken down.) Now restyled St. Pancras International (with a bland bran new entrance located between it and King's Cross), until the pandemic it was again crowded with passengers for Eurostar to the Continent and the old hotel once again was thriving.

Directly to the west of the main line stations on Euston Road is the British Library, whose opening in 1997 was an important milestone in the transformation of the neighbourhood. The work of Colin St John Wilson and his partner in life and in work, M J Long, the building was controversial in many ways—for its size (monumental, supposedly the largest public building erected in Britain in the Twentieth Century), for its cost overruns (no less monumental), and for its supposed failings as a working library (though in the end it seems to be functioning quite well in that regard). The original plans were for it to be even larger than it is, but as the costs mounted, the size was scaled back, leading to the concerns that space for users would be compromised.

The complaints preceded its opening and went on for years afterward. Much of the resistance to the new building came from academics who, like me, had cut their scholarly teeth in the old Round Reading Room of the British Museum. Now itself turned into a museum exhibit, more than once I have shown young visitors what was back in the day my favorite seat (when I arrived early enough secure it). Nostalgia is always a rose-colored fiction, and in truth the old reading room was a horrible place to work. There was a certain thrill to imagining one was sitting was where (for example) Marx had beavered away on *Das Kapital*, but as a research library, it had many failings. First, it was generally crowded, and if you didn't get an early start, you might not find a seat at all. The collections themselves were widely dispersed (I remember anything but fondly the long tube ride out to Colindale to read newspapers), and when a book had to be retrieved from remote storage, as often was the case, the wait could be lengthy. The staff members who accepted and filled the book requests were sometimes rude and nearly always incompetent. I recall that they had a particular fondness for stamping the paper request slips "DESTROYED IN ENEMY ACTION" when they were too lazy to search for a book; I once kept as a curiosity a stack of call slips for post-1945 imprints that over the years had been thusly dismissed.

The "new" library building has settled into its middle age quite comfortably. The vast plaza outside, which seemed stark and unfriendly when it was new, now in decent weather is filled with visitors. Inside, improbably enough, it manages to serve successfully both as a working research library and as a tourist attraction. The "permanent" exhibits display what one might expect—the Magna Carta, a Gutenberg Bible, a Shakespeare first folio, and other famous documents and books—and they are at times as crowded as any other of the main sights of London. However, I particularly recommend the café: it is huge and quite comfortable, a cut above most museum eateries.

The area to the north of Euston Road and immediately west of the Library is called Somers Town, one of the few London neighbourhoods bearing a proper name (it was built on land owned by Charles Cocks, the first Baron Somers). Proximity to the major thoroughfare that then was called the "New Road" (now Euston Road) spurred the construction in 1784 of the Polygon, an up-market development of 32 houses sited around a communal garden. It never fulfilled its posh ambitions, instead attracting refugees from the French Revolution as well as English radicals like Mary Wollstonecraft and William Godwin. After the later arrival of the railways on the east and west boundaries of the district, it quickly turned into a slum, notorious for both its overcrowding and the high proportion of foreign residents. (Dickens's *Bleak House*, set in the 1820s, has the feckless and penniless dilettante Harold Skimpole lodging cheaply in the Polygon.) Though the original buildings were long ago demolished and built over with council housing, the west side of Chalton Street retains something of its original character, and it still hosts a lively street market on Fridays. The council housing is the impressive group of blocks of flats that comprise the Ossulston Estate, built in the Twenties and Thirties by the LCC in a style best described as Art Deco meets Viennese modernism. They were ahead of their time not only in their design but for their steel-frame construction, and they were also innovative in that originally they were to house both council and private market-rate tenants, though in the end the private flat scheme never got off the ground. Of the three sections, Levita House (now a Grade II listed building) is particularly impressive.

On the western side of Euston Station is Drummond Street, boasting the highest concentration of Indian restaurants anywhere in London outside Brick Lane, but unlike that well-trod street, it is off any and all beaten tracks, seemingly unknown to tourists. These eateries are far cheaper than their more famous East End cousins, as well. Alas, Drummond Street is slated for partial demolition as part of the development of a new high-speed rail link to Birmingham, although whether that line ever will be built appears to be doubtful.

Back on Euston Road is one of London's oddest Georgian churches, St Pancras New Church. Built 1819–1822 to designs of a father and son team of architects, William and Henry William Inwood, it is in Greek Revival style. It was intended to serve the rapidly growing population of Bloomsbury and to relieve pressure on the existing parish church that is now known as St Pancras Old Church, some distance to the north. The new church was both huge, seating 2,500, and hugely expensive—costing £76,679. Faced in Portland stone, despite the accumulation of decades of soot, it still glows warmly in bright sunlight. Why a mélange of several well-known ancient Athenian buildings should have been the model for a modern Church of England place of worship is a mystery, but there is no doubt but that it produced a unique edifice. Most remarkable of its exterior features are the caryatids at the eastern end of the building, the work of Charles Rossi, that guard burial vaults designed to accommodate 2,000 coffins, though only some 500 spaces had been filled when this form of burial ceased. The churchyard proper is rather bleak, but at lunchtime on weekdays it hosts a stall serving what I reckon are the best falafel wraps in all of London. Don't waste money on the large one—the regular size is about as much as any human being can ingest at one sitting.

Interesting aside: the caryatids look like stone carvings, but in fact they are molded of Coade Stone, an artificial stone-like product invented by Eleanor Coade in Lambeth in 1769 and produced by the firm she led well into the 1830s. The product could be molded into intricate shapes and designs, and the molds reused many times, making it an attractive and cost-effective alternative to much more expensive stone carvings. The recipe—it is in essence a high-fired ceramic—was a great trade secret (although recently rediscovered), and Mrs Coade enjoyed a virtual monopoly of such products for a good fifty years. Other good examples of the firm's work are the keystones of the doorways of the terrace houses surrounding Bedford Square, the lion at the east end of Westminster Bridge, and the front of Twining's tea shop in the Strand. The St Pancras figures, however, were mistakenly made too large to fit into the available space, and Rossi had to cut out a small section in the middle of each figure. If you look carefully, you can see the cut lines.

Still further west along the Euston Road is the Wellcome Collection, one of London's little known but most interesting museums. The Wellcome Trust, whose vast facade dominates the south side of this section of Euston Road, was created by Sir Harry Wellcome in 1936, and it claims to be the world's third richest charity. Wellcome made his fortune in pharmaceuticals and the trust now funds biomedical research in the UK and all over the world. Sir Harry was a collector (more like a compulsive hoarder) of medical artifacts and of much else besides. At his death, a staggering 125,000 objects in his various collections were cataloged; some were retained by the new gallery, but most were given to other and more appropriate museums. Some of those that were kept now are permanently exhibited in the public gallery, which also mounts special exhibits on medical and public health themes. Entry is free and well worth an hour of any visitor's time. (The cafe is quite nice, too.)

Turning east and remaining on the south side of the Euston Road, detour onto Upper Woburn Place, walk past the church entrance, you will come to Woburn Walk. This may well have been the very first purpose-built pedestrian street in England—erected in 1822 by Thomas Cubitt. Cubitt was the most successful builder in Victorian London, and in the early 1820s he was active in the employ of the Duke of Bedford, developing for him large tracts of Bloomsbury. Many of the distinctive uniform brick-fronted terraces we think of as characteristic of Bloomsbury are his work. Woburn Walk retains its original plate glass shopfronts, and it is also notable for having served as the London *pied a terre* of William Butler Yeats from 1895 to 1919. (There is a statue of Cubitt in Denbigh Street, Pimlico, another district where he built extensively.)

Wander southward and westward and you will come upon the graceful crescent of Cartwright Gardens (home to several modest hotels) and you should soon enough be on Marchmount Street, which will take you south past the Brunswick Center. This was a bold architectural and social experiment designed by Patrick Hodgkinson, built between 1967 and 1972 in the brutalist style (featuring lots of exposed raw concrete surfaces—we'll see more of it soon enough at the Barbican) and intended to create a new kind of urban community, mixing together residential and retail space. The ziggurat-inspired terraces allowed direct sunlight into virtually every one of the 560 flats. It was intended for private sale, but in the end it was acquired by Camden Council to become some of the most desirable "social" housing in all of London. Now Grade II listed, and with most of the flats privately owned, the complex has been fully renovated and the shopping center is lively and bustling at all hours. I've walked through it well past midnight on week nights and it pulses with activity when most of London is as dead as the proverbial doornail.

Cut through the shopping center to Brunswick Square itself, named to honor Caroline of Brunswick, who in 1795 married the Prince of Wales (who later reigned as George IV). The marriage, by the way, was a complete disaster, but by the time that became obvious the square had already been named.

The square is a fairly undistinguished green space, but its eastern side abuts the wall surrounding Coram's Fields. This is a play area to which adults can enter only if accompanied by a child—and any child fortunate enough to visit will find a petting zoo, age-appropriate play equipment, and a long zip line. It is built on the site of the Foundling Hospital, established in 1739 by a retired sea captain, Thomas Coram, to rescue infants who were being abandoned by their mothers, for the most part unmarried and in some instances prostitutes. In early Eighteenth-Century London, thousands of unwanted and exposed babies were dying every year and the hospital is fruit of Coram's determination to do something about it. The Foundling opened in the 1740s and finally moved out of London to the countryside in 1935. The old hospital building was then demolished but only two years later the Foundling bought back a bit of the land on the north side of the square to erect the Georgian-style building that now houses the Foundling Museum. In addition to exhibits about the hospital, the museum contains one of the best collections of Eighteenth-Century English paintings, most donated by the artists. The top floor houses the Gerald Coke Handel Collection, devoted to the composer's life and work.

Though the hospital is no more (it has transformed itself into a charity that aids children), it does remind us that Bloomsbury has long had an institutional flavor—not far to the west are University College, University College Hospital, Birkbeck College, the University of London, and, a bit further south, the British Museum.

From the Foundling Museum walk southward, and as you leave the square, bear left (east) around the curve in the road to Guilford Street. Turn left (east) and walk past the entrance to Coram's Fields. Note the subterranean lavatories across the road at the top of Lamb's Conduit Street which is a pleasant lane of Eighteenth-Century brick terrace houses, now partly pedestrianized. The conduit itself, established by a 1564 gift of £1500 (then a vast fortune) by William Lamb (marked by a plaque but otherwise no longer in evidence), enabled the poor to draw water from the Fleet River. Do make time for a brief stop at the pub called The Lamb with its largely intact late Victorian interior.

Our destination, however, is Doughty Street, a little further to the east, a small stretch of road that runs south toward Theobald's Road, changing its name to John Street along the way. Number 48, one of the Georgian terrace houses in the middle of this row, is home to the Charles Dickens Museum, located in the only London house in which Dickens lived that still survives. It is furnished much as it would have been when Dickens lived there in the late 1830s. Do go in, and if you didn't refresh yourself in the café of the Foundling Museum, you can do so in the café here (and in decent weather sit out in the charming small garden). I confess that I have had a relationship with the museum for some years, so you might think me shameless in promoting it. But promote it I shall do all the same.

Dead ahead on Doughty/John Streets is Gray's Inn, one of the medieval Inns of Court, of which there are four survivors—Gray's Inn, Lincoln's Inn, the Middle Temple, and the Inner Temple. We will visit the Temple in due course, so for now we'll content ourselves by remarking that the inns of court are professional associations of barristers that function more or less like an American bar association, though they are also home to many lawyers' offices (called chambers), and they are also sites of legal education, as well as a great deal of informal fraternizing by members of the profession. Gray's, like the others, dates at least to the Fourteenth Century. They all sprung up in the early 1300s as the legal profession was changing dramatically. The pope recently had forbade the clergy, who often had legal training and acted as attorneys, to take any part in civil court proceedings; not long after, Henry III banned legal education within the City itself. But the law needs lawyers, and so several inns just outside the city walls were ideal gathering places for lawyers who needed to be close both to clients in the City and to the courts meeting at Westminster Hall.

Gray's is named after Baron Gray of Wilton, whose London home once stood upon this ground. Most of the buildings are Georgian or Victorian, and though the Chapel looks to be earlier, it was in fact severely damaged in the Blitz and subsequently was completely rebuilt. The gardens, known as the Walks, are very pleasant indeed, and on a bright warm sunny summer day they are well shaded by lines of mature London plane trees.

The western boundary of the Inn is Gray's Inn Road, surely one of the most boring of all inner London high streets, although there are the stirrings of gentrification just now visible. Turn left (north) on it and soon enough you will return to Kings Cross and descend again to the ever reliable Circle Line to continue the journey eastward.

Chapter 4

Farringdon

Farringdon Station—originally named Farringdon Street Station—was the first eastern terminus of the Metropolitan Railway, and from its platforms one still can see much of the original Victorian brickwork lining the tracks. The station now serves three of the shallow sub-surface underground lines—the Circle, the Hammersmith and City, and the Metropolitan—and it offers easy access to the main line station of the same name that is the only point in London where the north-south Thameslink rail service forms an interchange with the new east-west Elizabeth line. Once the City has recovered from the pandemic lockdowns, it should rapidly become one of the busiest commuter stations.

The first station building was in use only for two years; it was then relocated to allow the underground tracks to be extended to Moorgate, the first stage in the Metropolitan's mandated eastward progress. The present structure, dating from 1922, is an impressively robust example of early Twentieth Century station architecture, covered in off-white ceramic tiles and displaying the baked-on name "Farringdon and High Holborn," which it bore until 1936, when the "and High Holborn" dropped off everywhere except the building itself. If you walk around to the east side of the building, you will encounter another anachronistic ceramic tile sign, this for the "Parcels Office," the last trace of a delivery service run for a time by the Met to generate additional revenue. The place name Farringdon dates to the late 1300s and honors two prominent aldermen, William and Nicholas de Farindon, father and son-in-law goldsmiths.

Leaving the Underground station, you exit onto a pedestrianized section of Cowcross Street, so named because for hundreds of years this was the pathway along which live cattle were daily driven to slaughter in nearby Smithfield Market. The only mammalian traffic now, however, is bipedal. Directly opposite the Underground station is the striking, bran new Elizabeth Line (Crossrail) station. Turn left here, and then stop for a moment at the first turning to the left, Turnmill Street, bounded on one side by the wall that marks the eastern end of the Underground station. The name reminds us that hereabouts in ancient times there were several water mills along the River Fleet, which ran just to the west (and now is confined to an underground channel, which we shall visit presently). If you are on the tall side, or you can find a way to step up above street level, you can see over the wall into the station and what was once its goods yard.

The Farringdon area now is one of the trendiest in Central London, home to myriad architectural practices and the coffee houses, bars, and eateries that cater to the mainly young crowd who work here and live nearby. Supposedly Farringdon has the highest concentration of design professionals in the world, though I can't imagine how one might measure that to a certainty. What is beyond doubt is that it is—or, until Covid, was—filled during the working week with svelte, black-and-grey clad young people, and sundry others trying to look young, at all hours of the day and well into the evening. At the weekend, the street is fairly deserted, looking as if it were a party ready to happen but no guests have arrived.

The area in living memory had been light industrial and latterly fairly run down, home to businesses related to the wholesale meat market, like restaurant outfitters and wholesalers. Thanks yet again to gentrification, the Victorian warehouses all are now elegantly restored as offices and posh loft-style flats. To look at it now, one could hardly credit that this is actually the second wave of gentrification in these precincts: before the Smithfield live meat market was closed in the 1850s, these streets had been relegated to noxious trades like horse knacking and fish frying, and in particular the narrow lanes and rookeries off Cowcross Street were notorious for squalid overcrowded housing. ("Rookery" is an old name for London's ramshackle, maze-like slum neighbourhoods.) They all were torn down in the later Nineteenth Century.

We will follow Cowcross Street east to one of those narrow rookery alleys, a turning to the north (left) called Peter's Lane. Peter's Lane is a pedestrianized cobbled thoroughfare that exudes Victorian charm, the old buildings repurposed as offices, flats, and even a boutique hotel. Its present condition belies the fact that it once was the center of one of the foulest slums in all of London. (The newish hotel calls itself "The Rookery," which seems a rather tasteless choice, considering its origins.) We will walk the length of this short street, which merges into St John's Lane. This road is genuinely medieval— its slightly irregular path suggests as much—but most of the buildings are refurbished Victorian and post-war era. Now we are approaching St John's Gate, once the southern entrance to the Priory of St John (of which more in a moment). Just before the gate, there is a narrow turning to the east that is worth a moment's perusal—Passing Alley—whose original name, Pissing Alley, suggests how it was used by generations of monks returning to the abbey after a late night out. It still more than occasionally smells of the same activity.

St John's Gate was built in 1504 and I must say it looks very much as one imagines a late medieval abbey gateway ought to look—with a solid stone exterior, mullioned windows replete with stained glass, a crenelated roof, and a fan-vaulted covered archway over the road itself. Appearances, however, can be deceiving: what remains is largely a Victorian reconstruction of what the Tudor building then was thought to have looked like. Even the walls are *trompe l'oeil*: they look like thick stone but are made of brick and only faced in stone. The priory behind the gate disappeared at the Dissolution, distinguished by having been the very last monastic establishment seized by Henry VIII before he died. Queen Mary restored the monastic order, but the establishment soon after was dissolved a second and final time by Elizabeth I.

St John's Gate has led a chequered life since then. For a time in the reigns of Elizabeth I and James I it was home to the offices of the Master of the Revels, the court official responsible for censorship of the theatre, who over the years had licensed most of Shakespeare's plays. Later, in the early Eighteenth century, it housed a tavern run by William Hogarth's father; perhaps Hogarth's patriotic fondness for English beer and his disdain for foreign gin dates from his childhood spent here. *The Gentleman's Magazine*—the very first periodical to call itself a magazine—was published and printed in offices within the gate from 1731 until the early Twentieth Century. This journal was the invention of Edmund Cave, whose principal distinction prior to founding the magazine was to have been expelled from Rugby School for theft. From his print miscellany are descended the myriad general interest periodicals that we enjoy still today. Among its early distinguished contributors were Samuel Johnson, Jonathan Swift, and Cave himself under the paradoxical but euphonious pen name, Sylvanus Urban. In the late Twentieth Century, the gate was home for a time to one of the more distinguished of latter day periodicals, the *TLS*. I remember those offices well—they seemed by their very antiquity and eccentric floor plan something of a rebuke to Rupert Murdoch's News Corp., which had acquired the *TLS* more or less by accident when it bought *The Times* in 1981.

The gatehouse now houses a small but fascinating museum dedicated to the Order of St John. Back in the Twelfth Century, this priory was the English headquarters of the Knights of the Order of St John of Jerusalem, sometimes known as the Knights Hospitaller. The order had been founded to care for ill Christian pilgrims to the holy city but in time it became a large and powerful military establishment, from 1530 onward based in Malta. (The knights' rule over Malta lasted nearly 400 years, finally ending when Napoleon booted them out.) The order was revived as a charity in the late Nineteenth Century and it continues to this day as an ambulance service and international first-aid agency; its logo is a red Maltese cross, and you will notice various and sundry Maltese crosses feature as decorative elements on the building's exterior.

What lies before you through the archway six hundred years ago would have been the heart of the priory. As you walk through the arch, the street opens into St John's Square, and on its northern edge is the busy Clerkenwell Road, cut through overcrowded lanes and alleys by the Metropolitan Board of Works in the years 1874–78. Cross the road, and wander to your left, or west, and you will come soon to Clerkenwell Green. This is a quiet spot surrounded by various and sundry period and modern buildings, but it might better be called Clerkenwell Brown as there is not a single blade of grass or anything else green here to be seen. (There has been no green on the Green for two hundred years or more: Dickens made this very joke about the lack of green color in *Oliver Twist* in the 1830s.) Just ahead, a little further west, is No. 16 Farringdon Lane, and through a ground floor window one can glimpse what purports to be the clerks' well that gave the district its name.

The impressive Georgian building fronting the western side of the "green" is the Middlesex Sessions House, dating from 1784, where the Middlesex justices of the peace held sway until the formation of the London County Council in 1889. This was a convenient location for the county court of law, near the Inns of Court and close by several prisons, all now demolished. London outside the City boundaries then was part of the surrounding county of Middlesex, and as these metropolitan districts grew increasingly populous, the county was obliged to develop reasonably robust legal and penal systems, taking shape in court houses and jails. The building, or at least its exterior, stands yet; it is in the midst of renovation to create, in the words of its owners, "a curated mix of people and brands [who] will fill the elegant space—and imbue it with their passion"—in other words, a restaurant, bar, and shopping mall.

Clerkenwell has come up in the world over the past two decades, now solidly entrenched as one of London's hippest neighborhoods. And I must say that, as I stand on the green, it still feels more like a village than most of the other older Central London villages that have been absorbed into the general metropolitan sprawl. It survives as a bit of a quiet backwater as it is not a major through street, and its appeal is further enhanced by the architecture— still predominately Georgian—as well by the tangle of narrow pedestrian alleyways that run north from the eastern edges of the "village." There are also some attractive pubs here, including the Crown, dating from the 1720s, though the present building probably went up in the 1820s and the interior is late Victorian.

It is difficult to imagine it now, but Clerkenwell in the late Nineteenth and early Twentieth Century was home to several large light industrial concerns, including England's first Kodak factory, as well as myriad small workshops.

In particular it was the center of the watch, clock, and scientific instrument trades, which died out as recently as the Seventies, as I had good reason to discover first-hand. In the early Seventies I bought a small mantle clock shaped like Napoleon's hat for a pound at a street market, only to discover that it wasn't working—the mainspring was broken. A search in the telephone directory (which is how one located businesses before the advent of Google) suggested that I could find a replacement in Clerkenwell, so there I went. I wandered into a randomly-chosen closet-sized watchmakers supply shop that looked a thousand years old, only a few years younger than the shop assistant. He found what was needed (I think the cost was 50p) and he warned me to be very careful removing the clip that held together the tightly wound spring. Needless to say, I didn't follow his advice and the spring nearly took out an eye as it exploded. I went back a week later, to be greeted by his, "Ah, I told you, didn't I?" (Second time lucky: the repaired clock was working still when I gave it away a few years ago.)

On the north side of the green is the Marx Memorial Library, housed here since 1933 in an elegant Georgian building (mostly reconstructed) that was originally the Welsh Charity School. There was a prior connection of a sort to Marx or at least to the movement he inspired: by the 1920s, the building had become general office space and one of the tenants was the Twentieth Century Press, which published a newspaper for the Social Democratic Association, and which also had for a time published the exiled Lenin's political journal, called *Iskra* (Spark).

Indeed, Clerkenwell at the turn of the century was a seething hotbed of radical politics, domestic and foreign. Late Victorian and Edwardian Britain was for the most part quite tolerant of exiled revolutionaries—as long as they plotted to overthrow only their own governments and made no fuss locally. (Conrad's novel, *The Secret Agent,* provides a good portrait of turn of the century "revolutionary" London.) Supposedly, Lenin and Stalin first met in the Crown in 1907, though earlier dates have been proposed. (Neither strikes me as much of a drinking buddy but there you have it.) Trotsky was also in London early in the Twentieth Century and probably quaffed a pint or two at the Crown as well.

At the eastern end of the north side of the green is Clerkenwell Close, which opens onto the churchyard of St James Clerkenwell. The impressively large barn-like present building dates from 1792, when it replaced an earlier mediaeval structure that once had been the chapel of an Augustine nunnery. After the Dissolution, it was of course reborn as an Anglican church, but one of the few in London to retain the right to elect its own vicar, giving it a decidedly "low church" orientation. The interior is rather severe and unadorned, though a few monuments from the medieval church have survived.

Just beyond the church opposite the curiously named street Sans Walk is the site of the old Middlesex House of Detention, one of the area's several vanished prisons. Here in 1867 a Fenian plot to blow a hole in the prison wall and to extract an Irish republican arms dealer went disastrously awry, killing 12 and wounding over 100; the incident was henceforth known as the Clerkenwell Outrage. The prison was demolished in 1890 but its underground vaults and cells remain—and rather bizarrely are available for hire as an events space. (One wonders, what family celebration would be well suited to an underground prison as the venue?) Those same cells served as air raid shelters during the Blitz.

Continue north on Clerkenwell Close and just ahead lies Spa Fields, as you might guess once home to several spas, including Sadler's Wells, whose name lives on in the nearby theatre. This was once a much larger open space, of which only this small park remains. Spa Fields holds a special place in the history of English radicalism: here on 15 November and 2 December 1816, huge anti-government demonstrations were held. The first ended peacefully with a plan to deliver a petition to the Prince Regent, but after the second mass meeting, a few armed demonstrators exchanged fire with troops on standby near the Royal Exchange. Four leaders of the demonstrations were arrested on charges of high treason, but the trial of the first defendant ended in an acquittal and the other three were never tried.

Not far to the east, and just visible across the park, is the Spa Green Estate, designed after World War II by Berthold Lubetkin, a Russian modernist architect who had emigrated to London in 1931 and soon after established the firm Tecton, essentially a socialist architectural collective whose work was inspired by Soviet constructivism. Though Tecton lasted only a few years, its commitment to using modern materials and construction techniques, and its axiomatic belief that architecture could shape behavior for the better, strongly influenced the design of post-war council houses. Lubetkin—who had a prior connection to Finsbury Council, as we shall see presently—designed the site with generous common spaces and amenities that he hoped would support the revival of working class communities and turn residents into socialist utopians. Building on Spa Green began within a year of the war's end, long before most rebuilding was undertaken, and the estate opened in 1949. The flats were cutting-edge in their time, with modern kitchens and plumbing, even providing a balcony for *every* apartment. Recently renovated and refreshed, it is often thought of as not merely the first but the best of the post-war council housing projects.

Just a bit further to the west is Exmouth Market, once a neighborhood fruit-and-veg market that has been reinvented as a home to outdoor cafes and up-market street food. If you ignore the signage in English, you could almost believe yourself on a quiet square in Paris. This is a convenient moment to stop at a café for a treat, if you are so inclined, especially if it's warm enough to sit at a table outside. Try to sit with a view of the imposing façade of the Church of Our Most Holy Redeemer, a Catholic chapel built in the 1890s in striking early Italian Renaissance style but in bog standard London brick. It is the work of John Dando Sedding, though one of its most impressive features, the camponile, built later in 1906, was the work of his pupil, Henry Wilson.

Just past the church is Pine Street. Turn left and a short distance on is another and much earlier Lubetkin building, the Finsbury Health Centre, built for the Labour-controlled Finsbury Council, 1935–38. This is a bold statement in classic modernist idiom that is reminiscent of the work of the Bauhaus architects. Sensitively restored in the Nineties, it looks today as revolutionary as it must have done when it first opened.

Return to Exmouth Market, turn left, and a short stroll down the last stretch of the market brings us to the Farringdon Road. We are now literally standing atop the River Fleet, which flows directly under our feet. The Fleet rises in Hampstead where it is dammed to form the Hampstead and Highgate Ponds, but from there as it runs four miles to the Thames it is entirely underground. There is a grid here in the middle of the road at the intersection with Charterhouse Street where one can hear the river thrashing about below ground. For most of London's history, it flowed through the City unenclosed. Already by the time of Shakespeare, however, it had been reduced to a foul sewer, collecting human waste, animal carcasses, and every conceivable kind of rubbish. (Ben Jonson's "On the Famous Voyage" [c.1612] gives a nauseatingly vivid account of a boat journey down the fetid river.) The portion of the roadway that is now Farringdon *Street* was culverted in 1737 and became the home of Fleet Market, which lasted just over a century. The lower reaches were paved over in 1769 to create New Bridge Street, the entryway to the newly constructed Blackfriars Bridge. Here, where we now stand, Farringdon *Road*, was cut through this then densely populated area in 1845–46.

As one walks south on Farringdon Road, one can appreciate fully the depth of the Fleet Valley. For hundreds of years it was a huge impediment to the flow of traffic east and west through the City; horses moving in either direction struggled to pull heavy loads uphill. It now is elegantly spanned by the Holborn Viaduct. (Holborn was originally the [Hol]low Bourne or River, i.e. the Fleet.) This massive 1400' long structure, built in the late 1860s, runs level across the valley. But we will turn right (west) on Charterhouse Street just before we reach the viaduct, walking a short distance to Holborn Circus. Note in the center of the road at the circus the equestrian statue of Prince Albert (of whom more later). Our destination is Ely Place, a gated street opening to the north.

Ely Place is a short street of sedate and stately late Georgian row houses sitting regally behind massive, somber cast iron gates. It is built on ground where once stood Ely Palace, the London residence of the Bishops of Ely. The bishopal establishment survived the Dissolution, its substantial chapel then ceasing Catholic worship and commencing life in the Church of England. Elizabeth I sold off part the site to Christopher Hatton, who built a large house that eventually gave its name to nearby Hatton Garden (long the center of the retail watch and jewelry trade). The chapel, St Etheldreda (a Seventh Century East Anglian nun), dates from the late 1200s and has been many things in its long life, including a tavern, a prison, and a hospital, but in 1874 it was sold to one William Lockhart who, after funding its extensive restoration, reconverted it to its first use as a Catholic place of worship, in which capacity it serves still. It took a direct hit in the Blitz but since has been fully restored, although all of the Victorian glass was lost; the present windows date from the Sixties. It is open every day of the week and well worth a brief visit. Also worth a visit is the Old Mitre, a pub whose current building went up in 1773 but whose antecedents stretch back to Tudor times. Its well-preserved interior fixtures and fittings date from the early Twentieth Century. If it is after 5 (and it always is somewhere in the world), you might stop for a quick pint.

We will cross the road and walk east along the south side of Holborn Viaduct to enjoy the views down Farringdon Road toward the river. Note the dragons guarding the viaduct (we shall meet their cousins later), and note also the stairs down to Farringdon Street, though we won't go down them. Instead, pause on the railings and look below us off to the south, where on the east side of Fleet Street once stood the Fleet Prison, just north of what now is Ludgate Circus. Built in 1197 and demolished in 1846, it was twice destroyed and twice rebuilt (first in the Great Fire and then in the anti-Catholic Gordon Riots of 1780). By the early Nineteenth Century, the Fleet was a debtors' prison and home to what probably was the most corrupt prison administration in England, which was no small achievement. Prisons then were profit-making enterprises and the warden and warders sold everything from food and lodging to relative freedom—inmates could buy their way out of the prison proper to live in the surrounding neighborhood, known as the Rules of the Fleet. The Rules was also notorious for a considerable time for allowing clergy to perform clandestine and irregular marriages with impunity, until the practice was stopped by the Marriage Act of 1753. The Fleet's most famous inmates include John Donne, Richard Grosvenor (whose illustrious descendants are the Dukes of Westminster), and William Penn. Its most famous fictional inmates are Dickens's Mr Pickwick and Sam Weller; here they are imprisoned when Pickwick refuses to pay the damages assessed in an unjust breach of promise law suit.

Holborn was also the site of the world's first public coal-fired electricity generating plant, the Edison Electric Light Station. It opened in January, 1882, several months before a similar installation in Pearl Street, New York

City. The generator was nicknamed "Jumbo," after the beloved elephant celebrity of the London Zoo that had just been sold to P.T. Barnum, sparking great controversy. (The adjective "jumbo" meaning outsized appears to be an eponym from the elephant's proper name.) The plant was to provide power for street lighting on and around the Viaduct but it seems never to have been a commercial success and it closed in 1886. The neighborhood street lamps, by the way, all were converted back to gas. (There remain some 1,500 gas lamps in Central London, of which precisely 23 are in the City; the nearest to where you stand now are in the Guildhall Yard and Gough Square.)

At the eastern end of the Viaduct once stood the Holborn Station of the London, Chatham, and Dover Railway, now the site of the City Thameslink Station. Opened in 1874, until it closed in 1990, it allowed both local and main line services to enter the City via Blackfriars railway bridge and then to pass through Central London via a bridge over Ludgate Hill and the Snow Hill tunnel that connected to the Metropolitan Railway's so-called widened lanes (extra tracks) at Farringdon. In the Eighties when I sometimes stayed in Herne Hill in south London, I was able to take local service directly to Holborn Station and walk from there to the British Library in Bloomsbury. The new City Thameslink station that has replaced the old station is admirably efficient, but otherwise a large, graceless, and utterly forgettable structure.

Just past the eastern end of the Viaduct, and across the road, is St Sepulchre-without-Newgate, a large church—indeed now the largest parish church in the City—that looks convincingly mediaeval. It looks the part but what one sees in fact is a hodgepodge of reconstructions, the first completed after the Great Fire, which had destroyed the interior but left the walls and tower standing. The church stands catty-corner to the Old Bailey, named after the street it fronts and more properly the Central Criminal Court of England and Wales, an imposing Edwardian building erected on the site of old Newgate Prison. The notoriously unhealthy prison was built in the Twelfth Century near the "new" gate in the City walls; it like the nearby Fleet was destroyed twice and by the same events, the Great Fire and the Gordon Riots, and twice rebuilt. From here prisoners condemned to death were taken to Tyburn to be hanged until 1783; from that year public executions were held outside the prison gates until 1868, when they were removed inside the walls. (For a riveting account of a public execution in 1840, see Thackeray's essay, "Going to see a man hanged.") The infamous prison was torn down in 1904.

Look carefully inside the church and you will find a glass case enclosing a large hand bell known as the Execution Bell. The parish clerk was charged with ringing the bell outside the cells of those Newgate prisoners condemned to die the next day, urging them to repent. The vicar of St Sepulchre was also meant to be present at all executions, but the crowds were so massive that it was difficult for him to cross the road; supposedly a tunnel was built to ensure that he would arrive on time, though no trace of it remains. Among Newgate's better known inmates were Thomas Bambridge (ironically imprisoned here after he had served as warden of the Fleet Prison), Giacomo Casanova, Daniel Defoe, Ben Jonson, the pirate William "Captain" Kidd, the highwayman Jack Sheppard (who escaped from Newgate four of the five times he was there incarcerated), and Oscar Wilde.

The adjacent courts appeared first in the Sixteenth Century as the sessions house of the Lord Mayor and the Sheriffs of the City. An act of 1834 gave the court jurisdiction over *all* crimes committed in the City, and a further act of 1856 allowed it to hold the trials of selected major cases, crimes committed anywhere in England and Wales. By the time the prison was demolished, the law court already was serving as the most likely venue of all high profile criminal cases. The present court building itself is in the style of the typical turn-of-the-century jumble of neoclassical and baroque elements usually called "beaux arts," projecting mass and power, somewhat mitigated by the motto cut in stone over the main entrance: "Defend the Children of the Poor & Punish the Wrongdoer." Do look up at the gilt statue of Justice above the dome; she holds a sword in one hand and a set of scales in the other. (Despite the popular misconception, she is not blindfolded.) The building is actually owned by the Bridge House Estates—responsible for upkeep and repair of many of the Thames crossings—and maintained by the City Corporation, though administered as if it were part of the criminal court system. The Lord Mayor and aldermen retain the right to sit on the bench during trials but do not participate in deliberation and judgment.

We will turn north on the continuation of Old Bailey, Giltspur Street, presumably once home to high-end mediaeval spur makers. Giltspur Street takes us past St Bartholomews Hospital, founded in 1123 and said to be the oldest medical institution still located on its original site; some of its buildings still in use date to the Eighteenth Century. Don't miss the striking neoclassical St Bartholomew's Gate (1702), which displays above the entryway what is said to be the only public statue of Henry VIII in London, and who looks rather trimmer and fitter than he was. It is appropriate to honor Henry here, since after the Dissolution in an uncharacteristic act of generosity he gave the hospital to the City Corporation and thus ensured its survival. Through the gateway is the hospital's main square, laid out in the 1730s by James Gibbs, three sides of which are original. Despite its antiquity and rich heritage—it was here that William Harvey studied the circulatory system—the hospital was threatened with closure in the Nineties. It won a reprieve and it has been extensively recast as a teaching hospital specializing in cardiac diseases and cancer treatment. The hospital museum, just off the quadrangle, is free and open Tuesday to Friday. Friday afternoon tours (there is a modest charge) give access to areas normally closed off to visitors, including two large murals by Hogarth.

Giltspur Street terminates in an odd circular street called West Smithfield (though this spot isn't really west of anything). Before you now lies the vast complex of Smithfield Market, a.k.a. London Central Markets. It is not only the last remaining wholesale food market in the City but also the largest wholesale meat market in Europe, which you can confirm yourself if you visit early enough when it is in full swing (it opens at 2 a.m. and begins to shut down at around 7 a.m.) The two main structures date from the 1860s, and when built represented the fruit of a long campaign to rid the city of an entrenched nuisance. Originally a flat open space used for jousts and other games ("smeth" means smooth in Old English), from at least the Twelfth Century this area was the site of London's principal live meat market. By the early Nineteenth Century, thousands of live cattle and sheep every day were driven through the narrow crowded streets to the market to be sold, slaughtered, and butchered. (Dickens gives a vivid sense of the crush of animals and the horrific treatment they suffered in Chapter 21 of *Oliver Twist*.) Every sensible person felt the evil of the arrangement, but as it was a profitable enterprise for the City, there was little incentive for the Corporation to change it. A new live meat market was finally opened in Islington in 1855, and "old" Smithfield was then at last closed, to be replaced by the present structures and the "dead" meat market that opened in 1868.

The market buildings are the work of Horace Jones, for many years chief architect of the Corporation and also responsible for Billingsgate Market and Tower Bridge, *inter alia*. Note the cast iron frame, a hallmark of Jones's work for the Corporation. (The Poultry Market, future home of the Museum of London, dates from the 1960s.) Though the area around it has come up in the world and now boasts more trendy coffee bars and wine bars than pubs and old-school cafes, and while some of the out-buildings have been or are being redeveloped for other uses, the main facilities continue to serve their original purpose. (The Corporation has put forward a proposal to move the market to a new far distant site that would incorporate all of the other wholesale markets—New Billingsgate, New Spitalfields, and New Covent Garden—but securing approval will certainly take years and construction many years more.)

On the periphery of West Smithfield are two outstanding churches, St Bartholomew the Less and St Bartholomew the Great, both associated with St Barts Hospital, as their names suggest. The nearer to where we stand is the "Less," which dates from the Fifteenth Century, although the interior was much altered at the end of the Eighteenth Century by George Dance. It possesses two medieval bells still in their original bell frame—said to be the oldest structure of its type in London. For many years, it was the parish church of the hospital, but it is now merged with the "Great."

The "Great"—which has a legitimate claim to be the oldest parish church in the City—is across the road from the hospital complex, largely hidden behind its distinctive half-timbered Tudor gateway (incorporating an even earlier stone arch). It has the distinction of having survived both the Great Fire and the Blitz. It was partly demolished at the time of the Dissolution but what remains is mostly medieval and early Tudor. I recommend going inside for a few moments. It boasts that it was the very first parish church in England to levy an admission charge (not a "first" I'd have thought any church would wish to claim), but now it merely asks for a donation from visitors.

Running east-west just to the north of the "Great" churchyard is a street with the curious name, Cloth Fair. The name recalls its past as the spot where cloth was sold during Bartholomew Fair. That famous market has ancient roots—it was first chartered in 1133 (and Ben Jonson wrote an eponymous play set in it); it was at first a summer market mainly for cloth, but by the Nineteenth Century it was reduced to a few summer days only and mainly the site of cheap popular entertainments—and reputedly a magnet for petty crime. Such mass gatherings were considered both immoral and dangerous by our Victorian forebears, and the fair was suppressed once for all in 1855.

In the middle of this short stretch of Cloth Fair, take a narrow turning to the north, Kinghorn Street. A quick left on Long Lane and a quick right on Lindsay Street will take you to Charterhouse Street leading to Charterhouse Square. On two sides of the square (now a nondescript park) is the Charterhouse itself, the name an old Anglicization of the French "Chartreuse." Today the headquarters of Barts medical school, the Charterhouse was founded in the Fourteenth Century as a Carthusian priority. In 1537, the monks made the serious mistake of resisting the dissolution of their monastery: Henry VIII's response was to hang, draw, and quarter the prior and to imprison 10 of the monks, 9 of whom starved to death. The tenth hardly benefitted from his toughness as he was executed three years later. After passing through several owners, it was acquired in 1611 by Thomas Sutton, a well-connected and prosperous money-lender, who died just a few months later, leaving a will that endowed a chapel, an almshouse, and a school—one of the seven original "public" schools (as established by the 1868 act of Parliament). The school moved to Godalming in Surrey in 1872; the almshouse, home to 40 men, is very much still here. (There is a Tudor-era domestic building called Sutton House in Hackney, so named because it once was thought to have been built by Sutton, but in fact he lived nearby in a structure long ago demolished; the surviving house is owned now by the National Trust.)

A museum on the Charterhouse grounds was opened in 2017, allowing access to the chapel and presenting exhibits on the history of the institution, focused primarily on the almshouse. Tours that allow access to other parts of the site must be booked ahead of the visit. The site certainly looks authentically medieval, but much of what one sees is a 1950s restoration after extensive damage during the Blitz. The only traces of the departed school still visible now are tablets that commemorate a few of the many famous Old Carthusians, as alumni are known—among them Roger Williams (founder of the Rhode Island colony), Joseph Addison and Richard Steele, William Makepeace Thackeray, and Ralph Vaughan Williams. The museum has both a shop worth browsing for books on local history and a very pleasant small café.

From here, a short stroll westward on Charterhouse Street takes us back to Cowcross Street and Farringdon Station.

Chapter 5

Barbican

Barbican Tube Station opened as Aldersgate Street in 1865 as the Metropolitan Railway began its eastward march; it was later renamed Aldersgate and Barbican, and it became Barbican *solus* in 1968. The platforms and the interior of the station are very much as they were a century and a half ago. The station building has no real presence above ground, the last bits that survived the Blitz having been demolished in 1955. It was also a main line rail station until 2009—the disused tracks and a supernumerary platform are tokens of this past life.

The station exits onto the bottom end of Goswell Road, one of the busiest and dreariest streets in the City. (Its principal fame is as the home of the protagonist of Dickens's *Pickwick Papers*.) Don't be put off by unprepossessing urban blight that you see when first you exit—the environs of the station remarkably span the whole of London's history. It is rich in ruins that hark back to Roman times and it also is home to some of the most radical attempts to reconceive London as a modernist utopia.

As you emerge onto the street, a stairwell leads to a walkway above the roadway that provides direct access to the Barbican Estate. However, for now we'll postpone our visit to the Barbican Estate proper and instead walk southward along its western border on the continuation of the Goswell Road, an equally dreary Aldersgate. Somewhere along this stretch of road is the site of the original barbican, though no one is absolutely certain where. "Barbican" entered English from Old French around 1260, and ultimately it derives from the Latin *barbicana*. It is a fortified tower and very probably one stood on or near Aldersgate in the Thirteenth Century, perhaps on the site of an earlier Roman structure—or, then again, perhaps not. With or without a tower, this once was the northwest corner of the Roman walled city, and surprisingly robust remnants of the Roman fortifications are still to be seen. What is visible now actually displays two eras of wall building, one that ended when the Roman occupation ceased c.400 and the city was abandoned, and above it evidence of the rebuilding of the walls at the time of the resettlement of

Londinium ordered by Alfred the Great in 866. The later medieval walls and gates stood intact until the 1760s. Stow comments that from this tower "a man might behold and view the whole city towards the south, and also into Kent, Sussex, and Surrey," but I reckon in his day the air was clearer and there were no tall buildings (save old St Paul's) to obscure the line of sight.

The most evocative remaining bits of the Roman city wall are visible on the western end of the appropriately named street, London Wall, that marks the southern boundary of the Barbican Estate and more or less follows the line of the old Roman structure. For roughly 1500 years, this was the northern edge of the built-up area of London. It will take you about ten minutes to walk London Wall end to end, depending on the traffic lights, and it will give you a good sense of the scale of the Roman city, which at its peak had around 60,000 inhabitants. The best vantage point from which to see the wall itself is where London Wall at its western end intersects Noble Street, where accidental excavations that were a byproduct of a Luftwaffe raid uncovered a fairly intact buried section. Not far away, the bottom end of Aldersgate was the site of one of the medieval gatehouses. (When the walls were demolished in the Eighteenth Century the names of many of the old gates persisted—*videlicet* Aldgate, Bishopsgate, Broadgate, Ludgate, Moorgate, and Newgate.)

As you pass southward on Aldersgate, you may notice on the eastern side of the road a courtyard that leads to the Ironmongers' Hall. The Ironmongers are one of the original twelve City livery companies (of which more in a moment) and while their half-timbered home looks ancient, it dates only from 1925, its former home in Fenchurch Street having been destroyed by a German bombing raid in July 1917. (A useful reminder that London endured aerial bombardment in both world wars of the last century.)

The Ironmongers are but one of over a hundred livery companies, many, but not all, with medieval roots. "Livery" normally denotes a uniform, and early on (around 1300 or so), membership of a company afforded one the right to wear the clothes associated with that particular trade. Many of the older companies are no longer linked closely to their nominal trades (after all, there's not much of a demand for bowyers and fletchers these days), though others, like the Vintners, have never lost that close connection. There now are (as I write) 110 livery companies in the City, with the precise order of precedence at ceremonies and official gatherings determined by the date of its founding. The number of companies had reached 77 in 1746, and it stuck there for nearly two centuries. But in the 1930s, the Master Mariners were granted the privilege of forming their own company, since then joined by the Arbitrators, Fuellers, Lightmongers, Environmental Cleaners, Information Technologists, Hackney Carriage (a.k.a. taxi) Drivers, International Bankers, and Arts Scholars, among others. (This may be the only place in London where cab drivers come before bankers.)

Worth a little detour to the intersection of Foster Lane and Gresham Street is perhaps the grandest of all the livery halls, that of the Goldsmiths. The Goldsmiths were established at least as early as 1180 and are designated fifth in order of precedence. (The Mercers are first.) They have occupied this location continuously since 1339; the present building is the third on the site, designed by Phillip Hardwick (best known for the Euston Station Arch, controversially demolished in the Sixties) and completed in 1835. It sustained some damage in the Blitz but since has been fully restored. The goldsmiths still are responsible for assaying every object made from precious metal—gold, silver, platinum, and since 2010 palladium as well. This is, in fact, the very "hall" in the word "hallmark," since the assay process used to be carried out on site. (We will presently encounter two churches named after the patron saint of goldsmiths, St Dunstan. Each assay year, assigned a particular alphabetic mark that is stamped into the object, begins on May 19, St Dunstan's feast day, and runs for twelve months, spanning the usual January 1 calendar year break.)

Back across the busy road opposite Noble Street and accessible by an elevated walkway, a set of stairs leads down to one of the Barbican estate parking garages. The staircase is dark and clearly not much trafficked, but taking it to the bottom brings the brave pedestrian right smack against another substantial fragment of the Roman city walls, a bit that was also to be seen from the Roman exhibits within the adjacent Museum of London (soon to move to a new site). Look carefully and you may see a few of the distinctive, flat, tile-like Roman bricks. Their thin profile is immediately distinguishable from later, thicker medieval bricks. (Most of what one actually sees of the walls in fact is medieval.) A little further along London Wall is yet another section of the Roman fortifications, and also some ruined remains of St Alphage, the priory church of a nunnery on this site, later a hospital, and thrice damaged by fire—the Great Fire of 1666, another after a German air raid during World War 1 (leading to the demolition of all of the church but the tower), and again in the Blitz.

Climb to the top of the stairs and you now have entered the Barbican Estate proper. (You're near the entrance to the old Museum of London, now closed.) This is the Ward of Cripplegate, just north of the old city walls, named after another of the ancient city gates. A century ago, this district was the center of London's "rag" trade and, with its warehouses stuffed with highly combustible cotton goods, it suffered mightily in the Blitz. The prewar population of the ward had been several thousand; after the war it was less than 50. The destruction was almost total, and this provided an opportunity for reconceiving urban life that otherwise would never have been possible. Alas, the opportunity turned into something far less than success, if not quite a total failure.

The opportunity before the Corporation after peace arrived in 1945 was to replace what had been mostly slum housing—conveniently and completely swept away by German bombs—with modern, salubrious, and what we now would term "affordable" accommodation. First built was the Golden Lane Estate, designed by Chamberlin, Powell and Bon, at the northern end of the site, straddling the border with Finsbury, whose residents were allocated some of the 554 flats. (The borough boundaries were later adjusted so that the estate now falls entirely within the City.) They were built to house "essential" workers like nurses, teachers, police officers, and bus conductors, and accordingly rents were set low. Before this, council estates—what now is somewhat euphemistically known as "social housing"—had generally been built solidly but in a rather Spartan mode; this estate epitomized mid-Century Modern design and style, both in the overall architecture and in the details within the flats. The first phase opened in 1957 and it was completed in 1962.

Was the project a success or a failure? Probably something between: the main defect of the resulting estate is that it is fairly ugly—but the flats themselves were well-furnished, spacious, and within easy walking distance of most workplaces in the City as well as necessary amenities like shops and the tube station. The goal was to recreate a self-contained village-like urban community, and accordingly at first there were a nursery, a post office, a bowling green, and a pub to serve as focal points. Those are mostly gone now: only the pub remains.

If you walk north, following the signs for the Barbican tube station, you will come in time to the bridge where we began our walk. From here, you can see the Golden Lane Estate ranged along the east side of the Goswell Road. The flats now have been partly privatized and values have risen steadily as the City has become again a "hot" residential destination. The estate today is a divided almost equally between owner-occupiers and the remaining "council" tenants paying below-market rents. (The Corporation, however, retains the freehold.) The estate as a whole looks somewhat down-at-heel (at the time of writing); it appears as if essential maintenance is being done, but not a great deal more. Close inspection of window frames—always a good indicator of the state of a property—shows peeling paint and some rotting timber. The larger public plazas don't seem to have taken hold as living community space—perhaps it is the bare concrete that turns people off, but they generally are empty and residents seem to walk around them rather than through them. One evening I encountered two middle-aged men in the center of one vast area, sitting on folding chairs, smoking and chatting. It was the only time I've ever seen the space used.

The Barbican Estate was more revolutionary still, at least in principle. It was designed to be rented at commercial rates and thus aimed not at essential workers, but higher up the social ladder at the middle and professional classes.

Discussions about the site began in 1952 and the project finally was authorized in 1957. It was to be a virtual city in miniature, with 2000 flats, as well as its own gardens, ponds, fire station, schools, shops, and a cultural complex. A key to its macro-design is that it was to be completely automobile-free. The several buildings (including three high-rise towers) were accessed and linked by the elevated pedestrian walkways we have traversed—the offspring of Le Corbusier's "streets in the sky." Below, surrounding the huge estate at ground level, new roadways were designed to speed traffic through City while residents' cars were banished to the parking garages located at the periphery. Moreover, the elevated pedestrian paths were intended to be linked into a comprehensive system of walkways, dubbed "pedways," running all throughout the City. Only isolated portions of the system of elevated paths actually were built; the Barbican's—including some of the bridges that span nearby London Wall—is the most complete. (Other pedway bridges that carry pedestrians over busy main arteries are found at several places along Lower and Upper Thames Street.)

Construction of the Barbican complex started in the late Sixties and took ten years to complete. Ironically, during those years the tide turned decisively against high-rise apartment buildings in England. There had been a veritable epidemic of high-rise construction by local councils in the Sixties, and unfortunately many (though not all) of the tower blocks were disasters from the start, poorly designed and shoddily built. A case in point: Ronan Point in Ilford actually collapsed in May 1968, only a few days after it opened; four residents died. (This evokes the spectre of the Grenfell Tower disaster, a horrific fire in June 2017; but that had less to do with the original construction than with the provision of faulty appliances and the addition of sub-standard exterior cladding.) By the time the Barbican was nearing completion, high rise had gone from representing the utopian future to exemplifying the worst of post-war urban redevelopment: in fact plans were already afoot to demolish some of the council-built towers that had gone up only twenty or thirty years before. (Now, ironically, in a complete reversal of taste, mega-towers like the Shard or One Blackfriars offer the most expensive new flats in the city. And, strange as it is, a few of the old council-built towers actually are being sold off to be converted to luxury housing.)

And so it was no surprise that the reception of the Barbican complex at first was not warm—many were shocked by the trademark "brutalist" raw concrete on show everywhere, nor did anyone warm to the long, sometimes dark and deserted, pedestrian ramps that were the only way to navigate it. By an accident of unfortunate timing, it was all a bit too reminiscent of Kubrick's 1971 dystopian film "Clockwork Orange" (though that was mainly shot on the Thamesmead estate) and hardly likely to make residents or visitors feel safe and secure. It soon became a bit shabby as well: it was all too easy for

City to let maintenance slide as all the occupants were renters and so had no real sense of ownership.

Thatcher-era reforms to encourage renters to become owners in theory didn't apply here because although the Barbican was owned by the Corporation it was not council housing. Nevertheless in time tenants did gain the right to purchase their flats (at a substantial discount) and the majority did so. At the same time, the Museum of London and the late-opening Barbican Arts Centre began drawing in visitors and generating substantially more pedestrian traffic. Ironically, rapidly rising prices for the flats and the ensuing gentrification finally have transformed the estate into something much closer to the urban oasis its planners long ago had envisioned.

Speaking of the Museum of London, which (as I write) is at the southwest corner of the estate, it is well worth a long visit. It is closed now and in several years it will reopen at a new site a few streets away in Smithfield Market, leaving a shell that may or may not be redeveloped into a concert hall and the home of the London Symphony Orchestra, dependent on whether or not £300M can be raised entirely from non-government sources to rebuild it. The museum exhibits in its present incarnation were organized chronologically, beginning with prehistory and ending pretty nearly at yesterday. I was particularly fond of the Roman section, in part set up as a stroll down a typical street in Londinium, featuring what would have been ordinary retail shops and workshops at the time. Also not to be missed was the dynamic diorama of the Great Fire. Whether these exhibits will be part of the new galleries remains to be seen.

Even though the Barbican overall is more trafficked now than it was at first, the walkways and plazas still at times (like most Sunday mornings) are bereft of pedestrian traffic. And despite no doubt sincere attempts to signpost the pathways that crisscross the complex, it still is absurdly difficult for a visitor to walk from one end to the other. Indeed, there are areas that seem to have one way in and no way out—the secret escape route often requiring climbing well-hidden stairs to a different level walkway. Despite this, it very much is worth the effort to visit—both to experience this flawed attempt at an urban utopia and to enjoy some of the pleasing surprises—like the Barbican lake, complete with waterfall. Even more strange is to come across the church of St Giles Cripplegate at the center of the complex. This is one of the few surviving authentically medieval London churches, dating mainly from around 1400, though like so many city churches, it was damaged in the Blitz and heavily restored.

This is perhaps a good moment to pop into the Barbican Arts Centre, a sprawling complex that has a modest external footprint but once you are inside seems almost endless, containing a theatre and an art gallery as well as cafes, restaurants, and shops. (When I was last there, the star attraction was a robot bartender that made mixed drinks on demand.) Though the design of the interior space sports a very spare modernist idiom, it has been thoroughly humanized, very much like the lobbies of the equally severely brutalist National Theatre, and the space seems to attract a great deal of traffic without ever feeling crowded.

Alas, today's walk allows for no very easy way to cover the whole of this neighbourhood unless you double back to the Barbican tube station, which is what I will ask you now to do. (Best of luck if you have got lost in the maze of pedways, but look out for the familiar bar and circle Underground logo signposted here, then follow it and you can't go far wrong.) But as you approach the bridge that leads to the Underground station, you may notice a rather forlorn monument that consists of a 500-year old beech tree stump. This is what remains of Felix Mendelssohn's tree, or so it is claimed to have been; once it stood in Burnham Beeches in Buckinghamshire, a remote green outpost of the City Corporation, under whose shade the composer supposedly worked during a visit to England. The tree blew over in a storm in 1990 and the stump was installed here in 2005. (A replacement tree was planted in the original location.)

Take the stairs down to the street level and begin walking to the east along Beech Street (at first submerged in a rather uninviting tunnel under the Barbican complex), and continue past the next road junction, called Whitecross Street to the north and Silk Street to the south—the latter a nod to the Huguenot refugees who settled here at the turn of the Eighteenth Century. (Fann Street, once home of Huguenot fan makers, is just to the north.)

For as much as the Barbican shouts mid-Century modern, Beech Street continues as Chiswell Street, a remarkable survivor of the Blitz in what was an otherwise completely bombed out corner of the City. On the north side is a row of well-restored and quite elegantly proportioned Georgian terrace houses; on the south side is the old Whitbread Brewery, including the original red brick building, with a stone plaque commemorating its dedication by George III and Queen Charlotte in 1787. (It seems that royals were required to promote commercial enterprises in the Eighteenth Century just as they are in the Twenty-First.) Beer was brewed on site for over two hundred years, finally ceasing in 1976. Together with later extensions, the brewery is now an event space attached to (what else?) a nearby luxury hotel. The street that runs south along the eastern end of the brewery complex was once Grub Street, which has given its name to struggling hack writers everywhere. One of its past residents was anything but a hack: here Milton wrote *Paradise Lost*, and in his honor, Grub Street now has been renamed. Further along still, on the north side, little Finsbury Street comes to a gated end at the far side of the grounds of the barracks of the Honorable Artillery Company, which traces its origins to 1537 and remains an active military unit in the Territorial Army—although thankfully it no longer engages in on-site gunnery practice.

As long as we're stretching our legs a bit now, backtrack to the intersection with Bunhill Row, and a few minutes' walk north will take you to the Bunhill Fields Burial Ground. This was the burial place of Nonconformists or Dissenters, so named for their refusal to accept the tenets and forms of worship of the Church of England, as required by the 1662 Act of Uniformity, including at first Puritans, Presbyterians, Baptists, Calvinists, Quakers, and Unitarians, and later Wesleyans, as well. They could not be interred in consecrated ground in City churchyards within the walls, so this site just outside the walls was as close as Nonconformists could get. It is estimated that this is the final resting place of over 100,000 Londoners; about 2000 headstones and monuments are extant. It holds the remains of John Bunyan, Daniel Defoe, Susannah Wesley, and William Blake, among many others. It is a pleasant enough hour spent to locate them all. (The burial ground now is owned and operated by the City, but it is surrounded by the Borough of Islington.)

Carry on eastward across the burial ground and you'll pass the windowless back wall of the Georgian headquarters of the Honorable Artillery Company. At the far eastern end, on the other side of the City Road, is Wesley's Chapel, another classic Georgian structure built to a design of George Dance the Elder and in continuous use as a house of worship since 1778. It now serves as part of the Museum of Methodism, another part of which is John Wesley's house, next door. The collection of Wesleyana inside numbers 15,000 objects, quite a few of which are on display. Entrance is free (though donations are encouraged).

Dance is in fact buried nearby, in the churchyard of St. Luke's, at the north end of Whitecross Street on the other side of the City Road. The quickest way to get there is to walk north on Bunhill Row (passing the well-hidden entry to Quaker Gardens, the surviving section of a burial ground in use from 1661 to 1855, though these days in rather sad condition) and then to turn left (west) on the City Road. The now deconsecrated St. Luke's Church is an impressive building with a unique spire in the form on an obelisk, probably the work of Nicholas Hawksmoor, though the overall design is attributed to John James. The building you see is all the more impressive in that it was a roofless ruin abandoned for some forty years until in the late Nineties it was taken over and renovated by the London Symphony Orchestra to serve as a rehearsal space, supplementary concert hall, and recording studio. This has taken us past the north end of Whitecross Street, once a thriving Sunday market—such markets for groceries were necessary even on the Sabbath in the days before refrigeration—that still operates during the lunch hour on Thursdays and Fridays.

One more time, retrace your steps back to the Barbican Underground station. Now it is time to explore the area south and west of the station, which has its own fascinations. First walk south on Aldersgate, past the traffic roundabout, to the late Eighteenth-Century St Botolph's, now home to the City Presbyterian Church, and behind it, Postman's Park. The rather plain late Georgian exterior of the church belies its grand interior. The park adjacent to it was created in 1880 from the burial ground of the church and expanded several times to incorporate other adjacent disused burial grounds; the old headstones line the periphery, as one often finds in old city churchyards converted to public recreational spaces. The park is near the General Post Office and it was intensively used by postal workers on lunch breaks—hence the popular sobriquet that soon became its official name.

The gem within this park is the Memorial to Heroic Self Sacrifice, a long loggia that covers a series of oversize ceramic tablets. The tablets memorialize ordinary people who lost their lives saving the lives of others. This was a project first put proposed by the painter, George Frederic Watts, for Victoria's Royal Jubilee in 1887, and revived by the vicar of St Botolph's in 1898. When it first opened, four tiles, designed and executed by the art potter, William De Morgan, were in place; Watts died in 1904, and his widow continued the work, but after 1906, as De Morgan had abandoned potting, Royal Doulton was enlisted to produce the tablets. The project stalled in 1931 with 53 of the 120 spaces filled, and it seemed almost certain never to be revived—until 2009, when it was revived successfully by the Diocese of London in honor of Leigh Pitt, who "saved a drowning boy from the canal at Thamesmead, but sadly was unable to save himself."

Exit the park and walk north again on Aldersgate, and in a few moments were are back at Barbican Underground station, where our walk began and now ends.

Chapter 6

Liverpool Street

Liverpool Street Station was the first purpose-built interchange between the new underground railway and a main line station, designed from the outset to serve both as a station on the Metropolitan and as the London terminus of the Great Eastern Railway. But the work progressed unequally and almost predictably, the two parts were completed and opened several months apart. Also, unusually, the main area of the station—which like most of the main line station halls now is a shopping mall—is below street level. The station might well have been named Bishopsgate, as it fronts that busy thoroughfare which is far more trafficked than the little street after which it is named.

The Great Eastern Railway, serving East Anglia and the intervening suburbs, had reached London back in 1840 with its first terminus out in Shoreditch. But management's goal was to get as close to the city center as possible, and in 1847 toward that end the Great Eastern built a station closer to the City boundary on Bishopsgate. However, even that wasn't quite good enough, and so in1874 on a site even further west they built the present station. Happily, this coincided with the Metropolitan Railway's construction of its next eastward stage, and the two companies worked together to create a simple underground-main line interchange. Initially, there appeared to be more station than traffic, but that soon changed when the station became the entry point for the principal service to Cambridge, and by the turn of the next century Liverpool Street was reckoned to be one of the busiest stations in all of Europe. Since it is also now a stop on the new Elizabeth Line, it should get busier still.

A quick exit to the south from what technically is the front of the station (though it feels like a side door) will take you to Liverpool Street. (By the way, there's no connection between this street and the city of the same name; it was named to honor Lord Liverpool, Prime Minister from 1812 to 1827.) This land originally was the site of the Bethlehem Hospital, a.k.a. Bethlem and more commonly known as Bedlam, which eventually moved south of the river (and whose large utilitarian Georgian building now houses the Imperial

War Museum). Liverpool Street was then and is still a bit of a backwater, mostly used by taxis setting down and picking up rail passengers. It has somehow managed to retain amongst outlets of the usual retail chains a number of independent shops, like a newsagent, a cobbler, and a hair salon.

Liverpool Street does have one indubitable claim to fame—it was at number 46 that *The Communist Manifesto* was first published in February 1848. And it is home to the *Kindertransport* memorial sculpture, the work of Frank Meisler, himself one of the Jewish children sent from Central Europe to England just before the start of the Second World War. Over 10,000 unaccompanied small children arrived in London, virtually all of whom otherwise would have perished in the Holocaust.

One other local curiosity not to be missed is the Metropolitan Arcade, dating from 1912, and connecting Liverpool Street with Old Broad Street. This pleasant covered byway was for many years home to an interesting mix of shops and small restaurants. Owned by TfL, it was saved from demolition in the early Nineties and then sensitively rebuilt, but curiously it is not a listed building and thus it still is a likely candidate for redevelopment. For now, it is being operated as a food court.

At the bottom of Old Broad Street is Wormwood Street, and sitting atop a pedestrian bridge across it is an unusual sight that looks like the result of a tornado but in fact is a sculptural installation by Korean architect Do Ho Suh. As the official web site states, "The piece is a to-scale replica of the traditional Hanok-style Korean house adorned with a bamboo garden, that appears to have 'fallen' onto the bridge at an angle." The tableau of a house that's fallen from the sky onto a pedestrian bridge seems not to phase the average Londoner at all; most passers-by seemingly ignore it, as if that sort of thing happens every day.

Retrace your steps on Old Broad Street back to Liverpool Street, and turn right (or east) which in a moment will land you on Bishopsgate, which probably is one of the busiest places on earth. The street dates back to Roman times and takes its name from the medieval gate that was demolished in 1760; the surrounding Bishopsgate Ward is one of the largest and least populated districts in the City. The road years ago was lined with coaching inns, long gone, but it remains (as the A10) one of the major vehicular access routes to points north. This is the far eastern corner of the City itself, the boundary in places marked by those rather striking sculptures of a winged dragon bearing the City's coat of arms. A boundary marker is hardly necessary: the transition from the pavements that belong to the Corporation to those that are part of Tower Hamlets is immediately visible—the retail at street level instantly moves down market and the road traffic increases dramatically. But let us first walk south on Bishopsgate and almost at once we are at Heron Tower, the nearest of the cluster high rise buildings that today give this small corner of the City its distinctive and very dramatic character.

For the eastern end of the City nowadays is the nexus of striking changes to the London skyline. It is increasingly difficult to remember that until the 1980s, London was a very low-rise city, with rigid height restrictions enforced by the 1894 London Building Act. That law was in large part a response to the building of the fourteen-story Queen Anne's Mansions in Petty France, which supposedly had partly blocked Queen Victoria's view of the Houses of Parliament from Buckingham Palace. That legislation imposed a height limit of 80' in central London and, in doing so, preserved and privileged the visibility of the Houses of Parliament and St Paul's. Later, there were exceptions in other parts of London—for example, Shell Mex House at 80 Strand and Senate House tucked neatly behind the British Museum in Bloomsbury—but Westminster and the City itself remained remarkably low-rise well into the last century.

That changed in 1980 with the opening of the NatWest Tower (now called Tower 42) at 25 Old Broad Street, then the tallest building in Europe. For years it was the dominant, indeed the only, true "skyscraper" in the City. Controversial in its day, and now sold off and in redevelopment (a delayed consequence of the 2008–2009 banking crisis), it has since been joined and eclipsed by the Heron Tower (whose official name is 110 Bishopsgate), the Gherkin (sometimes prefixed "Erotic"), the Cheesegrater, the Walkie Talkie, and, just across the river, the Shard—not to mention several other giants further east in Canary Wharf. And several other projects over 600' in height have been given planning permission (though not all have broken ground and after Brexit and the pandemic some may never rise), including 1 Undershaft, which will top out at nearly 1000'. (We'll come back to the Gherkin presently.)

Views of principal historic monuments now in fact are protected by the Corporation's planning guidelines; indeed, the distinctive tapered shape of the Cheesegrater (122 Leadenhall) derives from an effort to preserve unsullied views of St Paul's from faraway Fleet Street. The City certainly does not come close to the density of high-rise buildings that gives such a dizzying quality to the cityscapes of New York and Shanghai, but there is no question but that the last forty years of construction have changed the pedestrian experience. When one stands at the bottom of St Mary at Hill, a quiet, stone-paved lane with a part-medieval Church, and looks up to the massive, looming facade of the Walkie Talkie, it is like viewing a fold in the fabric of space and time, one that collapses a thousand years into a single electrifying prospect.

Not far off is 20 Fenchurch Street, a.k.a. the Walkie Talkie, a mid-rise building that has a free rooftop garden (yes, *free*, though booking a timed ticket via the web site is necessary), generally open during regular business hours on weekdays and occasionally at weekends as well. The space is a rather futuristic interpretation of a "garden" but what you are here for are not the plants but the views. Panoramas open in all directions, including down river past Tower Bridge and the Tower all the way to the hill that houses the Royal Observatory in Greenwich. The rooftop also offers an unusual perspective on some of the taller nearby high-rise buildings.

Nearby is Houndsditch, a short bit of road that runs southeast from Bishopsgate to St Botolph Street behind Aldgate tube station; it terminates as a pedestrian alley behind the Heron Tower—at 230m presently the tallest building in the City itself, though only the third-tallest in London. Its exterior is difficult to see whole unless you get some distance away on Bishopsgate; its repeating diagonal struts have the look of a clever child's Meccano or Erector Set project expanded to monumental size. The lobby has a surprise of its own, a 70,000 litre aquarium, reputedly the largest private aquarium in England and said to be home to some 1200 fish.

Houndsditch is a fairly heavily trafficked one-way street, unremarkable now save for its name, with which it has been graced since at least 1275. No one is really certain how it attracted its canine association. It was perhaps as early as Roman times a broad ditch immediately outside the city walls and already then a favored spot for dumping rubbish, no doubt including dead dogs. Then again, it may just have been a place frequented by local pups; or, even more prosaically, a ditch belonging to an Anglo-Saxon named Hund. (A couple of possibly Roman canine skeletons were excavated nearby in 1989, but that hardly settles the matter.) By 1600, it was already completely filled in and the site of several bell foundries; later, when the Great Fire-induced demand for church bells faded, it was home to several cannon foundries; and eventually it became a center of the cheap clothing trade. By the early years of the last century, when the East End hosted a large Jewish population, 133 Houndsditch was the site of the Houndsditch Warehouse, a huge department store sometimes called the Selfridges of the Jewish Quarter, and uniquely among large shops open on Sundays, though strictly speaking that was illegal.

Here too in December 1910 the burglary of a jewelry shop by a gang of Latvian anarchists went very wrong: three police constables were killed, and a few weeks later, two members of the gang were cornered and died in what became known as the "Siege of Sydney Street." Thanks to the nascent newsreel industry, this was the first police siege to be captured on film, some of which features the current Home Secretary, none other than Winston Churchill. (All but one of the gang members were tried and acquitted, and the one conviction was overturned on appeal.) No trace of the Jewish Selfridges or the burgled jeweler remain, nor of the clothing and "novelty" shops that once lined the street; today it's mostly given over to offices and eateries, including the usual ubiquitous chain restaurants.

Stroll back northward on Bishopsgate and just past the station is One Fleet Place, a hideous office complex in the postmodern style. But directly across the road from it is the impressive facade of the Bishopsgate Institute, a registered charity that was established in 1895 to provide a public library and educational opportunities for residents of and workers in the City—all of which it continues to do quite actively. The building is the work of Charles Harrison Townsend, who also designed the nearby Whitechapel Art Gallery and the Horniman Museum in far-off South London. These three comprise all of his major commissions, and architectural historians have puzzled about what architectural style best describes them, Art Nouveau or Arts and Crafts. Neither, in truth, as he was a true original: the three buildings display a genuinely unique idiom, massive and yet light at the same time, that marks them all as the work of one hand and quite unlike any other contemporaneous designs.

We are now about to enter Spitalfields, the name a corruption of St Mary Spital, a medieval hospital (in other words, a lodging place for travelers). The area remained relatively undeveloped after the Dissolution, given over to small farms and market gardens. Eventually in the late Seventeenth Century it was built over to accommodate an influx of Huguenot immigrants, French Protestants who fled France after the revocation of the Edict of Nantes in 1685 (that decree previously had guaranteed them freedom of worship). By 1687, it was estimated that some 13,000 French emigres were living in Spitalfields and the surrounding parishes, and by 1700 perhaps as many as 25,000—but more of them presently.

We will cross the road and turn east on Brushfield Street. The street opens up into a large open space, Bishop's Square, owned by JP Morgan Chase and one of the largest "POPS" (Privately Owned Public Spaces) in London. The walkways and open plazas appear to be city streets like any others but they are in fact private property. POPS are more or less exactly what the name implies—spaces open to the public (often as parks or plazas) that *look* very much as if they are public parks, but are not. Developed first in New York in the Sixties, POPS are the result of tradeoffs that give developers something they want (more buildable square footage, improved access to the site, greater height) in return for creating what are in effect semi-public amenities, though often with private security overseeing them and sometimes weighed down by arbitrary rules and regulations. Canary Wharf is the largest of them and yet the entire neighbourhood now looks like and is experienced by users as typical public urban space—although if one looks carefully, one can find discrete signs here and there announcing that all visitors in fact are guests on private property.

This new office/retail project captured much of what had been the vast Old Spitalfields Market: only the eastern end of the original market buildings remains. Remarkably, Spitalfields and the surrounding area continue as a center of street market activity—hosting the Brick Lane, Petticoat Lane (Middlesex Street), Cheshire Street, and Columbia Road markets, all a short walk from where we stand.

Indeed, it's worth digressing for a moment to consider how very important markets have been to London's identity and to acknowledge the significant role they still play in the everyday life of the city. The first established probably was in Roman Londinium and may have been located near the site of present-day Leadenhall Market. When the City was resettled by the Saxons in the Ninth Century, markets must quickly have revived, and by the time of the Conquest several were thriving. There were, as yet, no dedicated retail spaces in London, and so markets served simultaneously as transportation depots, warehouses, and retail outlets. Some street names in the City still reflect *quondam* specialized markets—Bread Street, Honey Lane, Milk Street, and etc. (There is an exception to the rule: Leather Lane has no relation to animal hides but derives from the name of a local merchant, Le Vrunelane.)

By the early Eighteenth Century, shops had developed into something very much like their current form, and many of the street markets transformed themselves into places to serve the working poor, selling food and useful everyday items like candles and clothing. A select few became more specialized wholesale markets (Billingsgate for fish, Covent Garden for produce, Smithfield for meat, etc.). But in the middle decades of the Nineteenth Century, street markets began to be seen as impediments to traffic and thus dangerous impediments to progress. Some markets were "improved" out of existence by being closed entirely (like the Fleet Market) and others were moved into purpose-built and strictly regulated premises (Spitalfields, Covent Garden, and Leadenhall among them). It seems quite ironic that many of those buildings, no longer able to sustain their supposed market function, have become luxury retail shopping centers in the last 30 years or so, most focused more on tourists than local residents. Despite the transformation of some markets into high end retail malls, a few general markets located in lower-income neighbourhoods have survived and against the odds are flourishing, including Brick Lane, Deptford, and Walthamstow (said to be the longest street market in Europe). Despite the explosive growth and sirenic allure of on-line shopping, it seems many of us still crave the social dimension of shopping—the interaction with sellers, the ability to see and handle what we buy before we pay for it, the opportunity to haggle over price, and just the sheer pleasure of walking through the city, experiencing its sights, sounds, and smells. This is a mode of shopping as a form of community, as intensely social as online shopping is intensely solitary.

The new Spitalfields market building of 1887 that housed the vast wholesale fruit and vegetable traders was the work of the City Corporation. In

1991when the produce trade was moved to "New Spitalfields" in Leyton (the name trumping geography), this site was made available for commercial development. The market-like precinct that was built alas is devoted to high end retail and restaurants indistinguishable from any other shopping district in Central London. (One curious note: the excavations for the market redevelopment in the 1990s exposed a Roman cemetery and a lead sarcophagus that held the very first remains conclusively identified as those of a resident of Londinium, a young woman buried around AD 350.) What is left of the market hall, its eastern end, is open every day, generally selling crafts, clothing, and tourist souvenirs, but on Thursdays it is devoted to antiques. Foster + Partners were retained very recently to redesign the market stalls themselves, at the same time reducing even further the floor space available to sellers. More of the space is given over to stalls selling various ethnic foods and to seating for its consumption—in my view a sad loss.

Commercial Street, the eastern boundary of the market building, was the heart of Huguenot Spitalfields. Among the French residents were a number of master silk weavers, who occupied large terrace houses with huge windows on the upper stories to provide as much light as possible for their intricate work on the looms. The district's standing as the center of the silk trade was enhanced further by the arrival of Irish weavers in the 1730s. But the heyday of the silk weavers was short-lived, and from the middle of the Eighteenth Century to the middle of the Nineteenth, the trade suffered periodic crises (for example, when demand fell after the importation of cheaper calicos from India) and the neighbourhood began its slow, steady, inexorable decline. Jewish immigrants from central and Eastern Europe came next to Spitalfields, the large windows of the terrace houses as useful to tailors as they had been to weavers, and the area become the center of notoriously exploitative piecework clothing manufacture. By the time the district was made infamous as the site of the Ripper murders in the 1880s, it was one of the most overcrowded and worst slums in London. (Jack London's *People of the Abyss* [1903] provides a gripping account of contemporary life in Spitalfields.)

The most striking sight as one gazes across Commercial Street is Hawksmoor's masterpiece, Christ Church Spitalfields. This was one of the fifty "Commissioners" churches, so called from a 1710 Act of Parliament establishing a Commission for Building Fifty New Churches to accommodate London's growing population and its increasing spread outside the old city walls. (Only twelve of the projected fifty were ever built.) Spitalfields was just such a site, with its growing community of Huguenot silk weavers who, though Protestant, so far had ignored the Church of England by establishing their own houses of worship. Christ Church thus was not only intended to provide adequate seating in a Church of England church, but also to revive the authority of the state church in this very French emigrant community.

The church tower is a bold and unmistakable statement, fully 202' tall, and it can be seen from a considerable distance. The church, much altered by the Victorians, by the Sixties was empty and almost completely derelict, but gradually it has been restored to something close to its original grandeur. The interior now sparkles, as does the original and fully restored organ. The most recent renovations were to the crypt, completed in 2015, creating a delightful and capacious café that seems never to be crowded, despite its proximity to the heavily trafficked nearby market and shops above ground.

Turning north on Commercial Street, as we approach Folgate Street, the prow of a triangular shaped brick building comes into view. This characteristically Victorian block of flats looks quite ordinary, but it was revolutionary in its day. This was the first development built by the Peabody Trust, which had been founded in 1862 with a huge gift of £150,000 by George Peabody, an American-born banker who was determined to better the living conditions of London's working poor. He helped pioneer the provision of modern, clean, and affordable working-class housing; this building, opened in 1864, was the first fruit of that effort. Though this particular block of flats now is owned privately, the Peabody Trust continues to support its original mission, managing 27,000 properties that collectively house 80,000 people. (We'll encounter a monument to Peabody presently at the Royal Exchange.)

Turning left on Folgate Street leads us to number 18, the Dennis Severs House—surely one of the oddest of the legion of small museums in London. Severs was an American who in 1978 moved to this Georgian terrace house in what then was a thoroughly down-at-heels corner of a down-at-heels neighbourhood slowly being discovered by artists. (Gilbert and George had moved nearby about ten years before.) Severs restored the house, room by room, and as he did, he furnished each room as if it were in a particular historical moment and looking as if it had just a moment ago been abandoned by its residents. The house purports to tell the story of one Huguenot family, the Jervises (anglicized from Gervais) from 1725 to 1919. When Severs died in 1999, he left the house and contents to the Spitalfields Historic Buildings Trust, who maintain and operate it. If it is closed when you pass by (and it is open only very limited hours), check out their web site to get a good sense of what lies inside.

Retrace your steps on Folgate and Commercial Streets to Fournier Street, which runs east from Commercial Street along the north side of Christ Church. This street hosts many of the grandest houses once occupied by the master silk weavers, all with extra large windows on the upper stories. A detour to any of the adjoining streets reveals rows of charming Eighteenth-Century terrace houses that suggest why Spitalfields has been transformed from a slum to a very desirable residential district. Ironically, these terraces survived largely intact only because for so much of the Twentieth Century the district was so impoverished that no one thought there was any profit to be made by pulling them down to build on the same sites. The narrative of the successive waves of immigrants here—first Protestant Huguenots, then Irish weavers, followed by Eastern European Jews, and lastly Muslim Bangladeshis—is a familiar one, but one quite literally etched in stone. At very the end of the street is a rather severe Georgian brick building, now the Great London Mosque, but in its time a Christian church and latterly a Jewish synagogue.

Fournier Street ends at Brick Lane, still the heart of London's large Bangladeshi community (and note that many street signs are in English and Bengali). Sometimes called Banglatown, Brick Lane sensibly once was known as Whitechapel Lane until the area became a center of brickmaking. Appropriately enough, it terminates (though under the name Osborn Street) at Whitechapel High Street. It has long been associated with the first curry houses in London, and it still is full of Bengali restaurants, most of them now catering to the tourist trade. Bengal was one of the hives of economic activity in British-ruled India, and many young men from the Sylhet region worked in the ports and on merchant vessels, where they were known as Lascars (an Urdu word meaning soldier). Among them were cooks, who after they came ashore in London naturally enough continued doing what they knew best in a district not far from the docks. (Until the passage of the Commonwealth Immigrants Act in 1963, all commonwealth subjects had the unrestricted right of settlement in the U.K.) But one wonders for how much longer—the street displays incipient signs of gentrification, housing a few trendy night clubs and even a coffee bar or two. The area and surrounding streets also have become a well-known locus for graffiti art (some by the now world famous Banksy), and there are already a few proper art galleries at the northern end of the lane.

We will continue walking south to Whitechapel Lane. Across the road and to the east is Altab Ali Park, named after a young Bangladeshi man who was the victim of a notorious racist murder in 1978. The park once was the site of the chapel dedicated to St Mary for whom the neighbourhood is named, though little of it remains after its destruction in the blitz. Walk a short distance to the east (noting that we stand here on a broad, straight Roman road) to what once was the home of the Whitechapel Bell Foundry. This firm was founded in 1570, give or take a few years, though it settled into these premises only in the Eighteenth Century. One of its earliest products, a bell dating from 1588, still rings in the tower of St Clement Danes in the Strand. Astonishingly, bells were cast here until the foundry closed in 2016. The two most famous of its products—possibly the two most famous bells in the world—are the Liberty Bell in Philadelphia and Big Ben in the Palace of Westminster. (The name "Ben" properly attaches to the bell itself and not the clockworks or the tower.) By an odd coincidence both bells developed cracks soon after installation. At present, the site is owned by an American firm that is planning to make public some parts of the site but also intends to build a hotel here; the attempt by a group of London artists including Anthony Gormley and other celebrities to turn it back into a working foundry and heritage site seems to have failed. The premises are Grade II listed—meaning the exterior cannot be altered—but the interior can. It looks to be many years before its fate is settled.

Turn 180 degrees and retrace your steps past the Aldgate East tube station and you will have come to the Whitechapel Art Gallery, another of the small group of fascinating buildings designed by Charles Harrison Townsend. The gallery itself was founded in 1901 (of which more in a moment). The eastern half of the present complex was for many years a public library—a conventional Victorian brick building in Dutch revival style. The ground floor also incorporates the entrance to the Underground station. This was one of the many libraries, fountains, and other buildings given to the working poor of London by John Passmore Evans, a newspaper magnate and Liberal MP. The library closed in 2005 and it has been sensitively redeveloped as additional gallery space for the Whitechapel Art Gallery next door.

The main gallery exists only because of the heroic efforts of Canon Samuel Barnett and his wife Henrietta, who together had founded nearby the first University settlement house, Toynbee Hall, in 1884. The original building, Toynbee Hall, named after a recently deceased friend of the couple, is just around the corner—we shall see it in a moment. It was called a "settlement" house because it aimed to settle young, altruistic university graduates in working-class districts, both to teach in the community and to learn about the dire conditions in which residents lived and worked. Their effort was an offshoot of the transatlantic broad "Christian Socialism" movement to improve the lot of the urban working classes, many of whom in both London and large cities in the U.S. were recent immigrants. Part of this broader project was a desire to bring culture to the working classes—hence the Whitechapel Art Gallery. Its exhibitions from the start featured contemporary art, and it is now devoted to very contemporary, cutting-edge work.

Just ahead is Aldgate tube station (not to be confused with Aldgate East), opened in 1876 as the Metropolitan Railway inched slowly toward Tower Hill. It was meant to serve commuters from both nearby main line stations, Broad Street and Fenchurch Street, which accounts for its generous proportions. The original train shed survives, but it is hidden now behind a tile façade dating from 1926. The name mistakenly suggests an origin as the "Old" gate in the city walls, but more probably it was the Aelgate, Old English for the gate near where it was possible to buy ale. (The "d" is intrusive.)

Just around the corner at 52 Old Castle Street is the original building of Toynbee Hall, a good example of late Victorian "Tudorbethan" style with some design elements looking forward to the Arts and Crafts movement.

Aldgate also sports one of those rather impressively fierce City boundary markers in the form of a large sculpted dragon rampant. There are 13 of these beasts standing guard, in a few different sizes, all sited at principal routes into and out of the City, and many corresponding to the location of the ancient gates. The first two dragons were on display outside the old Coal Exchange, demolished in the early Sixties; though the building disappeared, the dragons were saved, and in 1963 they were mounted on plinths on the Victoria Embankment near Temple Gardens to mark the western City boundary line (and where they still stand). The Corporation found the design attractive, and so additional half-size replicas were produced and then installed on other major roadways at the city boundary. Why dragons, you may ask. The connection seems to be via St George, whose shield with a red cross resembles the City's coat of arms. Unlike the dragon that saintly George encountered and slew, the City's beasts seem very alive and well. (One of the dragons, however, is no longer in London: it has traveled all the way to Lake Havasu, Arizona, where it graces the reconstructed London Bridge.)

At the foot of this dragon, we will turn north on Middlesex Street, undistinguished six days a week but a star attraction on the seventh as Petticoat Lane. That actually once was its official name, changed in 1846, presumably to avoid any hint of impropriety. There has been a market here since time immemorial, but by the late Nineteenth Century it was dominated by Jewish merchants selling clothing. Ancient though it was, it had no official charter or sanction, and periodically there were attempts to shut it down, all of which happily failed. Finally, in 1936, it was authorized by an act of Parliament and its standing as a Sunday market officially confirmed. Though the London Jewish community moved away to the suburbs many decades ago, the Sunday market yet thrives, extending to over 1000 stalls on a good day. Nothing sold here these days is unique to the market, but haggling is still *de rigueur*. There is plenty of cheap clothing and also bric-a-brac (mostly junk, but you never know). Even though the surrounding neighbourhood has begun to gentrify, the market seems little changed from when I first visited in the Seventies. Whitechapel back then still had many Jewish businesses, and the attraction for me at the time was Bloom's delicatessen on Whitechapel High Street. There one could find hot salt beef (the closest thing to New York corned beef available) and decent enough fresh-baked bagels. Bloom's closed in 1996, though the branch in Golders Green held on until 2010.

Middlesex Street curls north and east back to Bishopsgate, more or less where we first surfaced at Liverpool Street Station, but we will turn left onto St Botolph's Street, which turns into Duke's Place, which turns into Bevis Marks, one of the odder London street names. (It is a corruption of Bury Marks, i.e. the boundary that marks the land owned by the Abbot of Bury St Edmond.) A narrow turning, Heneage Lane, leads to the Bevis Marks

Synagogue, founded in 1701—London's oldest surviving place of Jewish worship and still very much in use. It is open to the public very limited hours, and if you are fortunate enough to visit then, you will find a stunning interior in late baroque style that looks remarkably like the inside of a Wren church.

Now we are within the shadow of 30 St Mary Axe, a.k.a. the Gherkin. The building sits atop what was once the Baltic Exchange, which had been erected in grand neo-classical style that announced the importance of the owner, an entity that brokered and regulated freight movement at sea. It was nearly completely destroyed by an IRA bomb in 1992. Plans at first called for the façade to be restored, but damage was far greater than originally thought, and in 1998 English Heritage gave up the fight to save it. (The remnants that had been salvaged have ended up in, of all places, Tallinn, Estonia, where bizarre plans to recreate the original building appear to have stalled.) The cucumber-shaped building that replaced it is reckoned to be one of Norman Foster's masterpieces. It was at first called the Swiss Re tower, built to house that giant reinsurance firm, and later sold by them for a huge profit. After changing hands several more times, it is now owned by the Brazilian Safra Group. The name of the street derives from the medieval church of St Mary Axe, demolished in the 1560s; the eponymous axe, according to one legend, was used by Attila the Hun to murder St Ursula and 11,000 virgins, or, less dramatically, it alludes to the workaday axes used by the Worshipful Company of Skinners who were patrons of the church, or less dramatically still, it echoes the sign of a tavern nearby.

Turn down Bury Street and crane your neck to see the top of the pickle. But don't forget to look down where amongst the stone benches you will see a memorial to an unnamed teenaged girl who died in late Roman London and whose tomb was unearthed in 1995 as the site was being excavated; she was reburied beneath it in 2007. Walk round the south end onto Undershaft, and then take a narrow alley on the right, Great St Helens, past the church of that name, one of the largest parish churches within the City boundaries. Remarkably, St Helens survived both the Great Fire and the Blitz, only to suffer serious damage from IRA bombs in the Nineties. It has been fully restored, though some of the monuments were completely destroyed. Shakespeare was among its congregants in the 1590s when he lodged nearby. It is still very much in use, with several other parishes having been consolidated here and making its formal name a bit of a tongue twister: "St Helen's Bishopsgate with St Andrew Undershaft and St Ethelburga Bishopsgate and St Martin Outwich and St Mary Axe."

Continue past the church on Great St Helens and you will emerge onto the southern end of Bishopsgate. Just to the north is another medieval church, St Ethelburga's, which also managed to survive the Fire and the Blitz, only to be nearly completely destroyed by an IRA bomb in 1993. It has since been rebuilt (though little of the original fabric remains) and it now is the home of the Centre for Reconciliation and Peace, rather a noble response to its prior devastation. Among its famous congregants was Henry Hudson, who with his crew took communion here before setting off to fail to discover the Northwest Passage to China.

Across the road is the impressive façade of St Botolph's-without-Bishopsgate, site of a medieval church that lay just outside the city walls at the Bishop's Gate. This is the second St Botolph's Church we've encountered, and in fact there were churches of that name at every city gate as Botolph is the patron saint of travelers. The original church survived the Great Fire, but by the 1720s it was decrepit enough to necessitate it being taken down and replaced by the present structure. The structure is a good example of construction cost-shaving: the side facing Bishopsgate is faced with stone but the rest of the exterior is humble brick. The interior is more impressive, and note especially the font, where both Mary Wollstonecraft and John Keats were baptized. The churchyard is fairly large for a City church, and in it is the elegant late Georgian church hall that once housed a school; set into bays on the front exterior wall there are charming statues of boy and girl pupils. Alas, they are replicas, the originals now stored inside to keep them safe from vandals. Just a few yards further west is another interesting curiosity, the colorful, tiled entrance to what once were elaborate subterranean Turkish baths, opened in 1895 by James Forder Neville, who was something of a London Turkish bath mogul. The baths closed in 1954 and the premises at present are used as an event space.

Just ahead on Bishopsgate, you will see our starting point, Liverpool Street Station. And it is time to re-enter the Underground and press on to Tower Hill.

Chapter 7

Tower Hill

Tower Hill Station is a bit of a mess. Well, to be honest, that's a considerable understatement—it is a complete mess, and since the present station opened in 1967, it is mostly hidden below ground. Challenging to navigate though it be, it still moves tens of thousands of tourists in and out of the Tower precincts every day—some 22,000,000 users a year, most of whom are there to visit or at least look at the Tower, one of the most visited tourist attractions in London. It is also tantalizingly near to the Docklands Light Railway Tower Gateway Station—tantalizing because there is no direct interchange and it is not all that easy to walk from one to the other. It is also only a short walk from the main line station at Fenchurch Street, which serves commuter lines in the Thames estuary.

The Tower itself stands at what was the southeastern corner of Roman London, and indeed, in Trinity Square, just outside the main tube station entrance, there is on display a sizable section of the Roman city wall. Directly across the road, at the edge of the Tower moat, you can see ruins of the foundations of a medieval gatehouse. And just to the north, in Cooper's Row, is yet another impressive section of wall, the medieval stonework clearly visible atop the distinctive tile-like bricks of the Roman foundations.

Cross the very busy road to approach the Tower, and let us for now admire it from the outside—we won't enter at present, as it requires several hours for a proper visit. (The plaza surrounding it is almost always crowded with other lookers, many no doubt deterred by the £30 admission charge.) Until recently, here you might well have seen a vintage No. 15 bus go by. This so-called "heritage" route featured several refurbished 1950s Routemaster buses that retained their open backs, allowing seasoned travelers to hop on and off, even when the bus is moving. I never could resist jumping on and off the old Routemaster buses whenever I caught one, even though the practice is said to be dangerous enough to have been a major cause of injury a generation ago. Sadly, the heritage bus project was discontinued in November 2020, an early casualty of the Covid pandemic.

Riding these old buses always called up my memories of one of my very first journeys on a London bus in the Spring of 1973. I had taken the tube to American Express to cash a traveler's cheque, a necessary ritual in the days before ATMs, and afterward I boarded a bus to return to my lodging (which if memory serves, was a bed & breakfast, a.k.a. B&B, for which I believe I paid the princely sum of £1.35 a night). When the conductor came around, I had only a crisp new one pound note to offer him. He shook his head and said, "I can't make change for that, mate." He took the note and promised to return with change once he'd collected more fares, which he did, just in time before I reached my destination. That bus was a Routemaster, too, but there were still in those days aa few pre-war RT-series buses in service, as well, the last of them finally retired in 1979, when two-man buses were discontinued in the name of efficiency. The Routemaster was in production from 1956 to 1968, and once upon a time nearly 3,000 of them roamed London's streets. They served as the inspiration for one of (then) Mayor Boris Johnson's pet projects, the Thomas Heatherwick-designed New Routemaster double-deckers that debuted in 2011. They were at first, like the originals, two-man buses, but the conductors were a luxury axed back in 2016, and a year later Johnson's successor as mayor, Sadiq Khan, cancelled future purchases as the buses were simply too expensive. (They also roasted their passengers in the summer—the air conditioning system never worked properly—and they spewed too many pollutants.)

As for the Tower itself, what can one say that has not been said? Its construction started almost immediately after the Norman Conquest and for many years it was the tallest building in the City, whose primary function was to control London's unruly inhabitants rather than to protect the city from invaders. What is most remarkable is not only how well preserved it is—the White Tower is the oldest complete building in London—but that it has been preserved at all. The temptation to sell off parts or even all of such a huge site—12 acres—so centrally located at times must have been nearly irresistible. But resist temptation the Crown and the government did, and by so doing they preserved one of the city's treasured heritage sites and a huge tourist magnet, with nearly 3,000,000 visitors a year before the pandemic. (That's about 8,000 a day.)

The large pedestrian plaza outside the Tower entrance is a complex of shops, ticket halls, restaurants, and open spaces designed to contain, distract, and generate revenue from the visitors that flock to the Tower, day and night, every day of the year. Don't be put off by the merchandising mania, and press through to the plaza's western end to visit All Hallows by the Tower, which claims to be (and may well be) the oldest surviving church in London. Despite its proximity to the Tower, it offers visitors a remarkably quiet and relaxing contrast to the hustle and bustle around it; oddly enough, given its location and the crowds outside, it is often nearly deserted inside and even its small garden is often empty. If you wander in, you will find treasures that include a well-preserved Roman pavement and an early Saxon archway. The church boasts a few American connections: here William Penn (who founded the Pennsylvania colony) was baptized and John Quincy Adams (the sixth U.S. President) was married. (His father, John Adams, was at the time ambassador to Great Britain.) Penn's father we shall encounter again presently.

Retrace your steps and walk east past the Tower, and you will see directly across the road, tucked away near the Tower Gateway DLR station, the entrance to Royal Mint Court and the inelegantly named Johnson Smirke Building. This site was once a Cistercian abbey, sold off in 1538 at the time of the Dissolution. The buyer died not long afterward and in 1560 the Crown bought it back. It served various workaday royal functions until when in 1806 it was designated as the site of the Royal Mint. The severely neo-classical structure of the present building was designed by James Johnson, who died and was replaced by Robert Smirke—hence the building's compound name. The mint left these premises in 1967 and site was partly redeveloped into a slapdash office block. The office leases now have fallen in and the site is being redeveloped yet again. If you push on to the north, the back side of the mint is Royal Mint Street, which continues further east into Wapping as Cable Street—the site of a "battle" in 1936 to which we will talk about presently.

You now should by now have seen a sign welcoming you to the London borough of Tower Hamlets, and you've now crossed a very meaningful border. The name "Tower Hamlets" has legitimate medieval roots, but it fell out of use for a few hundred years until it was revived in 1965 in an effort to create a common identity for the new large London borough that was being created by the merger of the old boroughs of Bethnal Green, Poplar, and Stepney. Together they comprised the heart of an extended district that in Victorian times had become notorious as the "East End," for more than 100 years synonymous with extreme poverty, crime, ill health, and overcrowded sub-standard housing.

The roads from the Tower to the north and east leading in and out of Tower Hamlets are not easy to cross—the traffic is very heavy, as the intersection joins a major feeder road into Central London from the east and to the south connects with the approach to Tower Bridge—and the layout and timing of the traffic lights favor vehicles over pedestrians. It is difficult not to read this as a not very well coded message—if you, a visitor to the Tower, should think to walk this way, *don't*.

And yet, though no tourist unbidden is likely to take this short journey, it is worth a moment's pause to consider the somewhat puzzling persistence of historic inequities in Tower Hamlets. Though the worst slums of the old East End are long gone, the borough remains one of London's poorest local authorities: it ranks not only as one of the most deprived boroughs in London but in several respects it is one of the most disadvantaged local authority areas in all of England. Despite its location at the heart of one of the wealthiest metropolitan areas in the world, 39% of children and 50% of older people here are considered "income-deprived" (current bureaucratic double-speak for "poor"). On this measure, it has one of the lowest average incomes of all local authorities in England and it suffers from one of the highest unemployment rates. As if this were not enough bad news, it has one of the lowest male life expectancy rates in London—to be born and live here will cost you over six years above ground compared to the average in (say) Westminster. Furthermore, Tower Hamlets numbers among the worst local authorities in quality of housing, and (obviously this is not unrelated) it is the second most densely populated borough in England.

To be sure, the East End has for many years been the City's poor cousin. It became notorious for its poverty with the publication of Charles Booth's massive nine-volume survey, *Life and Labour of the People of London*, issued between 1892 and 1897, including incredibly detailed maps that illuminated the social and economic condition of the city, street by street, and even house by house. There were at about the same time best-sellers that exposed life in the East End as well—Arthur Morrison's *A Child of the Jago* (1896) and Jack London's *The People of the Abyss* (1903), whose title conveys in a single word its powerful message. In fact, many European and American cities have the same east/west socio-topographical divide, largely because the prevailing winds in the Northern Hemisphere tend to blow from west to east. Thus "better" suburbs often were located in the west to capture fresh air, while a host of noxious but necessary trades (such as tanning, brickmaking, and lime burning) were located as far east as was possible, along with the cheapest and least desirable housing.

Part of the explanation for the enduring poverty of the East End in the Twenty-first Century, despite so many efforts to ameliorate it, has to do with its more recent explosive population growth through immigration—in 1986 the borough had 150,000 residents but it is now home to 320,000. (Just for comparison, in 1901 it was 580,000.) It is the fastest-growing borough in England and one of the youngest. International migration helps to drive the growth—in recent years before the pandemic around 14,000 people from other countries moved here. (The net increase was about 10,000 international residents *p.a.*, as some also move out.) Roughly 35% of residents are Muslim, the highest proportion in any local authority in England (and considerably more than the 27% who identify as "Christian").

Yet, as the Tower Hamlets working paper cited above remarks, "not all deprived people live in deprived areas, and not everyone living in a deprived area is deprived." Case in point: Tower Hamlets also is home to Canary

Wharf, which has brought an astounding 120,000 new jobs to the borough (half the total number), generating fully 75% of the borough's business revenue. Canary Wharf is also home to a large number of new housing developments with prices in the range of £10,000 a square meter and up.

We won't visit Canary Wharf, but we can see it clearly from this vantage point. It began as a single mega-tower built over filled-in portions of the West India Docks. The Conservative government had kick-started the development process by undertaking to build the DLR, the Docklands Light Railway, providing the district with an essential transport link to the City. As the line was to run almost all above ground, it could be built quickly, whilst the tube would (and did) arrive only many years later. The developer was a Canadian firm, Olympia and York, that completed the project at the very moment that the property market for office buildings collapsed. They promptly went bankrupt and lost control of the project, but they bought it back in 1995 as the property market rebounded and began its unprecedented recent almost uninterrupted three-decade long rise. It now ranks as one of the most successful development projects of modern times, with 16,000,000 built square feet of office and retail space, including a vast shopping mall, a cinema, and even a branch of the Museum of London, as well as substantial residential accommodation. (One can actually walk to Canary Wharf from the Tower via the Thames River pathway, but it would take the best part of an hour and it involves a few puzzling detours where the pathway simply disappears.)

From the northeast corner of the Tower site, cross the road via the tiled subway tunnel, and you will emerge at one of the entrances to St Katherine Docks. (By the way, you now are on private property; this entire vast site is another of the larger POPS in London.) London acquired its commercial docks relatively late in its life as a port—the first was the Howland Great Dock in Rotherhithe, opened in 1699, and despite its success, it was a full century before the second was built—the West India Docks in 1802. Much of the traffic in the port then passed through the Pool, the stretch of the Thames just east of London Bridge, whose narrow arches formed a barrier for larger ships that could not pass under it into the city. Ships sometimes lingered there for weeks or even months before cargoes were unloaded into the smaller vessels that plied the river between merchant vessels and the wharves and warehouses ashore. Not only was this system absurdly inefficient, but it led to fairly substantial losses through pilferage, thievery, and chronic corruption. The purpose-built docks sped loading and unloading while offering extensive warehouse accommodation, and they did so in a secure environment that reduced cargo losses.

St Katherine's was opened in 1828, at the end of a great wave dock-building, and, sited as it was adjacent to the Tower, it was the closest dock to the City itself. Its construction was a massive endeavor: 1250 houses were demolished and some 11,000 residents displaced, for the most part, poor dockworkers and their families. Unfortunately, this development set a pattern for a number of later large Nineteenth Century urban redevelopment projects: while property owners were generously compensated, their tenants were given nothing beyond the shove. Moreover, as railways, railway stations, and new roads were built in the middle decades of the century, often they were located intentionally in the "worst" (a.k.a. poorest) neighbourhoods. The theory (perhaps I should rather say, the rationalization) behind this practice was that opening poor neighbourhoods to fresh air and sunlight would relieve overcrowding and make them more salubrious. In fact, the law of unintended consequences was very much in play: since public transportation was non-existent or at best wholly inadequate, and expensive, displaced workers still needed to live close to their places of employment, and so these large "improvement" projects more often than not increased overcrowding as the houseless residents moved into nearby already overfull slums and rookeries. The notion that alternative housing should be provided to those forced to leave their homes is a very Twentieth Century idea.

With a bit of imagination, these now-gentrified docks themselves provide us still with a sense of what London was like when it was a working port city. The Riverside neighbourhoods to the east of the Tower—Wapping, Shadwell, Ratcliff, Limehouse, and Millwall—were for five hundred years active day and night with ships coming and going, loading and unloading, served by armies of casual labourers who lived in what generally were appalling conditions nearby. Here too were communities of foreign seamen, Han Chinese from East Asia, Lascars from the Indian subcontinent and Southeast Asia, and Africans from Guinea. All this came quickly to an end with the advent and rapid ascendency of shipping containers—surely one of the great transformative inventions of the late Twentieth Century—and the arrival of the huge cargo vessels that carried them. By the end of the Seventies, the working port had moved east to deeper waters at the Tilbury docks with its spanking new container facilities.

Yet despite their proximity to the center of London, St Katharine Docks had never been a financial success. Badly damaged in the Blitz, they never fully recovered, and they were closed altogether in 1968. Their subsequent redevelopment is often attributed to Thatcher-era privatization, but in fact the project was conceived and begun under the auspices of the very left-leaning Greater London Council, though the last parts were completed only in the 1990s. There is no question but that the GLC, in recognizing the potential of the derelict inner London docks for commercial development, laid the foundations for a remarkable transformation of the entire maritime East End.

This dockland redevelopment established the precedent of using expedited planning permission and limited government funds as seed money to spur private investment. These particular centrally located docks were perfectly suited to host a marina, hotels, restaurants, and upscale housing. To see them now on a weekday, filled with office workers, or on a weekend, packed with residents and day trippers, it is difficult to imagine the blight into which they had deteriorated only forty years ago. Equally a measure of success, I suppose, is the price of an apartment here—it will set you back close to a million pounds for a compact one-bedroom flat.

Walking further east, past the western edge of St Katherine's, is Wapping—the name possibly alluding to a marsh that was drained in the early modern period. (*Wapol* means marsh in Old English.) It was once was home to countless inns and other businesses catering to sailors. The London Docks were built here between 1799 and 1815 and they forced out about half the district's population. The northern boundary of this sprawling area is Cable Street, so named because it was here that great lengths of hemp were twisted into ships' ropes.

It was also the site of the "battle of Cable Street" on Sunday, October 4, 1936. Oswald Mosely's fascist Black Shirts, modeled on Hitler's SA, or the Brown Shirts, planned a march that day through the heart of the mostly Jewish East End. A coalition of Jewish, socialist, Communist, and anti-fascist groups marshalled 20,000 people in the streets to stop it. The battle ensued when police tried to remove the barricades that the protesters had built; hundreds were injured and scores arrested, but the fascists were stopped. The area suffered badly during the Blitz, but Wapping was to see yet another epochal battle in 1986—this time between the print unions and Rupert Murdoch's News International, publisher of *The Times* and *The Sun*, among others. Murdoch moved the firm's printing works from central London to a new automated facility here and simultaneously laid off most of the staff, prompting a strike. The ensuing endurance contest was seen by both sides—and by the Thatcher government—as part of life-or-death struggle to break the power of print unions. The challenge Murdoch faced in the Eighties was to print enough copies to meet demand, impossible with restrictive union work rules. This chronic shortfall was very real: I can remember when I first lived in London that if one didn't buy a Sunday paper before 10 am, they'd have all sold out. (Ironically, the challenge to newspapers lately is to find anyone who wants to buy a print copy at all.) In the end, Murdoch won and the print unions never fully recovered. The printing works moved yet again in 2012 and the site was sold for redevelopment.

The docks here themselves had already closed in 1969 and the site was purchased by Tower Hamlets, intent on building council housing, but the funding never materialized. Sold off yet again in 1981, Wapping has become another landmark of gentrification. To my taste, what was built there is all a bit sterile: there are some old warehouses repurposed into flats as well as new residential construction made to look like the old warehouses repurposed into flats, but there are very few shops or restaurants and generally very little pedestrian or vehicular traffic. However, there are three ancient riverside pubs to visit, the Captain Kidd, the Town of Ramsgate, and the Prospect of Whitby, the last dating from 1520—supposedly the oldest surviving riverside pub in the city. These pubs used to be a bit rough around the edges when I first lived in London, but all their edges now are gilt. Somewhere on this stretch of river (no one knows the exact spot) is Execution Dock, where for four centuries those sentenced to death in Admiralty Court were hanged, including William Kidd, the legendary pirate after whom the pub is named. The last public execution here was in 1830.

There is one hidden gem of a structure on Wapping High Street, the Wapping Rail Station. This is the north end of the Thames Tunnel, a remarkable pedestrian underground river crossing designed by Marc Brunel, begun in 1825, then in 1826 taken over by his son Isambard Kingdom Brunel (as you may recall, the designer of Paddington Station). Construction was not continuous: there were long periods when it was suspended after fatal accidents (which happened all too often) and there were also recurring shortfalls in funding. But thanks to Brunel's revolutionary new tunneling shield, it was finally finished in 1843 (at the staggering cost of over £600,000). But linking as it did Wapping to Rotherhithe, neither being particularly attractive, and with a penny toll, the tunnel was never a going proposition financially. Finally, in 1865 it was sold to the East London Railway, who laid down tracks in it, and it has been a rail tunnel ever since. From 1884 to 1905, it was used by both the Metropolitan and the District Railways. Since then it has served a changing array of commuter lines (presently as part of the London Overground system), but the tunnel itself, still very much in daily use, has worn well.

It is time now to turn westward along the river pathway, keeping as close to the river as possible, threading your way through St Katherine Dock, and skirting the Tower to its south. This is our first stroll along the Thames Path. (The sections within London are part of a mostly continuous pathway along the entire length of the river, from its source to the sea, nearly 200 miles long.) There have been bits of the river accessible to pedestrians for some time—for example, on the Victoria Embankment—but the effort to embrace the river as an integral part of the urban fabric only coalesced in the Eighties and the path was largely complete by 1996. During this time, commercial traffic on the river virtually ceased, and so obsolete and abandoned warehouses and wharves suddenly became prime sites for redevelopment. Walking the path now—amidst the luxury flats, hotels, restaurants, pubs, buskers, and crowds of tourists—it is difficult to believe that the river in living memory was a dark, lifeless and dangerous place.

The Thames Path takes you under Tower Bridge, often mistaken for London Bridge by tourists. The massive faux medieval structure was roundly criticized as an architectural monstrosity when it first opened, but over the years it has settled comfortably into its site near the Tower and its status as an iconic synecdoche for the city itself. It used to be possible to walk across the bridge on the skywalk, but now that is used as an exhibit space. The engine rooms—housing the machinery that raises and lowers the central span—at times are open to visitors, and well worth the price of admission, which includes the opportunity to stand atop a glass floor in the upper walkway.

As you walk along the Tower's southern side facing the river, you will pass the Traitor's Gate, an archway over a water gate that allowed small boats to deliver condemned prisoners (and others) to the Tower without attracting notice. And not far past the bridge is the Custom House, a monumental early Nineteenth Century building that once was responsible for the collection of all customs duties in London. The stone-faced side fronting the river is best seen from the South Bank, but it's impressive enough from where you are standing now. At this point, we will turn north, away from the river, and continue on Byward Street to Mark Lane, possibly named after martens, a small fur-bearing animal that reputedly was made into coats here.

Just a bit further on is Hart Street, home to St Olave Hart Street, another of the handful of medieval churches that survived the Great Fire. It was saved from the flames by William Penn senior, the father of the founder of Pennsylvania, who ordered the houses surrounding the church to be blown up, creating a fire break that, thanks also to a lucky shift in direction of the wind, proved sufficient to preserve it. It was not so lucky in the Blitz, but it was restored relatively quickly after the war. St Olave, who was also King Olav II, is the patron saint of Norway; he joined forces with the English in 1014 and defeated the marauding Danes in what is known as the Battle of London Bridge and supposedly the church is built on the site of the battle. (Olav is better known for Christianizing the Vikings.) This was Samuel Pepys's parish church and inside, next to his tomb, is the touching monument he erected to his wife, Elizabeth. Another Elizabeth, the first monarch of that name, celebrated a thanksgiving service here in 1554 on the occasion of her release from imprisonment in the Tower, an event memorialized in a stained glass window. The pulpit—attributed to Grinling Gibbons—survived a direct hit from a German incendiary bomb in 1941. The ancient bells of the church—cast by the Whitechapel Foundry—were not as fortunate: they melted, but the metal was saved and recast into new bells in the 1950s by the very same firm. They are regularly rung for Sunday services. The churchyard also is the burial site of a very unfortunate Inuit native who had been brought here as a hostage by Martin Frobisher after the first of his three unsuccessful voyages in search of the Northwest Passage to China.

A little further north, via a short stretch of road called London Street, is Fenchurch Street Station, something of a hidden gem. Built in 1854 to serve the eastern counties, its tan brick façade is largely intact, only the canopy at the front having been altered. When the original station building opened in 1841, it was the first and for a time the only railway station actually within boundaries of the City itself.

Return to Hart Street, via London Street, and carry on East on the street that is called Crutched Friars. This has been its name since the Fifteenth Century, after a small friary whose brothers wore a cross on their habits. (Crouched is an archaic term for crossed.) A right turn on Cooper's Row (the name memorializing coopering or barrel-making, once one of the most essential London trades) takes us back to Tower Hill Station.

Onward to Monument!

1. Paddington Station. Paddington was the western terminus of the first underground railway. When the main line railway train shed opened in 1854, it was the largest in the world, a marvel of Victorian engineering spanning 102'6."

2. Little Venice. Little Venice is a picturesque corner of what once was a network of canals linking London to the midlands; now it is a desirable berth for houseboats.

3. Regent's Park. Without doubt this park contains the most variety of all of central London's green spaces, home to everything from a rose garden to a boating lake to the London Central Mosque to the London Zoo, as well as formal gardens like this one.

4. British Library Forecourt. Nearly 30 years in the making and derided when it opened in 1998, this vast, severely modernist monument manages to function as both a working library and a popular tourist attraction.

5. St John's Gate. This impressive medieval-looking structure stands on the site of what was the southern entry to Clerkenwell Priory, but what survives is largely a Victorian reconstruction.

6. The Barbican Estate. The Barbican estate is a vast 1960s experiment in modernist architecture and urban living. Inspired by Le Corbusier's "city in the sky" it separated pedestrians from vehicular traffic with a network of elevated walkways. Initially unpopular, its three high-rise towers have become fashionable and very desirable.

7. Roman City Wall, Noble Street. This long section of the Roman and medieval city wall was exposed by a German bomb during the Blitz; the original Roman tower or Barbicana probably stood nearby.

8. Bunhill Fields. Located just outside the City boundary, from 1665 to 1854 this was the principal burial ground for London's Nonconformists, over 120,000 of whom were interred here. About 2000 headstones and monuments remain.

9. Christ Church, Spitalfields. Nicholas Hawksmoor's masterpiece towers over Spitalfields. It was nearly derelict in the early 1960s and in immediate danger of demolition, but after decades of work it is now fully restored.

10. Tower Bridge. Completed in 1894, the faux-medieval design was ridiculed at the time, but since then it has become one of London's iconic landmarks. Tourists often mistake it for London Bridge.

11. St Katherine's Docks. This was the first of several large redevelopment projects that turned derelict industrial sites into vibrant residential and recreational districts. Privately owned, it functions very much as public space.

12. The Monument. Erected in the 1670s, the Monument memorializes both the Great Fire of 1666 and afterward the city's astonishingly rapid recovery and rebuilding; it is 202 feet tall and the same distance from the baker's shop in Pudding Lane where the fire is believed to have started.

13. River Terrace. This sign, semi-obscured by shrubbery, located just to the north and east of London Bridge, marks the entrance to a terrace overlooking the river, the marooned survivor of a never-completed 1960s scheme to create a network of elevated pedestrian walkways throughout the City.

14. Bank of England. The massive windowless outer walls of the Bank give the building a grim aspect; designed by Sir John Soane, they were intended to withstand attacks by dangerous mobs of rioters.

15. St Mary le Bow. Legend has it that only those born within the sound of the Bow church bells are true Londoners. The church was destroyed in the Great Fire, rebuilt by Wren, heavily damaged in the Blitz, and restored in the 1950s, when the present bells all were cast.

16. The Blackfriar Pub. This remarkable Arts and Crafts early Twentieth Century masterpiece was threatened with demolition in the 1960s but it was saved by a campaign led by the Victorian Society and its founder, Sir John Betjman.

17. Millennium Bridge. The striking design is a collaboration of architect Norman Foster and sculptor Anthony Caro, but when the bridge opened in June 2000, it wobbled, and it was closed after only 2 days to allow a stabilization system to be installed. It reopened, wobble-free, two years later. The walkway offers stunning views of both St Paul's Cathedral and (here) the Tate Modern.

18. Watling Street. This roadway anchors a small warren of pedestrian alleys within sight of St Paul's. Watling Street is *a* Roman road, but not *the* Roman Watling Street, the main highway from the coast, which ran somewhere to the south and crossed the Thames at Westminster.

19. Dragon Boundary Marker. This dragon, one of a pair, marks the City boundary on the Victoria Embankment. These beasts originally guarded the Corn Exchange and were moved here when that building was demolished in the 1960s. Other half-sized replicas were cast and installed at various City boundary points. Thirteen are still extant.

20. Temple Round Church. This unusual round church—one of only four in England—was built by the Knights Templar in the 1100s. The area around it has been home to attorneys since the Fourteenth Century and now contains two of the four Inns of Court.

21. Savory Chapel. Originally this site was part of the London residence of Peter, Count of Savoy; later it was home to John of Gaunt. The first chapel on this site was burned down in the Peasants' Revolt of 1381; this one was completed in 1512 to serve inmates of the hospital (hostel) for the poor founded by Henry VII.

22. Jewel Tower. One of the two remaining medieval structures once part of the Palace of Westminster, it was built around 1365 to house Edward II's valuables. (The other survivor is Westminster Hall, where Elizabeth II lay in state.)

23. St James's Park. Opened to the public by Charles II, this is the oldest royal park. The pelicans nesting at the eastern end of the lake are descendants of birds given the King by the Russian ambassador in 1664.

24. Sloane Square Underground Station. The River Westbourne, which rises in Hampstead and empties into the Thames, flows above the tracks and station platforms encased in this iron culvert, an ingenious solution to the problem of the underground railway needing to cross the river.

25. Saatchi Gallery. The Saatchi Gallery, a leading venue for contemporary art, some of it owned by Charles Saatchi, anchors the redeveloped Duke of York Headquarters. The site served various military purposes from 1801 to 2003, when it was sold to the Cadogan Estates.

26. Albert Memorial. Queen Victoria insisted on a grand memorial after Albert's sudden death of typhoid fever in 1861, and while it took over a decade to design and build one to her liking, the result is impressive, if architecturally incoherent. Albert is depicted holding the catalogue of the Great Exhibition, arguably his principal legacy.

27. Design Museum. This classic modernist monument formerly housed the Commonwealth Institute. It was left empty from 2004 as that entity was liquidated; the Design Museum renovated the site and moved into its new quarters in 2016.

28. Kensington Palace. This quintessential Georgian building, largely the work of Wren, is the most accessible of London's royal palaces. It is best known for its associations with Princess Diana.

29. St Mary Abbots Kensington. This is the very "church" that gives Kensington Church Street its name. The convincing medieval design and its somewhat dilapidated state suggest great antiquity, but the present building, by George Gilbert Scott (the first of three generations of this family of nearly identically named architects), dates from 1872.

Chapter 8

Monument

Monument is a curious station. A relative latecomer to the Circle route (opened in 1884 just as the Inner Circuit was being completed), for its first month in existence it was known as Eastcheap, named after the nearest major thoroughfare. Arguably, nowadays it isn't really a station in its own right—it functions as one end of a very large complex of underground passages and platforms centered at Bank, serving in addition to the Circle line the Northern, Central, and Waterloo and City Lines, as well as the DLR. (The first station actually named "Bank" opened in 1900.) The famous "travelator," the moving walkway linking the station's distant corners—reputed to be the first of its kind—opened in 1960. Back at the time of my first days in London in the Seventies, the station was always referred to as "Monument for Bank" and if memory serves it was so designated on printed system maps.

The monument in question is known simply as "*the* Monument" and it commemorates the Great Fire of 1666. The blaze raged from 2 to 6 September, and roughly three-quarters of the City within the walls was destroyed, along with a considerable section of Fleet Street outside the walls. It is astonishing still to consider the scale of destruction—virtually everything one can see from the top of the Monument was consumed by the epic conflagration. The losses included old St Paul's Cathedral, 87 parish churches, and 13,000 other buildings. Some 70,000 of the City's 80,000 inhabitants were made homeless.

No less impressive was the rapidity and scale of rebuilding. The fire ravished a city of wood and helped to create one of brick and stone. The Monument itself is a curious epitome of the late Seventeenth-Century sensibility that produced it: it celebrates the power of religious belief—an inscription on the base thanks God for stopping the blaze—and at the same time it signals humanity's growing faith in its own power, its pride in the rapid rebuilding expressed in neoclassical style and with engineering prowess that speak volumes about the growing confidence in humankind's powers at the inception of what justly is called "The Age of Reason." The Monument may nod toward faith, but it is rooted in rationality.

Designed by Christopher Wren and Robert Hooke, the structure is a very simple and elegant hollow stone Doric column. It stands on the site of the first church to go up in flames on the first day of the fire, and it is exactly 202' tall and sited exactly the same distance from the bakery in Pudding Lane where the fire apparently started. (Pudding Lane, by the way, is named not for sweet desserts but after the butchers in Eastcheap who sent their discarded offal down the street to the river to be carted away—pudding being an old synonym for entrails.) A deranged French watchmaker named Robert Hubert confessed to starting the fire and though it was quite obvious he was inno- cent—he was not even in London the day the fire began—nevertheless a goat to scape was needed so he was convicted of the crime and summarily hanged.

The climb to the top of the Monument (for a reasonable £5.80 admission charge) is challenging but it does offer a view that is quite expansive, despite all the new high-rise construction at this end of the City. The individual steps on the staircase are exactly 6" apart (7" is the more common pitch) so as to allow experiments involving readings of barometric pressure—every two steps obviously enough represent the distance of one foot. This no doubt was at the behest of Hooke, a "natural philosopher" (what we would call a scien- tist) of considerable renown. A further inscription on the base was added a few years after it was built, ascribing blame for the fire to Roman Catholics; even though the Catholic Hubert was demonstrably guiltless, the common view was that somehow it had all been a Papist plot. The inscription was effaced in 1830, a rare example of fake news being corrected, though it did take 150 years.

If one were to climb to the top (and you are welcome to do it, though be warned it is a tight squeeze in the narrow upper sections), one striking aspect of the cityscape on view would be the multitude of church steeples. The density of parish churches is a useful reminder that for the best part of 1000 years of London's history, the dominant institution in every area of everyday life was the Christian Church, first the Church of Rome, and, after the reigns of Henry VIII and his daughter Elizabeth, the Church of England. The church was at times not only London's principal but virtually its only functional public institution. To be sure, its primary mission was to tend souls, but the church also cared for the sick, supported the indigent, educated the young, and often acted as a *de facto* local government. The density of churches is also a useful reminder that, until the second half of the Nineteenth Century, this was one of the more densely populated parts of the city as well. We will visit several of the surviving parish churches a bit later in our walk.

If there were any logic to the naming of tube stations (and generally there isn't), Monument station would be called London Bridge, since it sits at the northern end of that busy landmark crossing. (That would give us two stations with that name, but as we have seen there is a precedent.) Standing on the bridge outside the Underground station, I am reminded that this is as good a place as any to reiterate the obvious—that London is built on the banks of a river. Not just any river, but a great and largely navigable waterway that has connected England to the world since ancient times. Indeed, the place that became Londinium probably was first settled by the Romans precisely because the river here was shallow enough and narrow enough to allow for easy crossing. The bridge spawned the city, though usually it happens the other way 'round. Over the centuries, the river has been a port, an essential part of transportation infrastructure, a water supply, an open sewer, a place of recreation, and even an invasion route—but always it has been the beating heart of the city.

The present bridge opened in 1973, replacing "New" London Bridge, built in 1831, which was sold off and improbably now sits on Lake Havasu, Arizona. ("Old" London Bridge was demolished and turned into rubble in 1831, the market for superannuated Thames river crossings being as yet undeveloped.) There has been a bridge of some sort here since around AD 50, when the first Roman crossing was built. After the Roman bridge fell into disrepair, there may have been no bridge for a short time, but a wooden bridge was definitely there as early as AD 1000. The first stone structure, dating from 1209, was the fabled medieval bridge (forever falling down in the nursery rhyme), a project of Henry II, who built at its center a chapel dedicated to Thomas Becket, an act of penance for having had him murdered not long before. The Crown subsequently sold the right to build houses on old London Bridge to help defray the cost of operations and repairs. Many of these houses were built and, as they were wider on their upper stories, they overhung the roadway, turning it into a dark tunnel. They were fire hazards as well. The southern gateway had an added function—displaying on pikes the heads of traitors after their execution, a custom that lasted into the Eighteenth Century and apparently was something of a tourist attraction. In 1282, the Crown granted the City Corporation—or, rather, a charitable trust controlled by the City—the charter for maintenance of the bridge; Bridge House Estates have cared for it ever since (along with other Thames crossings that have been added to its portfolio over the centuries). The trust invested wisely over the years: revenue has exceeded expenditures for quite some time, and in 1995 the trust gained permission to use the accumulating excess funds for charitable purposes, which it continues to do today.

Since the precincts of Southwark at the southern end of the bridge were legally part of the City (known as Bridge Ward Without) from 1337 to 1978, I reckon we are entitled cross to the South Bank and to wander there for a bit—even though the Circle Line itself never crosses the river. Alas, walking across the bridge now, one is reminded that the southern end was the focus of the 3 June 2017 terror attack, when a van jumped the pavement to mow down pedestrians. The three occupants, after abandoning the van, stabbed people randomly as they ran through the area around the market. Before they all were shot dead, eight innocent people had been killed and 48 wounded. In the wake of this attack, and a similar earlier attack on Westminster Bridge, London's bridges all have been fitted with concrete and steel barriers to ensure that vehicles cannot leave the roadway. They are as little intrusive as such things can be, but it is impossible *not* to notice them. Such is the world we live in now.

Be warned: if you happen to cross the bridge on the last Sunday in September, you may encounter a flock of sheep. One of the ancient privileges accorded Freemen of the City was the right to bring livestock over the bridge and then to take the beasts to market without paying a toll. One day a year the right is asserted, generally with a flock borrowed from a farm in one of the home counties. The right of free passage became meaningless when the live meat market at Smithfield closed, but it has been revived in recent years as a charity fundraiser. (Freemen also are accorded the privilege of being hanged with a silken rope, but that perk too has lapsed with the abolition of capital punishment.)

In ancient times, Southwark—often called the Borough, though legally it wasn't one—attracted all sorts of less than wholly respectable enterprises, all with the same goal: to escape the oversight of the City authorities. In particular, the Borough was home to many brothels and also to several theatre companies, actors and prostitutes then accorded equally low rank. Many of the areas just outside but adjacent to the city walls were "liberties," areas that geographically were part of London but legally remained outside the jurisdiction of the city's various governing bodies. Here, in addition to bordellos and playhouses, were bearbaiting rings (preserved in the street name Bear Gardens) and all sorts of drinking establishments, as well as resident foreigners, debtors, and assorted felons on the run. Not all residents were shady characters: there were also entrepreneurial craftsmen and tradesmen who wished to operate outside the rigid City guild system. There were two common threads running through these trades and activities. One was the provision of semi-licit and illicit entertainments. The other was that in this place unregulated by the City, trades or manufactures that produced noxious waste or were otherwise unwelcome across the river could flourish. Southwark also had some of the city's worst slums.

There were quite a few other liberties near the city's boundaries, often with defunct ecclesiastical connections. And though the religious orders themselves vanished after the Dissolution, the liberties retained their equivocal legal and jurisdictional privileges for hundreds of years afterward. The last disappeared as lately as 1889. The "protection" afforded residents of the liberties varied—in some, one could avoid being arrested for even the most serious crimes.

In Southwark, prostitution was not only tolerated but completely legal, bizarrely conducted under the aegis of the Bishop of Winchester, who kept a London house and estate here and whose liberties encompassed most of what we now call Bankside. (This was the result of historical accident: when the Winchester bishopric was established it had the same boundaries as the old Saxon kingdom of Wessex, which at one time extended as far as Southwark.) Indeed, the prostitutes were known as Winchester geese, and a narrow street on the south side of Borough Market, Redcross Way, leads to a small grave-yard, known as Cross Bones, occasionally open to the public, unconsecrated ground where for many years it is said prostitutes were buried. (On the opposite bank, off Upper Thames Street, is Stew Lane, probably so named because it was where one took the ferry across to the Bankside bordellos; we will walk by Stew Lane later.)

Bermondsey, just east of Southwark, had a similar profile, but nowadays it is known to antiques collectors as the site of a weekly market that, for most of its life, was governed by the law of *marché ouvert*. That statute held that no one could question the provenance of goods sold here during daylight hours, which made the market an ideal place for stolen articles to be passed into circulation perfectly and irreversibly legally. Thus a pair of sterling silver candlesticks that were burgled in Surrey one evening could be sold openly here at six the next morning. Though the law is no more (hard as it is to believe, it was nullified only in 1995), the market survives, reduced in size, surrounded now by a much gentrified neighbourhood. (What is left of the antiques market today is held on Friday mornings; selling starts at 4 a.m. and if you're a serious buyer, it's best to go before 9 a.m.)

Closer to the bridge entrance is a very different kind of market, one selling good things to eat—Borough Market. Indeed, there has been a food market at the Southwark end of the bridge since 1014, or so the charitable trust that manages the Borough Market claims, allowing it to have celebrated its millennial anniversary a few years back. To accept that date as fact requires rather a long leap of faith, but even if the date is wishful thinking, no great harm was done by celebrating it. The first reliable mention of what is now the Borough Market actually is much later, in the Thirteenth Century, and though it has moved a few times, there most definitely has been some sort of food market at the southern end of London Bridge continuously at least since then.

In the Nineties, the market developed into a source for high-quality ingredients, imported delicacies, prepared foods, and takeaway snacks to eat on the spot, surrounded by a thick girdle of trendy cafes and restaurants. The wholesale market operates every week day; the retail market is open Wednesday through Saturday. Nowadays, it tends to be mobbed well beyond capacity with tourists, especially during the warmer months. Its discovery by tourists is a great disappointment to me personally because now there is always an enormous queue at Brindisa, the stall that serves my all-time favorite sandwich—charcoal grilled chorizo on a crusty roll garnished with rocket—once voted one of the top ten sandwiches in the world, and a delight with every bite. My wife discovered it and introduced me to it in 1999 or thereabouts. Miraculously, it still tastes just as good, despite its popularity. If you're lucky, while you feast on chorizo you'll be treated to a vocal performance by one of the market's fruit and veg traders, a fellow who might well have pursued a career on the operatic stage. No need to look out for his stall—his voice is such that wherever you are in the market, if he sings, you will hear him.

If you manage to find the northeast corner of the market, a gateway that provides access to Borough High Street through a short tunnel, look carefully at the bollards (the small pillars set into the pavement to protect it from vehicles) that mark the entry to the marvelously named Green Dragon Court. They are marked with the date 1813, when they were installed, and they are now officially protected historical monuments.

Nearby, at the northern tip of Borough Market, is Southwark Cathedral, which despite its legitimate antiquity has been a cathedral only since 1905. The present building, parts of which date to the Thirteenth Century, was for centuries the Church of St Mary Overie (i.e. St Mary over the water) and before that, prior to the Dissolution, the chapel of an Augustinian Priory. There may well have been a church on this site as early as Saxon times; indeed, the church claims it was founded in 606, though a much later date in the Ninth Century is equally likely. After the Dissolution, it was rededicated to St Saviour and it served as an ordinary parish church and part of the diocese of Winchester though it stood at the entrance to the City.

The building itself is largely a Nineteenth Century reconstruction, with a few incorporated earlier bits here and there remaining. It suffered only modest damage in the Blitz, but if you look carefully, there are chips made by German bomb shrapnel visible on the outside walls. It's worth a look-in to see the tomb of the poet John Gower and also the Harvard Chapel, built by Harvard alumni to honor the founder of the university, John Harvard, who was born in Southwark and baptized in this church. Harvard's father knew the Shakespeare family (the poet's brother is buried somewhere nearby) and the Bard almost certainly attended services in the church quite often, as the Globe Theatre was only a stone's throw away.

A short detour westward along the river will take you to the Golden Hinde museum, whose main attraction is a replica of the vessel of that name, captained by Sir Francis Drake, that circumnavigated the globe between 1577 and 1580—the first English ship to do so and the first time that any single vessel completed such an arduous journey. The ship began its travels named the Pelican but it was rechristened in mid-voyage to honor Drake's patron, Sir Christopher Hatton, whose family crest included a golden hind. (A hind, by the way, is an adult female deer.) What is most striking about the exhibit, however, is how very small the ship was, roughly the size of a London double-decker bus. Crammed aboard were 80 crew members, 56 of whom survived the journey, along with all their gear, and considerable quantities of provisions, including livestock. To imagine for a moment embarking on a journey of long but indeterminate duration across uncharted seas and at endless risk of peril—from the weather, from disease, from the Spanish, and from indigenous people encountered in places unknown and uncharted—is to appreciate the courage (and no doubt the desperation) of those who ventured all on voyages like this.

It was not the thirst for adventure alone that led men to sea—there was also the prospect of acquiring untold riches. Drake's voyage was notable not only for its circling of the globe but for the seizure of a Spanish treasure ship off the coast of Ecuador. The gold and other precious cargoes were valued at £360,000—a whopping return of 4700% to investors, including the Queen, whose share was sufficient to pay off the entire national debt and still leave a substantial sum over. In Drake's day, there clearly was no great distinction between government service and private profit; the two were inextricably intertwined. Nowhere was this more visible than in the empire building of the East India Company, founded not long after Drake's voyage in 1600 and for 250 years a profitable quasi-state in its own right. In the centuries to come, no other voyage of exploration came close to achieving Drake's rate of return, but the allure of the sea and the promise of riches beyond measure continued to fuel what we now call the Age of Exploration (though we might just as well dub it "the Age of Exploitation").

Just west of the vessel, Pickfords Lane quickly turns into Clink Street, a reminder of the prison that stood here from the Twelfth to the Eighteenth Century and that has given its name to prisons in general. The building is long gone and what is on the site now is a private museum geared toward frightening young children and impressionable tourists. The jail that once was here served as a private prison for the Bishop of Winchester, where he could detain debtors and heretics, and as prisons then allowed inmates to pay for better lodging and food, it was probably also a considerable source of his revenues. Also worth a moment's perusal are the scant ruins of the bishop's palace, visible from the street.

A bit further westward is the Globe Theatre, a fairly faithful reconstruction of the Globe as Shakespeare knew it. This complex of buildings, including an indoor theatre, is so much a part of London's cultural scene now that it is difficult to recall that it exists solely because of the dream—dare I say, the obsession—of one man, the American actor and stage director, Sam

Wanamaker. He had fled the States in the red scare of the early 1950s to avoid being blacklisted in Hollywood and he made a successful career in the U.K. I met him in 1974, just a few years after he had embarked on his crusade to build a replica Globe on the South Bank, near the site of the original. We were both guests at a lunch party organized by my landlady at the time; I reckon she thought that as we both were American transplants, we would strike up a friendship, but it didn't happen. The playhouse was completed in 1997; Wanamaker had died in 1993 and so he never saw it.

It is time, however, to retrace our steps to the Cathedral. Walk past the front of the building and climb a set of stairs that will return us to Borough High Street. Cross the busy road (wait for the lights, though it takes an eternity for them to change to green) and just behind the row of shops is Guy's Hospital. This institution was founded 1721 by Sir Thomas Guy, a bookseller who had made a fortune in the South Sea bubble; it was initially meant to serve as a home for the incurables discharged from nearby St Thomas's Hospital. St Thomas's (where Keats did his medical training) left Southwark for its present site in Lambeth in the 1860s, displaced by construction for the viaduct that carries trains from London Bridge to Charing Cross. The original St Thomas's was an infirmary staffed by Augustinian monks and nuns and possibly renamed after Thomas Becket at the time of his canonization in 1173. Not to be missed is the Old Operating Theatre, built in 1822 in the garret of the adjacent church, also called St Thomas's, to provide a space adjacent to a ward where surgery might be done on female patients out of the sight and the hearing of other inmates. (There must have been constant screams during surgery, as there was no anesthesia in use until 1847.)

Nearby, in a court off Borough High Street, is the George, London's last galleried inn. There were in early modern times many other galleried inns all over London, among them the nearby Tabard, where Chaucer begins the *Canterbury Tales*. (The inn is long gone but Tabard Street remains.) The George dates back to an unknown medieval origin, but the present building went up in 1672 after its predecessor had burned down. Only one of the original three sides remains, the other two having been demolished to build warehouses for London Bridge station. It is now owned by the National Trust who operate it as a pub and restaurant. The food is standard pub and mid-market restaurant fare, decent enough, but it is best visited on a warm day when you can enjoy a cold drink from the bar at a table outside in the sun.

As we walk north on the High Street, ahead of us is the low rail bridge that carries trains from London Bridge westward to Cannon Street and Charing Cross. Just before the bridge a turning to the east opens into a vast plaza that houses the new entrance to the main line London Bridge Station. This was the terminus of London's very first railway, which then ran only as far east as Greenwich. The main line station opened in 1836 and it has been rebuilt several times, most recently over much of the last decade. The present station replaces a jerry-built hodgepodge of platforms, entrances, and exits that was a daily nightmare for commuters and confused visitors, ill-befitting the fourth busiest rail station in the UK. The redevelopment certainly is an improvement in terms of efficiency, and it also created a new stop on the cross-London Thameslink service, but inside it takes shape as yet another cookie-cutter shopping mall cum food court, indistinguishable from new rail stations any-where else in the UK. The associated Underground station is unremarkable except to note that it is one of the busiest in the network and the only London tube station that retains "London" as part of its name.

More impressive than the station is the extraordinary building that rises behind it, dubbed "the Shard." At 95 stories and just over 1000' in height, it can be seen from almost anywhere in Central London, except when one is standing directly under it. It is the tallest building in the U.K.—with its dra-matically tapered form it looks the part—but a veritable midget on the world scene, ranking as I write as only the 96th tallest internationally (and destined to fall lower on the list as other megaprojects are completed). The Shard is an excellent example of the increasingly common starchitect-designed tow-ers (in this instance the work of Renzo Piano), buildings that function both as working commercial enterprises and tourist attractions. In truth, this one looks better seen from afar when one can appreciate its distinctive tapered shape, resembling a shard of glass. Glass it has aplenty—some 600,000 square feet of it. It is also, like many other recent mega-developments in Central London, designed for mixed use—housing restaurants, high end shopping, offices, exclusive penthouse residences, and a luxury hotel (the "luxury" tag entirely superfluous as every new London hotel nowadays is in that class). The viewing gallery at 800' has become one of the city's most popular tourist attractions despite a ticket price of around £30. And, like many of London's other "named" high-rise buildings, it now is foreign-owned, in this case by a group of Qatari investors. The Shard is either loved or loathed—no one can be neutral about a thousand-foot building in the middle of the metropolis—but whatever your judgment of it as architecture, there is no question but that it has transformed London's skyline.

A walk back across London Bridge affords a prospect of many of those other relatively new named skyscrapers, but also a moment to reflect on T. S. Eliot's lugubrious description of morning commuters walking from the sta-tion into the City in *The Waste Land*:

> A crowd flowed over London Bridge, so many,
> I had not thought death had undone so many.
> Sighs, short and infrequent were exhaled,
> And each man fixed his eyes before his feet.

Flowed up and down King William Street,
To where Saint Mary Woolnoth kept the hours
With a dead sound on the final stroke of nine.

We've moved on in some ways from 1921, when these lines were written: for one thing, we are no longer in the dark shadow of a world war, as were Eliot's contemporaries. But if we observe that pedestrians now stare at the screens of smart phones instead of their feet, it's a fair enough picture of rush hour gloom for the 400,000 or so who commute into the City each and every work day, or who used to do so daily before the pandemic. We too will flow over London Bridge but we shall defer our visit to St Mary Woolnoth for another hour or so.

At the City end of the bridge take a set of stairs that drop down to the Thames pathway, and a short walk further east along the river you will see a mysterious concrete platform. A sign (often obscured by shrubbery) displaying an outsized hand pointing upward indicates our destination. Climb the stairway behind the sign and you will find yourself enjoying one of the finest views of London's riverfront. This is another abandoned fragment of the "pedway" system of elevated walkways that we encountered in the Barbican and along London Wall. At one point in time, in the Sixties and early Seventies, new developments in the City were required to include bits of what was to be an extensive walkway system, and this was one of them. The pedways plan fell apart before it could be fully implemented, but there are isolated parts of it still to be enjoyed.

We will leave this platform by walking to the north, taking us to the Church of St Magnus the Martyr, which stood directly at the entry to old London Bridge until 1831 when the new bridge required different road access a short distance to the west. The first church on the site probably dated from the late Eleventh Century, though which of the several martyred saints named Magnus it honors is not all that clear. Given its location, it is no surprise that it was one of the first churches to be swallowed by the Great Fire and soon after it was rebuilt by Wren.

St Magnus is distinguished by its ornate baroque tower, its early Eighteenth Century organ, and an interior that survived the Blitz with only moderate damage. Outside, note the huge clock hanging from the tower, the gift of a city alderman in 1709, inspired by his own inability as a young lad working in the neighbourhood to know what time it was. St Magnus is the guild church of the Plumbers and the Fishmongers, though of course the nearby wholesale fish market, Billingsgate, and any traders mongering fish, are long gone. The porch houses a remarkable ancient relic—a timber from a Roman wharf, found in nearby Fish Street Hill in 1931. It's a solid piece of sturdy English oak, and in rather good condition considering it was buried for the best part of 2,000 years.

Recalling that this church was rebuilt after the Great Fire by Wren, it is worth noting that he was responsible not only for rebuilding St Paul's Cathedral but also no fewer than 51 parish churches in the City, of which 23 survive. As you visit them, you begin to notice that he had a toolkit of architectural features and decorative motifs—for example, neoclassical columns, cherubs, and floral swags. No doubt Wren had teams of craftsmen who could produce them all in their sleep. And while his church interiors often include these somewhat predictable baroque decorations, where Wren really shone was in his use of space. Each church has a different footprint, determined by its history and by happenstance, fixed forever in their irregularities by the decision after the Fire to respect all existing property boundaries; and yet, all these limitations notwithstanding, he managed to maximize what he could not change by creating what we experience as great interior expanses even on the smallest of sites.

We now will cross busy Lower Thames Street via the pedestrian bridge over it, another fragment of the pedway system, emerging onto Pudding Lane, bringing us again within sight of the Monument. At the top of this lane is Eastcheap, the major east/west thoroughfare north of the Monument, which carries on eastward to the Tower as Great Tower Street. This was once a thriving commercial neighbourhood, the eastern counterpart of Cheapside, but now it is something of a retail dead zone. Even though this street connects the Tower and London Bridge, it is rarely as busy as you'd expect—perhaps because only one bus route (our old friend, the 15) traverses it. Recently, however, despite the pandemic, it has developed a vibrant restaurant scene and it is often crowded in the evening, even on weekdays.

As I have already noted, the area immediately surrounding the Monument is exceptionally rich in churches. Walk down any street and you are likely to stumble across at least one of them, or the remains of one. A short walk north on King William Street is Eliot's St Mary Woolnoth, its impressive baroque facade designed by Hawksmoor to replace an unsuccessful attempt by Wren to patch together sundry parts of the medieval building that somehow had survived the Great Fire. At the end of the Nineteenth Century, the church was scheduled to be demolished by the City and South London Underground Railway to make room for a deep tube station at Bank. The resulting outcry produced one of London's earliest preservation campaigns and led to a change of plan: the station was built in the crypt (the bones were removed to the relatively new Manor Park Cemetery) and the church above it, its structure suitably reinforced by steel beams, was left *in situ*. The church suffered remarkably little in the Blitz, though as the interior has been much altered over the years not much that is original survives. Its massive front is most impressive when seen from the opposite side of Lombard Street. The interior is quite grand, too, and well worth a few moments' perusal; not to be missed overhead in the entry is an 1810 sign displaying a table of fees for various church services; interestingly, it then cost about twice as much to be buried in the church as to be married in it, though I'm not sure what conclusion to draw from that. The entry vestibule also rather improbably hosts a very small and very good coffee bar. Behind the church is a small shaded area where one can sit and enjoy a pastry and a cappuccino.

If you are not in need of refreshment, exit the church now and cross Lombard Street—named after the Italian bankers and moneylenders who congregated here from about 1300 onward—and turn north onto very narrow Change Alley, the name a shortened form of Exchange Alley. It was here in two coffee houses, Garraway's and Jonathan's, that the dealers in company shares who had been booted from the Royal Exchange gathered and conducted the trading activity that ultimately spawned the London Stock Exchange. Whether you think the advent of securities trading a good thing or the source of all evil, pause for a moment to reflect that on this very spot modern capitalism was born.

We emerge from the alley on Cornhill, which was once, as the name suggests, a thriving grain market. Just to the east is St Michael Cornhill, an interesting Victorian re-imagining of a medieval church built around a Wren-era building. Wren-era, and not Wren—the medieval church indeed was destroyed in the Great Fire but there is no indication that Wren was involved in its rebuilding afterward. Its care supposedly was the responsibility of the Drapers' Company, but in the middle of the Nineteenth Century it was found that funds earmarked for church maintenance had had been used for far other and quite inappropriate ends. Threatened with a loss of the revenues intended for upkeep of the church, the Drapers embraced anew their duties and they embarked on substantial renovations and improvements, first guided by George Gilbert Scott and then by his associate, Herbert Williams. If you want to see what the Victorians thought a medieval parish church should have looked like, here it is.

Not much further east is St Peter-upon-Cornhill, another interesting Wren church. It is entered from St Peter's Alley behind Cornhill, but its most interesting feature is the mostly blank stucco wall that faces Gracechurch Street around the corner. It is definitely worth a quick visit and is often open to the public, although it no longer holds regular services. Not far from here on Gracechurch Street (named after a medieval church that no longer exists) were for many years the premises of Ede and Ravenscroft, founded in 1689, who claim to be the oldest men's clothier in England.

Next on our list of local churches, a short walk further south and east via Fenchurch Street to Rood Lane, is St Margaret Pattens, distinguished by its name—pattens were wooden platforms that women wore over their shoes to avoid muddying them in the streets. The origin of the church name may or may not involve footwear (it more probably is associated with a medieval cleric named Patin), but however it came by its name, the church has had a long association with the Worshipful Company of Pattenmakers. In the entryway, you will find a curious small exhibit of various historically noteworthy pattens, including some of relatively recent manufacture. This is yet another Wren church, the only one he designed with a spire that is convincingly medieval in appearance—and one of the few City churches to survive the Second World War without any damage at all. The interior is quite Spartan, but remarkable for its canopied pews, probably dating back to Wren's era, one of which has carved on it the initials CW. This graffito is almost certainly not the handiwork of the architect . . . but then again, who can say for certain?

St Dunstan's Hill, leading south from Great Tower Street, takes us to St Dunstan in the East, or what is left of it after extensive bomb damage in the Blitz. The original church was partly destroyed in the Great Fire, and the various surviving bits were then spliced together by Wren. He added a tower in pseudo-medieval style, which was taken down in 1817 when it was found to be in danger of collapse and then rebuilt yet again. The tower and two of the walls still stand, now enclosing a lovely public garden that offers a quiet and delightful picnic spot on a warm afternoon.

St Dunstan's Hill, narrowing considerably as it winds down toward the river, leads to the Billingsgate Roman House and Baths, discovered in 1848 and now open for guided tours for a very few hours on a very few days of the year. But, unlike its more famous cousin, the Roman Bath in the Strand, this really *is* the site of a Roman bath house.

We now are on Lower Thames Street, and just ahead of us is Old Billingsgate Market. (Note here another of London's "gate" names, this one likely belonging to a man named Billing and that provided a river landing for small craft.) The ornate Victorian edifice that stands here, erected by the Corporation in 1875 to designs of Horace Jones, once housed the wholesale fish market that from times medieval enjoyed a monopoly on selling fish within a circle drawn around the City precisely six and two-thirds miles in radius. That distance was reckoned to be the furthest someone could walk to the market and then back again in a single day whilst carrying a basket of fish. The fish went to the dogs in 1982—by which I mean that the market was relocated to the Isle of Dogs, but the building remains, now serving as a special events venue. It is a very impressive monument to the scale and the quality of late Victorian civic architecture.

Just past the market, rising from the river bank, is Fish Street Hill, once a lively thoroughfare but now somewhat forlorn and little trafficked, which in a few steps brings us back to the Monument—and if you've not yet climbed to the top, now would be the time to do so. Once aloft, you can pick out from the observation deck the places you have just explored on foot. Reflect as you look around that the City now has protected the views of the Monument and several other landmarks (St Paul's, the Tower, etc.), guaranteeing not only that they will continue to be seen from various vantage points, but ensuring that one can also see the City from them.

Chapter 9

Mansion House

I have always been fascinated by fractals—if you slice a small cross-section of one, its structure recapitulates that of the whole. (At least that is how my non-mathematical mind understands it.) Some urban neighbourhoods are like that—for example, the area surrounding of Mansion House. It is as close to that relationship to London whole as any part of the metropolis. It's all here—the rich past, the complex present, and the potentially extraordinary future of this great city.

A bit of an oddity is Mansion House Station—beginning with its name, unchanged since it opened in 1871. The original station was erected by the District Railway, and for a time it was the eastern terminus of its line as the company struggled to complete the southern half of what was to become the Inner Circle. Perversely, it is several hundred yards from the Mansion House, the official residence of the Lord Mayor since the mid-Eighteenth Century, a bit of which can just barely be seen from the station entrance. The station—all underground now—sits squarely at the western end of Cannon Street, and its misleading name probably results from its proximity to the main line Cannon Street rail station, which had opened just a few years earlier. Two different Cannon Street stations with the same name might have been seen as unduly confusing (though there were already two disconnected Paddington Underground stations and very soon to be two separate Hammersmith stations as well). It is also sited absurdly close to the Underground station that later opened under the main line Cannon Street terminus, as was demonstrated a few years back when a man bolted from an eastbound train at Mansion House, ran out of the station into Cannon Street, ran to and then into Cannon Street Underground Station, and continued his journey on the very same train, which had only just arrived. And, a final oddity—the station possesses a very prominent disused third track for the trains that once terminated here.

What is indisputable is that the immediate neighbourhood provides a window on several thousand years of London's history. Walk across the road (be alert, it's a complicated intersection) and just north of the station is the eastern end of Watling Street, which shares its name with the Roman Watling Street. Confusingly, this is a Roman road, but not "the" Watling Street; its name actually derives from the corruption of the Anglo-Saxon Athelingstrate (roughly translated as Princes Street). This short roadway once was part of a Roman road that ran from London Bridge through present-day Cannon Street and continued westward as Ludgate Hill and Fleet Street. The actual Roman Watling Street was south of the Thames and crossed the river much farther west, possibly at Westminster. Laid down around 47 AD, give or take a year, it followed a grassy track that had been used by native Britons for some considerable time before the Roman invasion, running from the Kentish coast through what is now Canterbury on to St. Albans and thence to the Midlands and the North. Though it was not a major highway, our little Watling Street certainly exhibits the features typical of Roman roads—it is relatively wide, very flat, and ramrod straight. (Back in the Eighties, I spent a few months living in a cottage near Felsham, a village in Suffolk, behind which was a wood that surrounded a bit of well-preserved Roman road. After nearly 2000 years, the buried foundations were still so tightly compressed that no trees would root in it, and one could walk easily enough through the tall grass that grew from the roadbed—an enduring monument of Roman civil engineering!)

Though this Watling Street is not really a Roman name, the immediate precincts just north of Mansion House are particularly rich in Roman connections and there are even some traces of the Roman city visible still. Just to the east of the Underground station and running to the north is a short street called Walbrook—as the name suggests, a paved-over rivulet, but in Roman times a free-flowing stream emptying into the Thames. Here in 1954 excavations for a new headquarters for the head office of the Legal and General insurance company (arguably one of the dullest and shabbiest pseudo-modernist buildings ever erected in London) uncovered a Roman temple devoted to the worship of the god Mithras. What exactly the mystery cult of Mithras was is a mystery still, although it seems to have been popular with military men. The temple certainly was popular with Londoners—after 400,000 of them had queued to view the temple, it was moved several hundred feet west to a site on Queen Victoria Street, where it was open to passers-by (and the elements) for nearly 60 years. The dreary office building now is gone, replaced by the striking European headquarters of Bloomberg LP, who have moved the temple back to the site where it was first excavated (and where it had slept unseen quite peacefully for two millennia). The temple now sits in a little private museum under the main building, about 20 feet below present street level—demonstrating how in a densely populated city the very ground under our feet rises over time. As for the museum, former New York Mayor Michael Bloomberg is to be congratulated for supporting the project, and the gallery wins my praise for demonstrating how modern technology can create a much richer museum experience. Entrance to the museum is free, but it must be booked in advance, although I've found that at slow times the staff occasionally will allow walk-ins.

Make your way back to Watling Street. Here you will come upon the bronze, life-size statue of a shoemaker, reminding us that traditionally these precincts were the home of the cordwainers—makers of shoes from new leather, as distinct from cobblers, who repaired them or made new ones from inferior hides. (The term "cordwainer" is etymologically related to cordovan, a kind of shoe leather.) The Worshipful Company of Cordwainers, founded in 1272, is another of the surviving livery companies of the City, celebrating its 750th birthday in 2022. The Cordwainers have lost their hall, but we will walk past several surviving livery halls presently.

Watling Street fell into disuse over time but it resurfaced (literally) in the 1670s during works associated with Christopher Wren's rebuilding of St. Mary-le-Bow, another medieval church lost to the Great Fire. Walk westward along Watling Street a short distance to the intersection with Bow Lane, the major cross-street. Turn right or north and just ahead of us Wren's church still stands, though much rebuilt after damage in the Blitz.

Arguably, we now stand at the very center of London—tradition holds that the only true Londoners are those born within sound of this church's bells. The bells still are rung daily (though the sound doesn't carry very far now) but what are struck are not the originals—those bells went in the Great Fire, and the second set, their replacement, dating from 1762, was destroyed by a German bomb in 1941. The third and most recent set dates from 1956. There is an American connection here, too—John Smith, later the saviour of the Virginia colony, was a parishioner, and a statue of him stands in the forecourt of the churchyard. (He is buried a short distance away in the churchyard of St Sepulchre-without-Newgate.)

The church interior displays rather ornate baroque decoration, virtually all of it dating from the post-Blitz restoration. The church is fronted by a modest little square, sometimes home to a flower stall and in warm weather to tables for the church café, rather a good one of its kind. Along the church's south wall is an alley that leads back to Bow Lane. The lane and the courts and alleys around it are much as they were in the Eighteenth Century—narrow, dark, and filled with small shops and public houses. (Well Court is particularly atmospheric.) This is one of my favorite corners of London, especially on a weekend morning when it is virtually deserted.

Just across Cheapside and a few steps north on King Street is a striking medieval building still very much in use—the magnificent Guildhall, dating from the first half of the Fifteenth Century and said to be the only non-ecclesiastical and non-royal medieval stone building still standing in the City. It has been the seat of London's government for 600 years, more or less.

And it has been severely damaged and then restored more than once: it was partly burned and then reroofed after the Great Fire, and after that roof was destroyed by the Luftwaffe, reroofed again as recently as 1954 to a design of another of the architectural family of Scotts, Giles Gilbert (best known as the architect of the Battersea Power Station and the designer of the once ubiquitous red telephone box). Flanking it are two newer buildings—one on the west side that houses City offices, the Guildhall Library (open to the public), and several small museums, and on the east side the Guildhall Art Gallery. Do stop in at the Gallery—which is free of admission charge and well worth a visit. Be certain to see the lower level: the gallery sits atop a Roman amphitheater that was discovered as the site was being excavated for the present building and that is now part of an extraordinary exhibit in its own right.

As you walk through the streets around the Guildhall, should you hear what sound very much like horses hooves clattering on the pavement, you will not be dreaming. You now are near the base of the officers and horses of the City of London Police Mounted Branch. The nine officers and their mounts operate out of premises on Wood Street, just west of the Guildhall. (At the bottom end of Wood Street, where it meets Cheapside, there are three row houses built shortly after the Great Fire whose ground floors comprise what are some of the oldest shops in London.)

The fourth side of the Guildhall precinct is the church of St Lawrence Jewry. The first medieval church on this site, as the name suggests, was built over what had been London's Jewish ghetto. The church was destroyed in the Great Fire, the church was rebuilt by Wren, and then, after extensive damage in the Blitz, again rebuilt in the 1950s. The street named Old Jewry is nearby and connects Gresham Street with Poultry. Though the place name has survived nearly a thousand years, the medieval Jewish ghetto itself was relatively short-lived: Jews, ever useful to monarchs as bankers and tax collectors, were first invited to England in 1070 by William the Conqueror, but at the end of the Thirteenth Century the entire community—by then several thousand people—was expelled from England. (Stow to his credit recounts the successive waves of persecution and royal thievery that were visited upon England's Jews in the years leading up to their expulsion.) England remained closed to Jews until Cromwell welcomed them back in 1656. The Jewish community, centered now not in the City but further East in Whitechapel, subsequently prospered and grew steadily in numbers.

St Lawrence Jewry serves as another useful reminder that London has also always been a center of immigration. On our walks through Spitalfields and the East End, we have remarked successive waves of migrants in modern times—among them the Huguenot French, the Irish, Eastern European Jews, Italians, Jamaicans, South Asians. From its beginnings, London has been a magnet for immigrants. New residents arrived in various ways, including by conquest (Roman and Norman) and some, against their will, cruelly enslaved, but most in search of economic opportunity.

In the early days, the contribution of immigrants was not only cultural but demographic: without vast numbers of new residents, internal and foreign, London would never have grown as rapidly as it did, or perhaps not at all. Until the middle of the Nineteenth Century, London was a sink of mortality, with annual deaths far outnumbering births. Infant mortality in particular was shockingly high, probably over 50% for the poor, but a scourge for all. Queen Anne, to note one particular instance, suffered through eighteen pregnancies; twelve infants were stillborn, five died as children, and her only surviving child died as a young man, ensuring that she was the last Stuart monarch. By the time of Anne's reign, in the early 1700s, the inflow to London was on the order of 10,000 people a year, most from the surrounding countryside. Immigration literally was the city's life blood. (And, I would argue, it still is.)

Walk down Old Jewry to its termination at Poultry and just across the road and quite literally underfoot at the very eastern end of Cheapside on the south pavement (just opposite the entrance to Tesco) is a plaque commemorating the Great Conduit. This was a pipeline built in the early Thirteenth Century to convey water from Tyburn Springs—roughly where Bond Street Tube station now stands—to the City. It passed through Charing Cross and down Fleet Street, across Fleet Bridge, and, now under pressure from gravity, flowed from there all the way to Cheapside, where it was collected in cisterns and made available free to all and sundry. It was in use for over four hundred years until it was destroyed in the Great Fire.

Poultry, where you stand now, is a good vantage point from which to consider successive waves of architectural style by studying the buildings surrounding the Bank intersection. Now that the area has been limited to bus and bicycle traffic during the day it's a bit easier to stop and look around without being run over. The buildings around the Bank road junction—the Mansion House, 1 Poultry, the Royal Exchange, the Bank of England, and the old Midland Bank—effectively showcase the last 250 years of London's development in shorthand form.

As you face east, on your right is 1 Poultry, a rather garish postmodern icon that replaced the Victorian premises of the jeweler, Mappin and Webb, and that also eliminated altogether several small ancient streets. The developer had originally planned to build a tall, American-style glass and steel skyscraper designed by Mies van der Rohe—it would have been London's twin of Seagram House (375 Park Avenue in Manhattan). The high modernist design was deemed too radical for London. Planning permission was denied and what ultimately was built, designed by James Sterling, is a massive carbuncle clad in pink stone that looks like an Ettore Sottsass Memphis chest of drawers gone wrong.

On your left, nearer to where you stand, is Edwin Lutyens's headquarters for the Midland Bank, built between the wars but harking back to Edwardian classical solidity (if not stolidity). It recently has been sensitively converted to a hotel—the exterior may be massively bland but the art deco interior, home to a tea room and cocktail lounge, is a visual treat. (Visit late in the afternoon and splurge on a drink in the stunning bar.)

Mansion House itself was built in the mid-Eighteenth Century to provide an official residence and suitable event spaces for the Lord Mayor. There were Lord Mayors in office more or less continuously from 1189, but there was no provision for a residence or even office space. The new building, to designs by George Dance the Elder, was a statement—its scale a forceful demonstration of the vast wealth, power, and prestige of the office and the city it governed. The Palladian building—criticized even at the time—seems far too large and too tall for its constricted site. Though much altered, the building continues to display power more than grace, but in so doing it serves as a good symbol of the City itself. Note the impressive sculptural pediment, which displays the City personified as a matron trampling upon envy. The interior is more successful: the vast Egyptian Hall seats 500 at dinner quite comfortably and it still is used for formal events, one of which I was lucky to attend in 2012. In addition to its own opulence, Mansion House is home to a marvelous collection of Dutch paintings, the gift of Harold Samuel, sometimes open for viewing by the public.

Poultry itself is the eastward continuation of Cheapside, once called West Cheap (balancing East Cheap, which we trod on our Monument walk.) "Chepe" is Anglo-Saxon for a place of trade, and medieval Cheapside was home to one of the principal markets in London—nearby street names like Poultry, Bread Street, and Milk Street were places where merchants specializing in those goods congregated. Roman Londinium within the walls likely was all but abandoned after 400 A.D., and the original Anglo-Saxon settlement, dating from the 700s, was actually some distance to the west, near today's Aldwych. But by the early Tenth Century, the old village at Aldwych had been abandoned in its turn and the ancient Square Mile was resettled and grew rapidly. The market on Cheapside must have sprung up not long afterward to serve its burgeoning population. Markets were the cutting edge of retail activity in their day; the cutting edge now (or perhaps as we enter the digital age one edge back from the cut) is One New Change, an upscale shopping mall at the western end of Cheapside. We won't visit it today, but it is fairly typical of its kind, replete with outposts of all the usual posh chains. Charley Dickens remarked in the late 1870s that Cheapside somehow had remained one of London's principal shopping streets for five hundred years; we can add 150 to his number and make the very same claim.

Some of the goods sold in the medieval market at Cheapside would have been landed a short distance south on the riverbank at Queenhithe, just beyond Mansion House Underground station. Supposedly it is the only remaining medieval wharf on the banks of the Thames—for now note its location but we will visit it later. Walk a few hundred feet westward, just past the point where Poultry becomes Cheapside, to Queen Street and its immediate continuation across Cheapside, King Street, a curious consequence of the Great Fire of 1666 and its aftermath.

By destroying most of the city within the walls, the Great Fire presented the Corporation with a unique opportunity not only to imagine but to create a very different London. Wren (and others) came forward with grand plans for a very different city; his would have created a grid pattern of broad streets with twin focal points at St. Paul's and the Royal Exchange. But the need to rebuild quickly necessitated selecting the simplest way forward, and that was to respect all existing property boundaries and to leave in place all the existing streets. The only widespread concession to improvement in the rebuilding was to widen the main thoroughfares—and to create just one new north-south road running from the Guildhall to Queenhithe and the river—King Street and its continuation as Queen Street.

And so we have London as it is—a modern city superimposed on a medieval street plan. Not that the fire did not force other changes: while property boundaries and the streets remained largely the as they had been, the houses newly built were required to be constructed of brick and stone, not wood. One novel product that came into being in the aftermath of the conflagration was an innovative and soon to be very popular invention, fire insurance. London's first property insurance company, Phoenix Assurance, appropriately named for the bird that rises from its own ashes, dates from 1680. London has been a center of the world insurance industry ever since. (The competing insurance companies each marked their clients' houses with visible plaques so that their proprietary fire companies would know which ones to save and which to let burn—one such plaque that dates from the early Eighteenth Century may be found on a house in Goodwin's Court, off Leicester Square.)

It is an interesting thought experiment to imagine London if Wren's grid plan had been adopted; it was designed only for the City itself, but it almost certainly would have set the pattern for the further development of the West End as well. London as Wren reimagined it would have resembled nothing so much as the Paris of Haussmann's *grands boulevards*, with broad prospects of impressive stone-faced buildings stretching on for miles. The sometimes annoying habit that London's main thoroughfares have of changing their names every few hundred feet (for example, from where we stand begins the westward sequence of Poultry, Cheapside, Newgate, and Holborn, all in fact the very same road) would have become a thing of the past, consigned to the dustbin of urban history along with all of the narrow winding lanes, the inconvenient intersections where multiple streets converge (like Seven Dials), and the (now) picturesque and sometimes surprising street names.

Directly opposite where we stand, near Bank and to the left of Mansion House, is the elegant neo-classical facade of the Royal Exchange. London has always been an *entrepôt* for, a producer of, and a market selling consumer "goods" (in the marketplace, there apparently are no "bads"), and on this spot from the 1560s merchants gathered to transact business in premises built by Sir Thomas Gresham. (Gresham is best known for Gresham's Law, which actually was formulated two hundred years after he died by one Henry Dunning McLeod.) Gresham had been impressed with the Bourse at Antwerp and thought London's merchants would benefit from a similar safe space to transact their business somewhere other than the street or an ale house. How right he was! His exchange quickly housed both wholesale transactions involving merchandise and the buying and selling of company shares, serving as a commodity trading floor and a stock exchange all in one. Retail space was added to the Exchange as early as 1660, when two stories were erected atop the existing building, in effect creating the first shopping mall in London, only a few years later to be destroyed in the Great Fire. Rebuilt quickly, that second edifice was also destroyed by fire in 1838, when the third and present building was erected. The exchange fell on hard times after World War II, and after languishing empty for years, it was renovated in 2001, successfully revived as an upscale shopping and dining venue.

You no doubt will have noticed at the front of the building the huge equestrian statue of the Duke of Wellington. Rather oddly, he is hatless and sits atop a saddle without stirrups, a curious omission. (Wellington attended the unveiling of the statue in 1844, so presumably he did not object to the peculiar features.) To the rear of the building are monuments commemorating George Peabody, founder of the Peabody Trust, and Baron Paul von Reuter, founder of the international news agency that still bears his name. Reuter, like Peabody, was an immigrant: he was born Jewish in Germany as Israel Beer Josephat, and all in one year, 1845, he moved to England, converted to Christianity, changed his name, and married. (His title, by the by, is German, but by order of Queen Victoria it is recognized and heritable in Britain.)

Also tucked immediately behind the Royal Exchange is an elaborate Victorian water fountain, a bronze statue of a mother tending to two small children atop an even more elaborate stone plinth girdled by benches. Public fountains like this remind us that ensuring a reliable and adequate water supply to the growing city was always a major challenge—let alone to supply it fresh and clean. For most of the early modern period, water was supplied mainly by private companies—some piped in water from the countryside while others drew it directly from the increasingly polluted Thames. Most made some minimal provision for free pumps or cisterns, but by the middle of the Nineteenth Century, as the population of London exploded, demand far outstripped supply. The inadequacies of London's water supply came to the fore in the 1850s—not only was most of it filthy, and (somewhat later) known to be contaminated with disease-causing germs, but there simply wasn't enough of it for London's poor, working or otherwise. The water companies—there were 6 north of the river and 4 south—were very profitable and so they had no economic incentive to change the *status quo*.

As was so often the case in Victorian England, when government was reluctant to solve a pressing social problem, private philanthropy attempted to meet the need. Hence this fountain, erected by the Metropolitan Free Drinking Fountain Association, founded in 1859, a product of the zeal and the bank account of Samuel Gurney, an exemplary instance of the mid-century self-made man. The association's self-appointed mission was to provide clean, safe, and *free* water to human Londoners and also to their equine and bovine companions. (Gurney was part of a respected family of Norwich bankers, made infamous in 1866 by the collapse of their limited liability banking concern, Overend Gurney, just one year after they had sold shares to the public at a substantial premium; Samuel Gurney, like most of the family, seems to have escaped the bankruptcy without significant personal loss.)

The association wasted no time—it built and opened its first fountain in Snow Hill in the same year it was founded. Ultimately, it erected hundreds of fountains and cattle troughs in London (a fine example of the latter stands at Clerkenwell Green), many of which, like that behind the Royal Exchange, survive—though now mostly dry. After only a few years in operation it claimed that it was providing water to 300,000 Londoners daily. Remarkably, the foundation is still extant, although with a slightly altered name, hard at work providing drinking fountains to schools and supporting clean water projects in developing regions of the world.

This is a good opportunity to take a short walk to the East on Threadneedle Street, which soon brings us to number 30, the rather modest exterior of the Merchant Taylors' Hall, home to yet another City livery company. Its charter dates from 1327 and, portions of its original medieval hall survive. It is said to be the oldest livery hall still in active use. The building's spare exterior belies the rich interior, and to see the kitchen in full swing, with its towering ancient wall overlooking, is a treat indeed, one which I enjoyed thanks to the hall's ever-helpful beadle, Andy Fell.

Retail establishments in the streets around Bank these days include branches of the chains that are prominent on every high street, among them both the obligatory "local" supermarket and the global coffee chain (you know the brands). Yet for the most part City shops and restaurants remain small and there still are quite a few "independents," especially those purveying what might be called slow "fast" food, much of it Asian. Variations of Vietnamese *banh mi*—itself a productive fusion of France and Vietnam—are particularly popular at the moment; a good rule of thumb that I cribbed from Anthony Bourdain is to turn up at lunchtime, when the streets are full of local office workers, and then look for the establishment with the longest line out the door. The "chef" of one eatery on Bouverie Street I that favor comes from Paris and his fillings are both scrupulously fresh and quite original; go early before the best ones sell out. And even in the common spaces of One New Change, amid the luxury brands, a sort of market has sprung up some days of the week where small stalls sell interesting ethnic ingredients as well as food to consume on the spot. The irony of a street market setting up inside a shopping mall is striking, abundant proof that what goes around comes around, sooner or later.

The City's global power today more than anything else is in the realm of finance—and so it is surely no accident that immediately opposite Mansion House is one of the pillars of the world's financial establishment, the Bank of England. Founded in 1694 by the new monarchs, William and Mary, as an expedient to fund a large government loan, the Bank met first in borrowed premises, but before long it became associated with this site. The City had been a center of banking and financial activity since the early medieval period; after all, the import, export, and buying and selling of consumer goods from all over the world requires a robust financial system to support it all. But even so, the creation of the central bank (one of the first in Europe) marked a new era for London, and this, its first permanent structure, is suitably monumental.

The present building is impressive seen from a distance, but to pedestrians walking beside it at street level its grim, windowless exterior wall is rather forbidding. It is so by design: the exterior is a response to the anti-Catholic Gordon Riots of 1780 when the bank was attacked by a large mob, successfully repulsed by troops but with great loss of life. This is all the work of Sir John Soane, who signed on as the Bank's architect in 1788. Soane laboured on the site for the next 45 years (most of his work was hidden behind the walls), surely one of the longest architectural commissions of all time. Very little of his design other than the exterior wall survives. His own house in Lincoln's Inn Fields, which we will visit on a later walk, is a museum that preserves his sprawling residence as it was when he died; displayed in it, among other treasures, is an 1830 watercolor by Joseph Michael Gandy that features a cutaway view of the rabbit warren of offices that Soane created behind the Bank's outer walls.)

Gone are the days when U.K. banks were required to maintain a physical presence close to the Bank of England so that cheques and other financial instruments could be settled in person. But in 1986, the previously staid world of English banking was turned inside out by the "Big Bang," the first and most important of a series of acts of radical deregulation. Financial services now make up something like 12.5% of the UK economy, and fully half of that contribution comes from London. The reach of the City is more global than ever—even after Brexit, London consistently pips New York as the number one banking center in the world—with the Square Mile (and its Canary Wharf annex) its heart and soul. At least so far, the impact of Brexit is less disruptive than many had feared and expected.

Cross the complex set of pedestrian lights to King William Street and walk south. Note the small turning on the right, Sherborn Lane, wholly unremarkable except for its name, which is an early euphemistic version of Shitburgh Lane, probably the site of a common privy. Cross Cannon Street opposite number 111, which houses and displays at street level a rather non-descript block of limestone that probably once was part of a Roman building but somehow as early as the Twelfth Century had taken on the name of *the* London Stone. Supposedly (and suspiciously like the story of young King Arthur) the rebel Jack Cade thrust his sword into it as his ragtag army entered London in 1450. (Despite the auspicious beginning, Cade's rebellion failed and he was mortally wounded in battle.) Various theories about the stone's ancient use and significance have been put forward, most of them aptly characterized as speculative, if not completely daft. One of them predicts that if the stone were ever to be moved, London would suffer dire consequences. In 2016, the stone in fact was removed for two years to the Museum of London while the site was in redevelopment; is it a mere coincidence that Brexit followed? In any event, believers in the myth may breathe a sigh of relief as the stone has been reinstalled in a glass-fronted repository at the original address.

Turn west along Cannon Street and just past the newly rebuilt main line station, turn southward toward the river on College Hill, a remarkably intact corner of pre-Blitz London. The eponymous college—long defunct—was the College of St Spirit and St Mary, founded by Richard (a.k.a. Dick) Whittington, the original "self-help" paragon: supposedly born poor, he was four times mayor of London, but he is most famous for his cat, according to the popular story sold to a Moorish king to eradicate the rats that were plaguing him, thereby founding Dick's fortune—and providing fodder for countless holiday season pantomimes. Alas, Whittington was not born poor and he never sold his cat to a king. But wealthy and powerful he certainly was, and a ceramic plaque now marks the location of the house where he lived. (There is also a Whittington Stone in Highgate, where the young apprentice Whittington had fled from ill treatment in London, and where, hearing the Bow bells ring out the message, "Turn again," an impressive aural feat given the distance, he turned back, the rest, as they say, is history.) The almshouse also founded by Whittington, like the college, is long gone, but the impressive doorway of the Innholders Hall is still fronts College Street (the hall itself dating from just after the Great Fire), as is the charming little church of St Michael's Paternoster Royal, a largely intact Wren church on the site of its medieval precursor, destroyed in the Great Fire. And as long as we're exposing fake history, please note that the "Royal" in the church name isn't royal at all—it is a corruption of Reole, the town in Bordeaux that was the center of wine production when this was the hub of the wine trade in London.

Continuing oenological connections, at the bottom of the hill, turn right across the lower end of Queen Street (watch out for the Boris bikes racing downhill) and on the other side of Upper Thames Street is Vintners' Hall, now part of a newer development, Vintners Court. While it is unimpressive from the street, it is quite magnificent within. I cannot pass up the opportunity to note that the Vintners, together with the Worshipful Company of Dyers, are the only entities other than the Crown that are permitted to own swans on the Thames, the privilege commemorated in July by the now largely ceremonial practice of swan upping. In the old days, this exercise involved marking the birds by clipping their bills (and eventually eating them), but it is now a census to determine the state of the health of the swan population on the river. (You will be relieved to learn that they are thriving.) You are now at the pedestrian entry to Southwark Bridge, which has a vaguely Victorian look about it though it dates from 1921. If you have time, walk halfway across to savor the views up and down the river); then return to the river bank, take the stairs down to the river, and turn west along the river path. This takes us at last, and as promised, to Queenhithe.

This ancient wharf now is not much to look at—when the tide is out, it exposes a dreary rectangular patch of rubbish-strewn mud and gravel riverbank—but it is noteworthy for its survival more than its appearance. Located just to the west of Southwark Bridge, it may well have been in use as early as Roman times. (A mural on the low brick wall along its eastern boundary recounts its long history.) It became the "Queen's" hithe or quay when Matilda, wife of Henry I, was granted the revenues of duties imposed on all goods landing there. The royal or at least governmental connection continues: as a protected ancient monument, the site is now in the hands of English Heritage. The river foreshore—defined as the zone uncovered between high and low tides—is still regarded as Crown property. Amateurs used to be able to engage in mudlarking (as scavenging on the riverbank is called) along the Thames without permission, but now a permit (available online) is required as is the payment of a substantial fee. I've done some larking of mud here myself, so I can attest from experience that all sorts of interesting bits and pieces turn up on a daily basis, ranging from Roman glass to medieval nails to Chinese export porcelain to Victorian wine bottles, and quite literally millions of white clay pipe stems and bowls, not to mention endless plastic beverage containers of more recent manufacture. (Be aware that an appropriate museum should be consulted about any found object of significant historical value.)

Continue westward, although this requires a dogleg detour to High Timber Street. (This is the only discontinuity on the river path in all of Central London.) Walk westward past Stew Lane, which you'll recall probably took its name as a place to hire a boat to cross the river to consort with the Winchester geese, and continue past Trig Lane, said to be named after a medieval fishmonger. Return to the river via Broken Wharf. Now we are within site of the Millennium Bridge, designed by Norman Foster and at first disconcertingly wobbly, but now completely stabilized. These days it is almost always jam-packed with selfie-snapping tourists. Climb the long set of stairs on the south side of the bridge (there is a lift, but it's usually out of order) and enjoy the picture postcard perfect view of St Paul's (which we will visit on our next outing). Then turn 180 degrees and take in the massive profile of the Tate Modern, once a power station, and a sibling of its counterpart at Battersea. Turn again, like Whittington, to face the cathedral, and you will see just across the road and slightly to the west the College of Arms, its elegant red-brick symmetrical form still looking much as it did when it was rebuilt shortly after the original building burned in the Great Fire; it was also damaged by a fire again only a few years ago but appears to have been fully restored. Don't cross the street (unless you plan a bit of genealogical research to establish your right to a coat of arms), but turn right (east) on Queen Victoria Street. On the north side, at the intersection of Friday Street, you'll see a Police Call Box, painted bright blue—one of the last survivors of a network of these objects, all with direct lines to the nearest local police station. The system was useful in the era before the advent of the mobile phones that have made it completely redundant. And now just a stone's throw ahead of us is the tube station where we began now is.

And so there you have it—within a half-mile radius of the tube station, visible traces of every era of London's history, encompassing the Roman, the Anglo-Saxon, the Medieval, the Modern, and the Twenty-First Century city. This same small compass has served as the nursery, incubator, and principal nexus of London's wholesale, retail, and securities markets as well as its financial center. It may be an exaggeration to say that if you are tired of Mansion House you are tired of life, but if any one tube station opens a window onto both London's rich history and London's enduring greatness, it would indeed be Mansion House.

Chapter 10

Blackfriars

Our journey begins today in the vast, relatively new combined Underground and main line station at Blackfriars. The original Underground station here at first was named St Paul's when it opened in 1870 as the eastern terminus of the District Railway. Nothing of the old station above ground remains. The entire complex was rebuilt in a somewhat sterile postmodern vernacular in 2009–2011. The large, open entry hall is an impressive public space but it feels rather too capacious and monumental for the modest traffic passing through it; before the pandemic, even at the peak of morning and evening rush hours, it seemed underutilized, at times virtually deserted.

Blackfriars take its name from dark habits of the Dominican friars whose priory was located here on the banks of the Thames from 1276 until its dissolution by Henry VIII in 1538. This area, on the western edges of the medieval City, was in the Thirteenth Century open land that became home to several large religious communities: the first to settle here in 1225 just to the north, on Newgate Street, were the Greyfriars, the Franciscans; the Whitefriars—named after the Carmelites' habits—from 1253 were just to the west. All survive as place names, but little more than the names remain.

As you exit the station, bear left, and just outside is another of those grand Victorian water fountains erected by Samuel Gurney and the Metropolitan Drinking Fountain Association. This one dates from 1861 and though it looks intact, it is dry, as are so many of the other survivors scattered around the City. We are now standing on Blackfriars Bridge, lately disfigured, as are all the Thames crossings, by huge bollards and concrete blocks installed to prevent vehicular attacks on pedestrians. The whole of Blackfriars Bridge and a smidgeon of the road on the other side were long within the boundaries of the City (like the southern end of London Bridge). Do walk toward the southern end to see the massive cast iron coat of arms of the London, Chatham, and Dover Railway atop the remains of the old rail bridge.

As you now can see easily enough, Blackfriars is home to not one but three bridges—more accurately two and a half—across the Thames. (Arguably, the count is four if you include the pedestrian Millennium Bridge only a few hundred yards to the east.) The first road and pedestrian bridge here opened in 1769, at the time only the third crossing to span the river in the whole of the metropolitan area (the others were London Bridge and Richmond Bridge). That first bridge at Blackfriars was taken down in the 1860s and the present replacement opened in 1869. It is a fine example of Victorian engineering— elegant cast iron arches atop graceful stone piers, the heads of which have intricate high relief carvings of birds native to the river, and which are just visible from several cozy bays where pedestrians can sit and shelter from the wind (and, in my observation, if tourists, they mostly take photographs of themselves, and if Londoners, they smoke or canoodle).

The first rail bridge opened in 1864; the second, on a competing line and very much still in use, in 1886. There was no main line station at first—that was on the South Bank and called Blackfriars Bridge Station; the main line station as we know it came into being with the opening of the second rail bridge in 1886. The first rail bridge remained in service until 1985, when it was partly demolished, though its massive piers and bright red supporting pillars were left in place. This no doubt was an exercise in cheeseparing, but serendipitous cheeseparing: when the stations and the platforms were extended in 2009, the easternmost pillars were incorporated into the new South Bank station platforms to help support them. Those freestanding pillars that remain, painted bright red, are not easily overlooked. They have always looked to me as if they are the first phase of a grand structure that is about to be built rather than what they are, the forlorn remains of an old one that's been semi-demolished.

Also at the southern edge of the bridge and is a bran-new high-rise project, appropriately named One Blackfriars. At 170 metres (just under 570'), it dominates the mid-city South Bank skyline. The first developer on the site went bust; the second developer's web site boasted during construction that it was "[e]nvisaged as an awe-inspiring sculpture looking down on the River Thames." A more disinterested passer-by might call it an ungainly blob lurking over the river that looks dangerously unbalanced, as if, given a shove, it might just tip over. (The structure's mid-building bulge has also given the building it's informal name, the Boomerang.) Like so many other new buildings, it is sheathed in reflective glass. I must come clean: a glass skin is a *bête noir* for me. Back in the 1930s and 1940s arguably it was a bold and innovative architectural statement that highlighted new construction techniques, but nowadays it is almost invariably a cop-out, architects borrowing reflected images of the surrounding buildings to hide their failure to design something that would be both contemporary and distinctive. This tower is home to 274 luxury "apartments," which sounds much classier than "flats," very much like the Shard and a few other spectacularly tall mixed-use structures that are meant to comprise a "vertical city" (as the Shard calls itself). The price tags are equally sky high, another sign of the reversal of status of high rise buildings from the days when they were associated solely with soulless council housing. When it opened, some of the flats were meant to be affordable (they weren't) and the observation deck was to be open to the public (it isn't).

Retrace your steps along the bridge toward the station and immediately opposite the station entrance is a leading contender for the worst pedestrian intersection in London. Unfortunately, our route requires you to cross here to reach the north side of Queen Victoria Street. Several main roads come together at the bridge approach, and the pedestrian subway designed to separate foot traffic from vehicular traffic is a poorly signposted maze that almost guarantees that the few brave souls who use it will come out at the wrong corner and then be forced to cross the road anyway. Already confusing enough, in recent years the addition of bicycle highways and another set of traffic signals for two-wheeled traffic has made a bad crossing worse. The timing of the "go" signals seems to ensure that clueless pedestrians will be stranded in the middle of the road.

It is worth reflecting as well that at this point we stand on the eastern edge of the original Thames Embankment that ran from here west to Westminster. Built from 1865 to 1870, this was the work of Joseph Bazalgette, part of a massive civil engineering project to convey the bulk of London's raw sewage through huge underground outfall pipes to the eastern edges of the city, where it would serve as fertilizer on what still was farmland. This was designed to remove a goodly proportion of the human waste and other detritus in the river that had caused the Great Stink of 1858, when Parliament itself was driven out of Westminster by the awful stench rising from the Thames after a spell of hot, dry weather. It was in many ways an engineering marvel: the flow of sewage was entirely powered by gravity. (Later embankment projects, like that at Chelsea, added pumping stations.)

At the same time as the new Embankment solved the sewage disposal problem, it also regularized the Thames foreshore, providing a new, wide, and much-needed east-west thoroughfare connecting Westminster and the City. It was in the end one of the most important, impressive, large, and (against all odds) highly successful Victorian public works projects. It has for so long been so much a part of London's fabric that it is difficult to imagine what it replaced—a jumble of rundown warehouses and streets sliding (sometimes literally) downward into the water. The Embankment also incorporated a rail tunnel that allowed the construction of a key segment of the District Railway's eastern section of the Underground inner circuit. Sewers, roads, and railways were planned to have been built concurrently, but the perennially cash-strapped District fell behind and the opportunity was lost; in the end, parts of the new Embankment had to be dug up almost immediately to allow the District's tracks to be installed.)

If you do manage to cross Queen Victoria Street without sacrificing life or limb, you now will be standing at one of the architectural gems of London, the Blackfriar Pub. Built in 1875, in 1905 it was remodeled in an exuberant Arts and Crafts style, and it is mostly untouched, inside and out. But it was once at risk, and indeed the Blackfriar holds a special place in the history of the preservation of London's landmark buildings. It was slated for demolition in the early 1960s in connection with improvements to the rail line from the main line station into the City. A campaign led by Sir John Betjman and the recently founded Victorian Society saved it. The interior decoration, all on the theme of jolly monks enjoying themselves with food and drink, is spectacular. Every detail—from the carvings to the mottos to the lamps—is of a piece and relates to this pastoral vision of Merrie Olde England. The snug (the cozy inner parlor) is particularly inviting and rich in spoof monkishness; unfortunately, it now is exclusively a dining room and can be visited only for the price of a typical pub meal. I first visited it in the early 2000s, when it was usually empty every evening except Friday. It has become of late a popular after-work spot for City workers and it now even attracts tourists, so it is best avoided in the early evening and on weekends.

Walk under the railway bridge to the east of the Blackfriar and just past it take the first turning on the left, Blackfriars Lane. Walk up the hill and you will find yourself in a warren of small streets and alleys, many pedestrianized, that provide a bit of the atmosphere of the City before the Blitz leveled so much of it. The local street names, like Creed Lane, Friar Street, Pilgrim Street, and so on, bear witness to the vanished priory, as does the churchyard of St Anne Blackfriars, now a tiny park. Step inside the churchyard and immediately on your right you will see a small section of the priory wall, one of the few extant physical remains of the monastery.

Another august survivor is the Apothecaries Hall, half way up the hill, home of the Worshipful Society of Apothecaries, another of the City's livery companies. The Apothecaries were relative latecomers to guild status, founded as recently as 1617, having before that been housed within the Grocers' Company, and, before that, the Guild of Pepperers. In 1632 they acquired Cobham House, formerly part of the priory, to use as their hall, only to see it burn down in 1666. Rebuilt by 1672, and incorporating one portion of the original Thirteenth Century wall on the north side of the courtyard (clearly visible still), it looks today much as it did after extensive renovations in the late Eighteenth Century. Inside, the Great Hall, Court Room, and Parlour are virtually unchanged since the 1670s. The Apothecaries remain quite active in their original field of expertise—while they no longer compound drugs on this site as once they had done (that work finally ceased in 1922 but an unmarked doorway set into the building facade marks the location of the old druggist shop), they do offer various courses of medical education, conducting a broad range of postgraduate workshops and diplomas. They also have historic links to the Chelsea Physic Garden, formerly their working medicinal plant laboratory, and now operated by an independent charity and at some times of the year open to the public. (We will walk by it on our Sloane Square ramble.) The Apothecaries still own a few properties in the immediate neighbourhood—look for houses with a bright blue front door.

At the top end of Blackfriars Lane, the same street continues northward for a short distance as Ludgate Broadway (broad only in comparison to the adjacent narrow thoroughfares), but we will take the first turning on the right onto Carter Lane. (The name bespeaks its humble commercial origins.) Running parallel to Ludgate Hill, Carter Lane is a bit of a throwback, filled with small, family-run restaurants and a few old-school pubs. One small detour worth taking is a narrow lane on the right, Church Entry, at the bottom of which you will find Ireland Yard, the site of the last London home of Shakespeare. Or, at least, this is the last London property he *owned*; he purchased it in 1613 and immediately leased it back to the seller and a few years later he was dead. There is speculation he used it as a *pied a terre* on his occasional visits from Stratford, but that is probably wishful thinking. (There is a commemorative plaque but for some reason it is around the corner on St Andrew's Hill.) You'll also see here a not very impressive bit of stone wall that was part of one of the gates of the priority—hence "Church Entry."

At this point, you are in fact standing directly over what once was the center of the Dominican priory. Looking around, one can begin to understand why the dissolution of the monasteries and the Crown's seizure of their buildings and estates were so important to the city's development. The Dissolution was the largest transfer of property (and of wealth) in London's history. Late medieval and early modern London was often criticized for growing too populous too quickly. Indeed, several monarchs tried to counter the growth by prohibiting building outside the city walls, but these attempts inevitably all failed. As the city's population grew, overcrowding within the walls made it necessary that there be more and more development beyond the city gates. The land occupied by the monasteries and other church establishments located as they were just outside the walls, thus was becoming prime territory for new building. And whatever Henry VIII's motives may have been, in one fell swoop (or a series of coordinated swoops) he simultaneously provided vast tracts of land for new buildings and founded or enhanced the fortunes of many families who with their new wealth were able to build on it. It is hardly an exaggeration to say that the Dissolution created London's real estate market, which has never looked back. So if a one bedroom flat in the

City now costs the best part of a million pounds, you can blame Henry, the eighth monarch of that name.

Back on Carter Lane, another gateway just a little further on provides entry to the King's Wardrobe, now home to self-catering holiday flats. Inside the entryway are well-preserved Eighteenth Century brick terraces, but in the late medieval period this was a royal storage facility, more for arms and armor than clothing. It was destroyed in the Great Fire and never rebuilt; however the name survives as Wardrobe Place.

Just a stone's throw away now (quite literally) is the landmark that gave Blackfriars Station its first name, St Paul's Cathedral. There is no building more associated with London and no building in the metropolis more impressive in its own right than Wren's *chef d'oervre*. A good time to view the interior is when it is theoretically closed to tourists—during church services. My favorite time to visit is at Evensong on a week day, generally at 5 pm. Often there is choral or organ music, and while the sound fills the space, one has the opportunity to sit quietly and explore visually.

As you listen to the music, glance upward into the iconic dome. The cathedral is a magnificent blend of a medieval floor plan and neoclassical design, but the dome is for me the masterpiece of Wren's masterpiece. Pevsner called it the finest dome in the world. There are actually three layers to it: the interior dome; an outer dome rising 365' (no doubt an astronomical and architectural pun), high enough to ensure that it could be seen from virtually anywhere in the City; and a cone that lies between them, a massive tower of brick that supports the immense weight of the cupola—something like 850 tons. Sit directly under the dome and try to look up directly into the oculus; if the light and the angle are just right, you can see some of the intermediary brickwork. The dome's interior decoration—scenes from the life of St Paul—is stunning, and it so successfully blends actual architectural details with painted features that it is difficult to tell where the building ends and the painting begins.

Still, I have always found the interior decoration rather overwhelming; I prefer to see the cathedral from the outside. (And the best time for that is at night, when the cathedral is highlighted by very effective dramatic lighting.) Just outside the front of the cathedral is an impressive statue of Queen Anne, which is actually a Twentieth-Century copy of the original. To the right is Paternoster Square, the redeveloped area to the north of the church. It is worth pausing for a few moments here. Extensively damaged in the Blitz, this area was the site a number of undistinguished mid-century modern buildings that were built shoddily in the 1960s. Twenty years later, most tenants had moved on, and the Corporation was determined to redevelop the site all over again but to do a better job of it. The initial proposals, very much in contemporary architectural style, were publicly criticized by then Prince Charles as unsuited to a location so close to the cathedral, and after the ensuing fracas, they were abandoned. In the end, planning permission was granted for a design by Sir William Whitfield that mirrored the neo-classical style and the Portland stone building materials of St Paul's. (Charles has been both pilloried and praised for his architectural interventions, which also included forcing the redesign of a new wing of the National Gallery.)

As you leave the cathedral, immediately on the right is Temple Bar, a city gate rebuilt by Wren (although it had not been damaged in the Great Fire). Standing at the western boundary of the City, for two hundred years it served as a ceremonial entrance to and from Westminster, but since it was absurdly narrow, it was also an awkward obstacle for traffic on the Strand and Fleet Street. It was finally taken down in 1878, and the stones were sold to a wealthy brewer who rebuilt it in the garden of his country house. There it remained until 2003, when it was relocated here.

Through the archway of Temple Bar lies a large open plaza, the pedestrianized heart of Paternoster Square. When the development's design was first floated, there were doubts as to whether the space would function at all, but one has only to visit at lunchtime on a warm spring day, when each and every surface that can accommodate a human backside has one firmly planted on it, to appreciate that it is one of those rare instances where genuine community space has been created. If one were inclined to carp (and generally I am), one might complain that all of the many takeaway food options are branches of the same chains that can be found everywhere in Central London—but at least there are dining options, however predictable.

Leave the Square by walking back through Temple Bar, then turn right (west), and as you stroll down Ludgate Hill toward Ludgate Circus, which together preserve the name of another of the ancient city gates, note along the way the front of St Martin's Ludgate, another well-preserved Wren church. You now are entering the Fleet Valley. There is actually still a river here, long covered over, but as recently as the Eighteenth Century this section leading to the Thames was still on the surface, though by that time it was reduced to a foul, sewage-clogged ditch. At the very western end of Ludgate Hill begins the eastern foot of Fleet Street, once the center of Britain's newspaper world, of which more in a moment. Just visible ahead and to the left, hovering over the surrounding buildings, you will see the spire of St. Bride's—another post-fire Wren church heavily restored after damage in the Blitz and supposedly the site of a church founded by St Bridget in the Sixth Century. (Bride is a corruption of her name.) St Bride's spire was Wren's tallest on a parish church, and once you are familiar with its shape, it is often possible to pick it out from the skyline at many vantage points around the city.

Near this church, in 1500, the serendipitously named German immigrant Wynkyn de Worde set up one of the first printing presses in England; later he set up a stall in St Paul's Churchyard. The area quickly became the center of the publishing trade and here too in 1702 London's first daily newspaper, the *Daily Courant*, was founded by Elizabeth Mallet. Eventually, Fleet Street was home to almost all London-based and many of the national newspapers, large and small. By the middle of the last century most of the major dailies had built palatial headquarters here, though as print journalism has declined into near irrelevance, their grand buildings now mostly are home to financial and consulting firms. The *Daily Express* building—now the London HQ of Goldman Sachs—is arguably the finest Art Deco edifice in London, and the first building in the City to be entirely sheathed in glass. Though the newspapers all have left for greener (and cheaper) pastures, and the press is increasingly irrelevant to the production of news, the journalistic establishment in Britain still is and probably always will be referred to metonymically as "Fleet Street." (You may recall that Rupert Murdoch started the newspapers' exodus from Fleet Street in 1986 when he moved the *Sun* and the *Times* to Wapping.)

Pause on the southwest corner of the beginning of Fleet street to admire the late Victorian majolica tile front entry of the Punch public house (and stop in for a pint if you've time), and then turn south into Bride Lane, which will take you directly to St Bride's. The church and the churchyard are an oasis of quiet, miraculously just steps from one of the busiest intersections in all of London. At the time of my last visit here, an elderly homeless man who had set up camp in one corner of the churchyard was deep in conversation with a small group of tourists; inside, I found a box of paperback books for sale on the honour system, and I managed to score an Ian Rankin Inspector Rebus novel that I hadn't yet read to take on my next trans-Atlantic flight.

Though Fleet Street itself has lost most of what marked it formerly as the home of the press, there are still a few drinking establishments once frequented by the fourth estate that have survived its departure (including Ye Olde Cheshire Cheese and the El Vino Wine Bar). (The phrase "fourth estate" for the press, by the way, was coined by Edmund Burke, the other three being the common people, the hereditary nobility, and the clergy). But aside from these drinking holes and the grand headquarters buildings noted above, there is little here that you cannot find on any standard "high street" in London. One exception is the Old Bell Tavern, tucked into Bride's Lane behind the churchyard. Supposedly, it was built by Wren, though almost certainly it was not, but it probably was frequented by workmen rebuilding churches after the fire. The clientele today is more likely to be builders of web sites than builders of churches, but it is still packed on a Friday evening.

We are now close to Whitefriars Street, and a few hundred feet down the street, south of Fleet Street, is Ashentree Court (a lovely name, though there is no tree there now) which, after a dogleg twist, turns into the equally pleasantly named Magpie Alley. There is a good reason to detour here—the opportunity to see a small section of the crypt of what probably was the abbot's house within the Carmelite monastery. The ruins are below ground, accessible through a gate that is usually left unlocked, down a set of unmarked stairs, and visible through a long window. The building above them dates from the 1980s, but it sits on the site of what once had been the home of the *News of the World*, a Sunday paper that in 1950 achieved the largest sustained circulation of any newspaper in history, 8.5M copies; in some weeks, it sold a touch over 9M—about one for every four adult Britons. It was bought by Rupert Murdoch in 1969 (after a bruising battle with Robert Maxwell, a now nearly-forgotten media mogul later unmasked as a financial fraudster); under Murdoch's leadership it became known as "News of the Screws" for its aggressive coverage of the couplings (and at times throuplings) of celebrities and politicians. It was closed in 2011 in the wake of scandal—it was found that its journalists had been illegally hacking innocent parties' cell phones to juice up stories. It was then at the time still selling over 2M copies a week and shutting it down is said to have cost Murdoch's News Corp £240M.

It now is time to turn back towards Blackfriars Station. Walk on by way of St Bride's Passage, an alley just east of the churchyard that terminates at the opening of Salisbury Square. This is a small, quiet, and often deserted public space, once part of the London lodgings of the Bishop of Salisbury and the site of a theatre in the Seventeenth Century. Note the obelisk commemorating Robert Waithman, who rose from humble origins to become a successful linen draper; he went into politics as a "radical," eventually serving both as a Member of Parliament and Lord Mayor. Monuments to mayors of London are few and far between; this one seems to have been well deserved. (The City Corporation has proposed redeveloping Salisbury Square; let us hope they don't ruin it in the process.)

We are standing now atop what was the home of the Carmelites. After the Dissolution, this area, right down to the river bank, was one of the most notorious of the ancient liberties. It took on the name of Alsatia at some point, apparently because like Alsace it was disputed territory, but over the years Alsatia became a generic term for any lawless neighbourhood. Alsatia's status as a refuge for criminals and debtors (and that of the other liberties) was eliminated by act of Parliament in 1697, but perhaps not all that effectively, since a second act to eliminate them was passed in 1723. Though from that time no longer a liberty, its reputation as a den of petty thievery and crime persisted well into the Nineteenth Century.

Walk south from the square on Dorset Rise to the intersection with Tudor Street and turn left, which will take us immediately to New Bridge Street. From here you again can see Blackfriars Station just south of where we stand. Walk towards it, and as we approach the river, on our right is the massive, curved façade of Unilever House, begun by Lever Brothers in 1920 and completed in 1931 under the aegis of its new multi-national successor firm, Unilever, the result of a merger with a Dutch margarine manufacturer. At the time it was the most valuable company in the United Kingdom and the largest soap manufacturer in the world; the building is still the headquarters of Unilever and on rare occasions it is open to the public. The building is as grand as befits a leviathan of the business world, its curved façade best seen from the river at night when it is illuminated. The style is a cross of Edwardian monumental and Art Deco, though unfortunately most of the decoration is too high up to be seen from the pavement.

Cross the road to the station where we started our tour, but before we go inside, we have one final detour: just to the right of the station entrance, it is possible to take the stairs down to the river (there is also a lift, usually not working). Under the bridge, the Fleet River empties into the Thames, usually quietly, but in rainy weather with a bit of gusto. If you are lucky and the tide is out, you can see the mouth of the outflow tunnel. (This will be the last of our encounters with the underground Fleet.)

Walk east and linger for a few moments on the riverbank. Pleasant as this is, continue to walk eastward through a sort of galley park, and take the first set of stairs up to the street level. You will emerge onto Queen Victoria Street. Immediately to the east and rather isolated by a poorly designed road crossing is the striking Church of St Benet (a contraction of Benedict), the *only* Wren church both undamaged in the Blitz and unaltered by renovation. It is quite unusual for a City church and for a Wren church in that it is made primarily of brick, with only its decorative accents in Portland stone. It also contains within some of the finest surviving carvings of Grinling Gibbons. It is the official church of the College of Arms and also since 1879 the home of London's metropolitan Welsh Anglican congregation. It is open a few hours a week, courtesy of the Friends of the City Churches, and well worth a visit if you should be there at the right time.

But it is also time to walk west on Queen Victoria Street and to reenter the Underground. Onward to our next station, Embankment.

Chapter 11

Embankment

Embankment Station has had this name since 1976, but it started life in 1870 as Charing Cross, presumably to emphasize its location adjacent to the main line station which it was built principally to serve. The present station building, in a somewhat bland, non-descript neo-Georgian style, dates from the early part of the Twentieth Century. "Embankment"—which at various times before 1976 was only part of its name—is the more accurate if less useful tag, as the station was built in conjunction with the Victoria Embankment as the District Railway marched East toward the City. Given its proximity to so many tourist attractions, including Trafalgar Square and the National Gallery, one might expect it to be among the busiest stations: though it does often feel incredibly overcrowded, it served a mere 22,000,000 passengers a year before the pandemic, not a particularly impressive number for a central London station adjacent to a main line rail terminus.

Leave the station and walk north to Villiers Street, named after George Villiers, Duke of Buckingham, who owned York House (once the London residence of the Archbishop of York) in the 1680s when the palatial residence was demolished and this site was first developed. (Buckingham Street is not far away.) Villiers Street now is pedestrianized, and it offers nothing more than a dreary assemblage of fast food joints catering mainly to tourists. We will avoid it, turning sharply to the right to enter the splendid Victoria Embankment Gardens. This is one of four riverside gardens created when the Embankment was built, an instance of enlightened town planning if ever there was.

Wander through the garden in an easterly direction, noting along the way the plethora of monuments and statues, featuring both names you may recognize (like Robert Burns) and many you probably will not. Indeed, who now remembers Sir Wilfred Lawson, Robert Raikes, or General Sir James Outram, all honored here with statuary monuments? Of, for that matter, who recalls the exploits of the Imperial Camel Corps, also given its own monument. These tokens of past celebrity remind us that nothing is as fleeting as fame, and even those who achieve it in their lifetimes may be forgotten soon after. All the same, we will take particular notice of two of them. The first, York Gate, on the north side of the gardens near the entrance, technically is not a memorial but it preserves what was once the riverside entry to York House. It serves now to mark the location of the river bank before the Embankment was built, and it also a good exemplar of the robust neo-classical style favored for public structures in the first half of the Seventeenth Century. Further along, on the south side of the garden, is the gigantic Belgian Gratitude Memorial, built in 1920 to express the thanks of Belgium to Britain for harboring so many Belgian refugees during the Great War, a now mostly forgotten act of generosity.

Although almost invisible from within the gardens, outside and roughly opposite this place on the river bank is another monument, the curiously named Cleopatra's Needle. It was already 1000 years old when Cleopatra was born, and as far as anyone can tell, she had not the slightest connection to it, but it is named after her all the same. This immense granite obelisk was "given" to Britain in 1819 by the ruler of Egypt to commemorate Nelson's victories over the French, but as no one was prepared to pay for its transport to London or to arrange for its display, for decades afterwards it was left in Egypt. Finally, in 1877 a wealthy and philanthropic dermatologist named William James Erasmus Wilson agreed to cover the cost of moving and erecting it. The transport problem was solved when a sea-going iron cylinder was built around it, but it was far from successful as it foundered in the Bay of Biscay and was nearly lost (at the terrible cost of six seamen's lives). The following year, it was at last installed where it now stands, although the Embankment was the second-choice site after Parliament Square had been rejected. (It is actually one of a pair—the other was erected in Central Park in New York in 1881.) The obelisk is flanked by two impressive faux sphinxes, and inside the base is said to be a time capsule that contains, among other riches, photographs of England's most beautiful women and the text of John 3.16 in 215 languages—rather a slap in the face to the old religion of pharaonic Egypt. Do study the sphinxes carefully—one displays quite visible shrapnel damage from a World War 1 German bomb.

We will resist the temptation to linger on one of the garden benches, as it is too early in our walk to require a restorative pause—unless, of course, it is a sunny day when the floral beds are in full bloom. As you walk on, look northward past the gardens and what you regard is the site of the old Savoy Palace, named after the Count of Savoy, uncle to Queen Eleanor, who was given the land by Henry III in 1246. The land and buildings eventually came into the hands of John of Gaunt, the younger son of Edward III, reckoned to be the richest man in England after the king. In 1381, during the Peasant's Revolt, led by Wat Tyler, the palace and everything in it were completely destroyed. A hospital (what we would call a hostel) to house 100 poor and needy men was built on the site by Henry VII, but it was mostly demolished in the Nineteenth Century. Remarkably, one part of the hospital has survived although much damaged in a fire in 1864—the Queen's Chapel of the Savoy—but let us defer our visit to it and instead continue walking East on the Embankment.

Looming in the offing is Waterloo Bridge, designed by Giles Gilbert Scott in the 1930s and, rather astonishingly, completed in 1942 in the midst of the war, and no less remarkably the *only* London river span to sustain serious damage in the Blitz. It also enjoys the nickname of the Ladies' Bridge, as a goodly number of those who labored to build it were women recruited to replace men serving in the armed forces; some 25,000 women worked in construction across Britain although their contributions to the war effort were long ignored. The bridge has five long, graceful arches, clad in Portland stone, and in my eyes it is the most elegant of all the Thames crossings. It is best seen and appreciated from its underside, an example of form married to function as impressive as anything Le Corbusier designed. The bridge also provides a marvelous vantage point from which one can see both down river toward St Paul's and up river toward Big Ben—especially from a seat on the top of a double-decker bus. There is a set of steps cut into the side of the bridge here—climb to the top, walk to the center of the bridge, admire the views in both directions, and then return to the Embankment by the same stairs.

Just to the east of the bridge, now set back from the river bank, is the imposing façade of Somerset House. In the Sixteenth Century, this stretch of the Thames between the City and Westminster was a favored spot for residences of the wealthy and powerful, and it was here that the Duke of Somerset began to erect his palace in the late 1540s. He never lived to enjoy it, as in 1552 he was executed and his property seized by the Crown. Over the years, the house was occupied by various royals, but in 1775 it was slated for demolition to clear the site for what was to be a grand palace of government offices, modeled on the Continent where enlightened monarchs were establishing suitably impressive permanent homes for their civil servants. Among the government offices that eventually were housed here were the Salt Office, the Stamp Office, the Tax Office, the Navy Office, the Publick Lottery Office, the Hawkers and Pedlars Office, the Hackney Coach Office, the Surveyor General of the Crown Lands Office, the Auditors of the Imprest Office, the Office of the Duchy of Lancaster, the Office of the Duchy of Cornwall, and the King's Bargemaster's House, *inter alia*, as well as the offices of a few learned societies, thrown in for good measure.

The building—a vast four-sided edifice enclosing a large quadrangle—was largely the work of William Chambers, and it dragged on for over two decades. Chambers never saw it finished—he died in harness in 1796 before it was completed in 1801. For now, we will walk on, saving a peek inside for later on this walk—but do note the gentle arch in the center of the façade facing the river. When it was built, the building abutted the unembanked Thames, and this archway served as a landing place for boats bringing visitors by water. And although this is the "back door" to the complex, it is the most impressive of its prospects. If you do fancy a short restorative break, in good weather there is ample seating on the terrace, which is open to the public, and from it there is a fine view of the river as well.

Walking further east along the Embankment, we pass Temple Station. The station originally was called "*The* Temple," obviously enough taking its name from the Temple nearby, but at some point the article went missing. The station opened in 1870 as another part of the District's eastward extension from Westminster, and its neo-Georgian station building is more or less unaltered since it was built. The station's roof terrace is a small public park, and despite its location, it is usually empty, as one has to know it is there to find it; I recommend it as a quiet place to sit and enjoy the river view. Also do stop at the station entrance to look at the outdoors glass-encased wall map of the Underground system—a survivor from 1932 that must have been printed just before Harry Beck's iconic design went into production. No doubt it was preserved initially by oversight, but it is kept on now by design.

Just east of the station, at the end of the Embankment gardens (don't miss the statue of John Stuart Mill at the eastern end), Temple Place opens to the north. This is a curious little street that curves back on itself and turns west toward Temple underground station. Just at the turn is 2 Temple Place, a grand late Victorian town house built for William Waldorf Astor in 1895, and the moment one steps inside, it is easy enough to see that the cliché "no expense was spared" here was quite literally true. Astor could well afford it—he was reputed to be the richest man in America before he decamped across the Atlantic in 1891, having faked reports of his own death to escape the attention of the press. (The ruse didn't work for long.) The house was sold by the family when he died in 1919 and it since has passed through several owners. Miraculously, it survived a V1 flying bomb strike in 1944, and it has retained much of its original interior. Now operated by the Bulldog Trust (a charity that helps launch and promote other charities), it is normally closed to visitors, though it is open for a few months once every year to mount special exhibitions from small museums and arts organizations.

The Temple itself houses two of those curious legal institutions, the successors of the medieval Inns of Court, one of which, Gray's Inn, we have already visited. This one has roots in an earlier era when this was the London home of the Knights Templar. (The name refers to Temple Mount in Jerusalem, ostensibly the site of Solomon's Temple.) Founded in 1119 as a monastic order to defend the new Christian kingdoms of the Holy Lands, the Knights

Templar played an increasingly prominent role in the Crusades and very quickly accumulated wealth and property all over Europe. In London, they built a church—still on this site and remarkable as one of the few surviving round churches in England—and they also owned most of the land around it. The Pope, wary of their power and envious of their wealth, dissolved the order in 1312 and directed that their property should pass to the Knights Hospitaller; eventually the Temple did end up in that order's portfolio, but only after passing through a succession of other owners who had already rented out portions of the site to lawyers, who have been there ever since. The lawyers were attracted to this location midway between the City and the courts at Westminster, and thus it proved very convenient for them as they did business in both. By the 1320s, quite a few attorneys already had established themselves in the area, and over time, the Temple morphed into two distinct inns of court, the Middle Temple and the Inner Temple. (Almost needless to say, there is no Outer Temple.) Though the structure of the legal profession has been modestly modernized, all four inns of court are still home to legions of lawyers.

As you continue walking east, just ahead are the Temple gardens, a delightful oasis of peaceful green space, accessible those of us who are not Templars on weekdays from 12.30 to 3.00 p.m. At one of the garden gates notes is one of my favorite signs, indicating that it is open only to residents' dogs, all other dogs presumably being able to read sufficiently well to know they are not welcome. Running north-south through the heart of the legal enclave is Middle Temple Lane and what one can see as one saunters along its length offers a fairly good idea of how very privileged are the members of the legal profession in England. A short distance on, any turning to the right (east) will take you to the round church, now mostly an exhibit space, but well worth a poke around inside (there is a modest charge for admission). Back onto Middle Temple Lane and northward a few hundred feet along one exits to the Strand though a gateway just opposite Temple Bar, or more accurately the site where Temple Bar once stood.

You will recall that Temple Bar was the ceremonial entrance to the City from Westminster, with the Strand leading to it on the Westminster side and Fleet Street issuing from it on the City side. We have already seen the thing itself in Paternoster Square, but this was where it stood for several hundred years. The location is actually some distance west from the where the city walls ended as the boundary of the City here extended beyond the walls. (This was then and is still the City Ward of Farringdon Without.) While there probably was an actual "bar" across the road in the late Thirteenth Century, and various other gate-like structures were erected over the years, it is in its last iteration, almost certainly the work of Christopher Wren, that it is best known, not only as a set of elegant classical arches in Portland stone, but, as the

Nineteenth Century wore on, a tremendous impediment to the flow of traffic. (Dickens uses it as a consummate symbol of the hidebound incompetence of the City authorities in his novel, *Bleak House*.) One of the City dragons sits atop a pedestal where the arch once stood.

Cross the road, and almost directly opposite is Bell Yard, which continues north along the easternmost outer walls of the Royal Courts of Justice, of which more in a moment. Ahead of us is Carey Street; turn left on it and just a little further on the right hand side is a pedestrian entrance to Lincoln's Inn, the last of the four inns of court. You are entering the inn via New Square, built in the late Seventeenth Century (when it was "new"), and one of the inn's many architectural gems. The oldest building standing is the appropriately named Old Hall, which dates to the Fifteenth Century, though much altered. The oldest original part of the entire complex is the Gatehouse on Chancery Lane, built 1518–1521. Most of the buildings are open to the public only on rare occasions (though some spaces can be hired for special events); wander freely and admire from the outside for as long as you like, and then walk out the way by which we entered.

A little further along Carey Street, a short distance west, is the Seven Stars public house, one of the oldest in London (though there is as you'd expect some debate about that). The date 1602 is displayed outside, but probably the present building is a bit later, dating from the 1680s. What is indisputable is that there has been a drinking establishment here for the best part of 400 years, and every evening you will find it packed with ambitious young lawyers. (The interior, very late Victorian, is charming in its own way.)

Carey Street leads to Grange Court, which takes us past the London School of Economics, founded in 1895 by very left-leaning members of the Fabian Society, but now, improbably given its origins, a pillar of the international business establishment. LSE has developed a world class reputation: its global strategy is to be the best at what it does and then the world will come to it. The world has obliged: one third of its students are from the UK, one third from the EU, and one third from everywhere else.

Further on and off to the left is Clements Inn, now a set of offices, but once another of the inns of court, whose legal standing was terminated in 1903; the original building was demolished between the wars. We've now made nearly a full circuit round the Royal Courts, at whose impressive façade we soon will emerge. Best to cross the Strand to look back across it at the front of the building, designed by George Edmund Street who, like so many architects we've encountered, did not live to see his masterpiece completed. It was paid for in part with funds seized from the estates of persons who died intestate, a touch worthy of a Dickens novel, and rather an ironic commentary on the efficiency of the law in looking after its own interests at the expense (literally) of those it was meant to serve. The building is a wonderful example of what might be called Victorian fantastical medieval style, with turrets, huge stained-glass windows, and archways galore. It is said to contain over 1,000 rooms. Most of us know it as the backdrop for myriad British legal dramas on TV and film, or, if one has been unlucky in life, from the inside as a defendant. For the rest of us, it can be visited only by pre-arranged tour.

Across the road, on the south side, at 229 and 230 Strand, note two narrow buildings that may well be the oldest surviving houses in central London. Built in 1625, they predate the Great Fire and now, conjoined, house a branch of a Thai chain restaurant. One has a bowed front and the other features overhanging upper stories, both medieval builders' tricks to maximize interior space on narrow streets. They were damaged not long ago when a bus (a number 341, to be precise) crashed into them, but they appear to have been successfully restored. And don't omit a stop at nearby Twining, which has occupied these premises at 216 Strand continuously since 1706. When Thomas Twining bought it in that year it was already a going concern as Tom's Coffee House (no relation, apparently); it flourished under Twining, who eventually gave up the coffee business to focus on tea. (The firm started selling coffee again just a few years ago.) The shop is great fun to visit, and among the many blends of tea available (leaf or bag) is the classic Earl Grey, black tea enlivened by the addition of dried rind of bergamot, which many mistakenly believe to have been first made by Twining. In fact, it probably was first produced by Jacksons of Piccadilly, who as it happens were bought by Twining in the 1990s, though still for now maintained as a separate brand.

As we walk west again, one encounters two impressive churches islanded in the middle of the road, St Clement Danes and beyond it St Mary-le-Strand. St Clement Danes supposedly sits at the boundary of the Danelaw on the site of a Ninth Century Danish church, which explains the name, although there are other theories (including one that claims it marks the site of the massacre of a party of Danes, though one might think that was an event more likely to be forgotten than commemorated). The name Aldwych ("Old town" in Anglo-Saxon) was in use as early as the 1200s, and this is approximately the site of the Anglo-Saxon settlement, Lundenwyc, which thrived for a couple of hundred years after the abandonment of Roman London. By the time William the Conqueror arrived, there appears already to have been some sort of church on the site; he rebuilt it, and that building in turn was damaged heavily in the Great Fire. The tower was rebuilt, but at that point it became clear that the entire structure was unstable, and in 1682 it was taken down and replaced by a Wren design. The distinctive new tower came later, designed by James Gibbs. It was gutted by German bombs in 1941, and after extensive restoration, it was reconsecrated in 1958 as the Central Church of the Royal Air Force.

Return to the south side of the Strand (apologies for sending you on such a zig-zag route) and enter a narrow lane, Surrey Street. Start walking downhill toward the river and you will pass the immense tiled entryway to the abandoned Aldwych tube station, which was in use from 1907 to 1994. Just past it, nearer to the river, on the right you will see a small, dark turning called Surrey Steps. If the iron gate is open, walk through; if it is locked, as it often is, carry straight down to the Embankment, turn right and walk a few paces to the west, and then turn north again. (You are heading into the back end of King's College now.) We are in search of Strand Lane, which runs parallel to Surrey Street, at the top end of which, close to the Strand, is the fabled "Roman" Bath—so-called since the 1830s when it was mistakenly identified as a Roman ruin. Alas, it is neither Roman nor a bath—it has a much later and more humble origin as a cistern that was part of the infrastructure of a garden built by James I in 1612. Roman or not, it can be seen through an often-fogged and quite dirty window, or visited by appointment (courtesy of Westminster Council who now own it).

Just north of the "bath" and overhanging the street is St Clement's Watch House, which in the Eighteenth Century, despite its name, probably did not house the parish watch (an early local police force). Whatever its original function, the building does legitimately appear to be at least 250 years old. It incorporates a bit of brick wall that is believed to be the only surviving part of the original Somerset House still standing.

At the northern end of Strand Lane, Aldwych begins its semi-circular sweep. This oddly shaped street was created in 1903, and its distinctive crescent moon curve gives it a character all its own. St Mary-le-Strand is a little further west along the Strand, tucked below Aldwych. Cineastes will recognize it as the exterior of the church in the opening scenes of *Chariots of Fire*. (The church interior shown in the film is St Mary-le-Bow in Cheapside, which we visited whilst on our Mansion House walk.) There was once a medieval church dedicated to St Mary nearby that was unceremoniously pulled down in 1549 by the first Duke of Somerset to clear ground for the original Somerset House; he promised parishioners that he would build for them a much better replacement church, which he never did. The omission was repaired only in 1723, when the present church was built to a design of Gibbs as one of the fifty Commissioners' churches. It was lucky in the Blitz, avoiding direct hits and suffering only limited damage. Given the always heavy traffic around it, it's probably the noisiest church interior in all of London.

Back on the south side of the Strand opposite St Mary is the entry to King's College. King's was founded in 1829 by George IV (hence the name) and the Duke of Wellington to serve as a conservative Church of England counterbalance to the newly opened London University (now University College London) in Gower Street, a nonsectarian (a.k.a. "godless") institution inspired by the teachings of the ruthlessly rational Jeremy Bentham. A few years later both institutions were transformed into constituent colleges of the newly chartered corporate University of London, though in recent years both colleges have severed their connections to that umbrella institution and they have struck out on their own. They now grant their own degrees and quite successfully have become genuinely global research powerhouses. The original neo-classical structure survives as the King's Building.

The next entryway, a row of three archways along the southern side of the Strand, opens to the courtyard of Somerset House, which now we shall at last enter and explore. The courtyard is immense and largely given over to a playful set of fountains. In winter, it becomes an open air ice rink. Government offices started moving out of the building in the late 1980s when it was flagged for its future as a new center for the arts. The Courtauld Institute moved its magnificent art collection—principally Old Masters and Impressionists—to the North Wing, abandoning the pokey quarters in Woburn Square that it had shared with the Warburg Institute; the new home was less than ideal (temperature control was an issue from the first day) and it recently reopened after being closed for several years to allow a £50M renovation. The South Wing was for a time home to the Gilbert Collection of decorative arts (now permanently housed in the Victoria and Albert Museum) and to rotating exhibits from the Hermitage in St Petersburg. (The relationship with the Russian museum ended some years back.) The space currently is used for various and sundry temporary exhibits. The upper floors are rented at commercial rates to "creative" tenants. Remarkably, the whole enterprise receives no government funding (though in any rational polity it would be regarded as a cultural crown jewel).

Leave the courtyard, return to Aldwych, and continue westward. Once past the vehicle approach to Waterloo Bridge (traffic whips round the corner here so please cross the road only when the light is green!), on the south side of the Strand you will come to a small lane named Savoy Street that opens southward; turn here and continue on Savoy Row, then further south on Savoy Steps, and, as if by magic, a late medieval church will appear. We are back on the grounds of what once was Savoy Palace and we are looking at the only surviving bit of it. Even most Londoners seem not to know of the existence of the Queen's Chapel of the Savoy, a hidden gem that was built by Henry VII between 1490 and 1512. It is today part of the Duchy of Lancaster estate and it enjoys the status of "royal peculiar": in other words, its chaplain is appointed by and reports directly to the monarch rather than to a bishop. It has had its ups and downs over the years, and for quite some time it enjoyed the privilege of conducting marriage ceremonies without banns for couples in a rush to wed. (Banns were the formal announcement of a forthcoming marriage made in the local parish church on three successive Sundays, effectively requiring a month-long delay in the ceremony.) In its day, it was one of three chapels in the Hospital of the Savoy. When the hospital was dissolved in 1712, eventually over the course of the Nineteenth Century every other part of the complex was torn down to clear the way for development, but the Chapel remains.

As I observed on our starting out, the old palace name survives in all of the "Savoy" street names and in the present-day Savoy Hotel and Savoy Theatre. A short cut near the front of the chapel called Savoy Buildings is a narrow alley that gives a good sense of the myriad alleys and pathways that gave direct access to the river before the mighty Thames was embanked. Walk north on it to the Strand, and immediately ahead to the west is the forecourt of the Savoy Theatre and Hotel.

The theatre was built first, erected by Richard D'Oyly Carte in 1881 to showcase his wildly popular productions of Gilbert and Sullivan operettas. Not long after the theater opened, he purchased an adjoining property to house an electric generator that would power the house lights (his was the first theatre in England lit entirely by electricity), but he soon determined instead to build on the same site a luxury hotel, bankrolled by the profits from the operettas. It took five years but once completed it established a new standard of luxury for all posh hotels—for example, most of the 268 rooms had a bathroom *en suite*, unheard of in those days. D'Oyly Carte brought in Cesar Ritz to manage it. Ritz in turn hired Georges Auguste Escoffier (the inventor of Peach Melba, among other culinary delights) as head chef, and under their joint direction, after a few early stumbles, it became a rip-roaring success. The list of famous guests is virtually identical to the late Nineteenth and Twentieth Century *Who's Who*. (Years later, Ritz and Escoffier both were found to have been fiddling the accounts, and they were summarily sacked in 1898. Ritz of course went on to open his own hotel.) Do walk through the forecourt and have a look at the hotel lobby. If time permits, and it is late enough in the day, you could do worse than to visit the famed American Bar of the Savoy for a cocktail. (I recommend one-time guest Frank Sinatra's favorite tipple, Jack Daniels, ice, and water.)

The same forecourt is home to the entrance to the Savoy Theatre. D'Oyly Carte's theatre was rebuilt by his son, Rupert, in gloriously bold Art Deco style. Alas, it was gutted by fire in 1990, and after a tussle about the proposed high modernist design of what was first proposed as its replacement, it was rebuilt as a faithful replica of the 1929 theatre. Unfortunately, the D'Oyly Carte company itself, with its vast repertoire of Gilbert and Sullivan classics, is no more, although the theatre with its wonderful acoustics has been home to many classic musical revivals, including in recent years *Carousel*, *Fiddler on the Roof*, *Gypsy*, and *Funny Girl*. You may have noticed another peculiarity here: the forecourt contains the only semi-public thoroughfare in London in which two-way traffic drives on the right. (This ensures that taxis dropping off passengers at the theatre and at the front doors of the hotel don't conflict.)

Across the road, one can see some of the grand thespian palaces that make this the epicenter of the West End theatre district, principal among them the Lyceum, with its imposing colonnaded façade. There are several theatres hereabouts that seat 2000 or more, which usually means they are reserved for perennially popular musicals, the only fare that can fill houses so large. We shall continue walking westward on the Strand a few hundred feet to Southampton Street. Turn right and walk northward and in a few moments you will stand at the edge of Covent Garden.

Covent Garden—originally a walled vegetable garden belonging to the monks at Westminster Abbey, thus a Convent Garden—at the time of the Dissolution was given by Henry VIII to John Russell, the first Earl of Bedford. The fourth earl in 1630 commissioned Inigo Jones to build on this site a church and three terraces of houses around a central square or piazza. Despite the Italian name, the immediate inspiration for the design probably was the Place des Vosges in Paris, built by Henri IV from 1605 to 1612 and the first planned "square" in a Western European city. (It is in fact a perfect 140m square, and despite having endured a revolution, several wars, and two German occupations, it still looks very much as it did when it was built.) From this moment onward, the garden square and brick row houses were one of the primary building blocks in the development of residential London. Examples large and small, square, rectangular, round, up-market and down, abound—but this was the first.

Indeed, nothing is so closely associated with the streetscape of London than the brick terrace or row house, whether red, buff, or dark gray in color. The brick canalside houses of the Low Countries probably were the first of this type in Europe, but the first built in London were right here at Covent Garden. Terrace houses were soon to be (and still are) the most common form of London single-occupier residence. A number of factors lay behind their success: for one thing, after the Great Fire, all London houses were required to be built of either stone or brick and brick was cheaper. Moreover, terraces were the most efficient use of land possible, with no wasted space separating one house from the next, and building was possible right up to the property line on at least three sides. Examples range from the large town houses built around garden squares for the landed classes to (much later) modest four-room, two-story workers' houses (often referred to as "two up, two down"), sometimes built back-to-back with no garden at all.

The earliest surviving London terrace house is in Stoke Newington and dates from 1658; so little did the style change that it looks as if it could have been built at any time between then and 1800. Perhaps the most active builder in the immediate wake of the Fire was the economist and financial speculator

Nicholas Barbon (his surname Frenchified from Barebone) who was active building in the rapidly filling district between the City and Westminster. He was also instrumental in the expansion of the insurance business, not a bad strategy as his houses were poorly built and at least once a terrace that he'd built collapsed. (Barbon is further distinguished by his lengthy Puritan-inspired middle name—"Unless-Jesus-Christ-Had-Died-For-Thee-Thou-Hadst-Been-Damned.") He is said to have built over the last stretch of open land in the Strand. The later Building Act of 1774, also known as the Black Act, went so far as to specify the height, footprint, and overall size of terrace housing, partly determined by the width of the street outside. The act categorized buildings into four "rates," the first rate being reserved for town houses of the aristocracy and the fourth for humble mechanics and tradesmen. From this point on, houses on any given street were almost always all of exactly the same height.

However, Covent Garden itself remained a prime residential address only for a short time: before long, it had become one of the main sites of prostitution in London, perhaps because its covered walkways allowed streetwalkers to huddle there whenever it rained. The market for which Covent Garden eventually became famous grew slowly from just a few stalls that first had appeared in the 1650s; only in the 1830s, when a covered market was built, did it gain prominence as the most important of London's wholesale produce markets. I remember well from my first residence in London in the early Seventies the early morning crush of lorries, hand carts, and porters here every weekday morning. My wife worked nearby, and if she walked through the market on the way to the office, by the time she left she generally had an armful of whatever was in season, gifts from admiring stall holders. The area was also exempt from the usual pub licensing hours so that it could meet the needs of market porters for fortifying sustenance before dawn—in other words, this was one place in London where you could still get a drink early in the morning. This era ended in 1974 when the modern, purpose-built wholesale market of the same name opened at Nine Elms. But progress is a fickle god—the wholesale market has moved on once again and the Nine Elms site is now becoming an "it" destination in its own right after the opening of the new U.S. Embassy and the successful redevelopment of the nearby Battersea Power Station.

The covered market now caters mainly to tourists (the exception being Monday mornings when there is a small but interesting antiques and collectibles market). The shops inside the covered market include many of the well-known high street names. One corner, however, houses the London Transport Museum, a must-see for every child under or over the age of twelve.

As for the church at the western end of the market, St Paul's Covent Garden, the Earl was said to have told Jones that he wanted to erect a simple church not much better than a barn; Jones supposedly replied, "Then you shall have the handsomest barn in England." Jones chose a severe neo-classical style that mimics a Roman temple. Originally covered in stucco, it was refaced with Portland stone in 1789. The space immediately outside the church is a preferred location for Covent Market buskers, and rare is the time you will pass when there is not a bit of street theatre in progress. The soaring stone colonnaded façade is actually the back of the church; if you walk around to the other side, which is faced in plain red brick, you'll find the main entrance, which faces the church yard. Grinling Gibbons, who carved the pulpit, is buried here, and the church contains memorials to many famous personalities of the stage—Charley Chaplin, Noel Coward, Gracie Fields, Boris Karloff, and Vivien Leigh among them. Appropriately it is known informally as the actors' church.

Leaving the church by the church yard takes us to Bedford Street. Turn right and walk on for a short distance, and then turn left onto New Row, and this will take you to St Martin's Lane. Turn left and you will be walking southward past more of London's most famous theatres, one of which now houses the English National Opera. Soon enough, the magnificent profile of St Martin's-in-the-Fields comes into view—another Gibbs church in the neo-classical style and boasting an impressive spire nearly 200' in height. Gibbs' innovation here was to integrate the tower into the fabric of the building, rather than to place it outside the foundations and walls, a design much copied since. The church is impressively entrepreneurial—hosting a brass-rubbing center, a large café in the crypt, and several ambitious series of concerts. It is also a pioneer providing services for the homeless; it now aids 4000 homeless people each year.

It is worth noting, however, that Gibbs' contemporaries were barely able to see the church, hemmed in as it was by buildings on all sides until Trafalgar Square was laid out in the 1820s. The site had housed the royal mews, and after they were moved to the new royal residence, Buckingham Palace, George IV directed Nash to create a huge square to commemorate his coronation. Work was slow, and the king died before it was finished. Rather than memorialize the unpopular king, the decision was made to commemorate the perennially popular Nelson's great victory against the French at Trafalgar off the coast of Spain. Finally, in the 1840s, what now was officially named Trafalgar Square was built to the designs of Charles Barry, whose star was ascendant after the selection of his design for the rebuilding of the Houses of Parliament a few years before.

But while Barry was responsible for the overall layout of the square, other highly visible projects on the site proceeded annoyingly and incongruously with neither prior consultation nor his approval. At the very center of the square is the column atop which stands Nelson, designed not by Barry but by William Railton. The famed and beloved lions, by Landseer, came later, in 1867. The corners of the square gradually attracted four plinths, only three of which are topped with permanent statues (two Victorian generals and an improbably svelte equestrian George IV); the fourth plinth is now used for temporary exhibits of contemporary sculpture. The square itself is another of those tourist meccas that attracts crowds made up of people who are attracted by crowds of other tourists, a sort of tourist lemming effect. It also is often the locus of many political demonstrations in central London, offering both a large space for a crowd to gather and easy pedestrian access to Westminster.

Even before the square was completed, the new National Gallery of Art had already appeared on the north side. For some time, pressure had been mounting to create a national art museum on the model of several that already were established in rival European capitals. Enlightened Continental monarchs were generously turning their personal collections into national museums, but no English king was prepared to donate his own treasures to the nation. Several times, impressive, large private collections had come up for sale, any one of which might have been purchased to serve as the nucleus of a national museum, but the cheeseparers in Westminster blocked that, too. Finally, in 1823, the unexpected repayment of a Napoleonic war debt by Austria provided funds that could be used to acquire a relatively modest collection of 38 paintings that had been owned by the banker John Julius Angerstein. (Angerstein was a Russian-born, half-English financier and his collection was purchased in part with the profits of his slave plantations in America.) This was the core of the new museum, and when the collection rapidly grew, a new building to house it was commissioned to a design by William Wilkins. From the first it was a bit of a dog's dinner: the columns were recycled from Carlton House and the cramped site had only space behind the long façade sufficient to house a narrow, one-room wide gallery, and furthermore half the new building was to be occupied by the Royal Academy (which did not leave for its present home in Piccadilly until 1868). Much altered and much expanded, only the façade of the original structure remains.

The westernmost corner of the site is the Sainsbury Wing, a postmodern riff on neo-classical style by Robert Venturi and Denise Scott Brown. An earlier approved design in a bold modernist idiom had been cancelled after it was attacked in the press by Prince Charles—his scathing dismissal of the proposed building as a "monstrous carbuncle" captures the essence of his critique, which was taken up gleefully by the tabloid press. Whatever one thinks of the post-prince exterior now (it was meant to be bland and in that it succeeds), the interior is an undisputable success. Its best feature is the creation of a gallery that extends the main axis of the older building, now a continuous vista whose depth is enhanced by very convincing false perspective created by a series of columns of diminishing size.

The collection itself encompasses European painting from the medieval era to around 1900. It holds 2300 works, rather a small number for a leading national museum—the Louvre in Paris has 35000 art works and the Metropolitan in New York 13000. The majority have come as gifts, which means that a few areas are particularly rich and others are a bit thin. And while Tate Britain in the grand scheme of things is meant to house British art, nonetheless there are here works by Constable, Hogarth, Stubbs, Wright, and Turner. In any event, a proper visit would require many hours, if not days, so we will step inside only briefly. (And, although we will not visit it, tucked into the north side of the National Gallery is the National Portrait Gallery, the first of its kind in the world when it opened in 1856.)

Leave the gallery and wander southward on the pedestrianized square, and at its southern edge you will come upon an equestrian statue of Charles I, stranded on an island amidst heavy traffic. This is the original site of the Eleanor Cross that gives Charing Cross its name, and it is still the point from which all distances from London are officially measured. (The actual cross was demolished by an angry anti-royal Parliament in 1647, and reputedly its stones were crushed to pave part of Whitehall.) If you turn left and walk east, you now will see in front of Charing Cross Station a supposed replica of the original cross, though probably it is quite a bit more ornate. The station building and the adjacent hotel (built in a sort of down-market French Renaissance style) date from the 1860s. This was the terminus of the South Eastern Railway, which from 1868 to the late Twentieth Century offered the shortest and fastest trains to Dover and, via its ferries, travel onward to the Continent.

We will skirt the station to the east, and walk back down Villiers Street, which takes us to our starting point, Embankment Underground Station.

Chapter 12

Westminster

I try to stay away from the crowds in Westminster as much as possible, but there really must be a Westminster walk in this series. Even though this part of Central London is overrun by tourists and even though its vehicular traffic is in perpetual gridlock, it still is very much the center of government and the site three of London's most iconic and historic buildings—the Palace of Westminster (a.k.a. the Houses of Parliament), Westminster Abbey, and Buckingham Palace. So concentrated are the organs of government here—it is home to Parliament, the principal ministries, and the Supreme Court—that "Westminster" is a universally understood synecdoche for the British government itself. All the same, the crowds make it difficult to stop, step back, and look around—so I recommend a visit on a weekend morning when most government offices are closed, and early enough in the day to be a few steps ahead of the tourist hordes.

Technically, Westminster is not a London borough at all but the City of Westminster, though in practice now the legal distinction is entirely moot. Its boundaries encompass most of the West End, stretching on its southern border along the river from Pimlico to Somerset House; it continues north from Somerset House to Primrose Hill and Maida Vale; then west to Kilburn; and south back to the river along the border with Kensington and Chelsea. All in all, it comprises a goodly chunk of Central London. Yet despite its very central location, it is a remarkably green borough: within its borders are all of St James's, Green, and Hyde Parks, almost all of Kensington Gardens, and the lion's share of Regent's Park.

The Westminster Underground station opened in 1868 as the eastern terminus of the District Railway (though it remained that for only two years). It was modified a number of times to accommodate more traffic and longer trains, and then completely rebuilt in the Nineties when the Jubilee line was first made operational and Portcullis House (the then new office block housing 213 MPs and their staff) opened. A portcullis is a heavy metal (usually iron) gate, often the entrance to a castle, that can be raised and lowered, and since the Nineteenth Century it has been the semi-official "branding" logo of Parliament. The faux medieval style of Portcullis House is to my eye not a great success; the chimneys (actually cooling towers) that are its most distinctive feature are disproportionately large. The best that can be said for its overall blandness is that it doesn't diminish the visual impact of Parliament's historic home across the road.

The deep tube station beneath us is, by the way, the deepest in London. The excavations for the new station required that the foundations of the clock tower housing Big Ben (which properly denominates the bell, not as most wrongly assume the clock) be reinforced; even so, when construction ended the tower had sunk what was deemed an acceptable 35 millimeters or about an inch and a half. The rebuilt station has a very postmodern and decidedly functional esthetic, all concrete and stainless steel, but somehow the overall effect not as sterile as that suggests.

The tube station serves what we might call Westminster proper, the area around Parliament Square. This was the site of the Benedictine "west minster" (or abbey) as early as the Tenth Century, at the time a rural site far to the west of the City itself. The first king crowned in the Abbey was the Saxon Harold in 1066—though his reign was rather cut short (as was he) at the Battle of Hastings later in that same year. The palace at Westminster became the favored home of England's kings around the year 1200, and it has been the seat of government continuously ever since. Not much of the ancient complex of palace buildings survives—a fire in 1834 destroyed all but Westminster Hall, which dates from 1097, and where Elizabeth II lay in state.. Westminster Hall is open every weekday, free of charge, and it is worth stepping in to admire the soaring hammerbeam roof. (It also houses special exhibits from time to time; entry to them is free but by timed ticket.)

Across the road is the venerable Abbey, but we won't visit just yet; however, we will pause to admire the exterior of the church tucked, as it were, under the wing of the abbey, St Margaret's. It was founded in the Twelfth Century by the Benedictines to serve as the parish church for the ordinary local folk who were crowding into services in the monks' own much grander church. The present building dates from the reign of Henry VII, and it is said to be the last church built in England to be decorated as a Roman Catholic place of worship. It was almost demolished in the 1540s by the Duke of Somerset (no friend to ancient churches, as we have seen) who wanted to repurpose the stone to build his new palace in the Strand; supposedly he was fought off by armed parishioners. This may well have been the first "demonstration" in Parliament Square, which has seen many of them over the centuries (though generally less successful). For several hundred years St Margaret's was the parish church of Parliament itself, a formal relationship that ended in 1972 when it was turned over to the Abbey. The church contains some fine, old stained glass windows, but I suggest for now admiring them from the outside—entry requires a combined ticket to the Abbey itself, and we are not yet ready to look inside.

Just west of Parliament Square and St Margaret's is the Jewel Tower, dating from 1366 and now managed by English Heritage. Turn around as you approach the tower, and if this view of the Palace of Westminster seems familiar, it is because virtually every political correspondent on television is filmed standing before it for the evening news. I suggest you pause for a good look at the tower; you can enter for about £6, but it's rather disappointing inside. The buildings on the west side of the tower, behind the brick wall, belong to the Westminster School, one of the most prestigious (and seriously academic) of the elite "public" schools in Britain, and beyond it is Dean's Yard, which can only be accessed from a gateway outside the front of the Abbey—of which more presently.

More interesting is the walled garden just ahead, the College Garden, the abbey's private preserve, once the monks' medieval medicinal herb plot, and now open to the public free of admission charge several days a week. If you can manage a visit on a day when it is open, by all means wander in, and don't miss the opportunity to see two smaller associated gardens, the Little Cloister Garden that features a fountain, and St Catherine's Garden, containing a few ruined bits of the monks' infirmary.

Continue walking westward from the Jewel Tower to Great College Street. Turn right and walk past Little College Street to an inverted T-junction with Barton Street, named after the actor, Barton Booth, who built its first houses; it is one of the few London streets named after a person that bears a Christian and not a family name. This short, curiously shaped street (it becomes Cowley Street as it makes a 90 degree turn) contains a number of well-preserved early Eighteenth-Century row houses; if it should seem familiar, it is because you may have seen it before—it is often used as the backdrop for period films and TV series. Its past residents include T.E. Lawrence and John Gielgud (both of whom are honored by blue plaques), and it is sometimes considered to have been the home of Virginia Woolf's fictional character, Clarissa Dalloway (no plaque for her, however). Barton Street and the streets nearby are favored residences for MPs, as they are within the sound of the Division Bell. When the bell (actually, quite a few bells strategically placed in hotels, pubs, and restaurants as well as inside the Palace) is rung it signals that a vote is to take place, and members have exactly eight minutes to get inside the House. At that time, the doors are locked and any MP who arrives later misses the vote and presumably faces a shellacking by the party whip. (The major political parties have their headquarters nearby as well, for obvious reasons.)

Walk straight on Cowley Street a short distance to Great Peter Street, named after the oft-forgotten patron saint of Westminster Abbey. In the mid-Nineteenth Century this area was known as the Devil's Acre, one of the most overcrowded and miserable slums in all of England. Victoria Street was cut through it in 1851 in part (it was argued) to open the neighbourhood to light and air. Unfortunately, like many urban renewal projects since, the new street worsened the housing crisis it was meant to ameliorate: it displaced 5,000 residents who were forced to move and who mostly packed themselves into the remaining nearby slums just behind the shining new developments, further overcrowding them. The contrast between the seats of government and the great church on the one hand, and on the other the horrendous poverty abutting them, did not go unremarked. Eventually, starting in the 1860s, decent housing for the district's working poor was built by the Peabody Trust and other private philanthropists, including Dickens's close friend, Angela Burdett Coutts, heir to a banking fortune. (Coutts and Co., a private bank, is still extant and located in the Strand near Charing Cross.) Most of these well-constructed blocks of flats were built as hollow rectangles, enclosing open common spaces in their centers—a plan that remains attractive to city dwellers today. The Peabody Trust still manages several of the buildings hereabouts and this is one of the largest estates it maintains.

A slight detour southward will take you to Smith Square, until recently home to Conservative Party Headquarters, but best known as the site of the Church of St John's, Smith Square. Completed in 1728, it is another of the fifty Commissioners' churches, this one designed by Thomas Archer. Early on, it was known as Queen Anne's footstool—the story goes that when she was shown the design, with its distinctive four corner spires, she kicked over her footstool and said that it looked just like that (and frankly it does). Dickens more inventively compared it to a prehistoric monster lying on its back. It was severely damaged in 1941, and it languished in its ruined state until the early Sixties, when the Friends of St John's raised funds to turn it into a concert hall, in which role it has served quite successfully ever since. By fortuitous accident, the acoustics are marvelous, and it is one of the principal venues for classical music performances in London.

We will leave Smith Square via Great Peter Street, here lined on both sides with blocks of Peabody flats. Continuing westward you will pass on the right a narrow lane called Strutton Ground, home to a small but lively weekday street market. Despite the encroachment of trendy coffee shops and wine bars all over Westminster, this street somehow retains a number of modest, old-fashioned businesses, including a few very inexpensive eateries and a bakery. It looks and feels very much as it did when I first encountered it in the Eighties, though even then it was something of an anachronism. I find something very pleasing about the street's persistent refusal to gentrify (which probably has much to do with its proximity to the moderate income residents of the Peabody Estate).

Turning south at a small but quite busy roundabout we come to a well-proportioned early Eighteenth-Century brick building, the Grey Coat Hospital, that houses part of the Grey Coat School, a famous charitable institution. It has an unusual history: founded as a school for boys in 1698, it went co-ed in 1701, and then in 1874 it became an all-girls school. It has expanded into other premises, but the original building is still in used for the lower grades. Indeed, Westminster was especially rich in charity schools in the Eighteenth Century: there were also Black, Blue, Brown, and Green Coat schools, the last giving name to nearby Greencoat Place and Greencoat Row.

Just ahead is Artillery Row—once actually used for gunnery practice—but note the fascinating shop windows of J. McCarthy Ltd., a jeweler and silver-smith who have been there since the beginning of time (well, at least since 1932) and a wonderful place to browse antique jewelry. At the bottom of Artillery Row, turn left and continue west on Victoria Street, past what was the House of Fraser department store, which once was the Army and Navy Stores. The Army and Navy was one of the pillars of the Victorian retail establishment, founded in 1871 as a cooperative society owned and operated by army and navy officers. It specialized in solid, dependable, and durable goods at reasonable prices, as well as merchandise suitable for use in the colonies, and as such it not only prospered but it expanded across the globe, with overseas branches in Bombay, Karachi, and Paris, as well as others in provincial English towns. In 1934 it turned itself into a limited liability com-pany, and later in 1973 it was acquired by House of Fraser. The name was finally retired in 2004. It recently closed, a victim of the pandemic and the rise of internet shopping.

Not much farther along Victoria Street, Westminster Cathedral comes into view. Properly known as the Metropolitan Cathedral of the Precious Blood of Our Lord Jesus Christ, it is the mother church of Roman Catholics in England and Wales, built at the turn of the Twentieth Century. For most of the Nineteenth Century this had been the site of a prison, the Tothill Fields Bridewell, upon whose foundations the cathedral was built—surely one of the odder efforts of building recycling. It is a vast structure—enclosing some 54,000 square feet—in a blend of Neo-Byzantine and Renaissance Revival styles. The banded brick and stone of the exterior is very pleasing, more so for me than the opulent interior that sports a surfeit of pseudo-Byzantine mosaics that have been a work in progress ever since it was built.

Retrace your steps on Victoria Street back to Artillery Row, and cross the road onto its northward continuation, Buckingham Gate. Just ahead is Caxton Street, and at the west end of this short street is the Blewcoat, a charming early Eighteenth-Century building that once housed the Bluecoat School, another of the area's charity schools. For many years the boys were required to wear a blue coat, memorialized by the statue of a boy in uniform in an alcove above the front door. The building is owned now by the National Trust, and up until recently, it was run as a gift shop. The premises now are leased to a fashion designer who is open only by appointment.

Walk eastward via Caxton Street and you soon will pass the St James's tube station entrance. If you have difficulty remembering the spelling—that distinctive double "s" is confusing—don't be overly concerned, as the station has officially been called St James Park and St James' Park as well as St James's, the current preferred version. The station is on the ground floor of 55 Broadway, completed in 1929 as the headquarters of the London Underground Electric Railways Company, in 1933 taken over by the new London Passenger Transport Board (which later morphed into London Transport and now TfL). The Art Deco building, designed by Charles Holden, uses a rotated cruciform plan to make maximum use of an irregularly shaped site. When it opened it was the tallest office block in London (but only for a brief time). The building is a bit too self-consciously grand for my taste; it would have looked quite at home in Mussolini's Rome or Ceausescu's Bucharest, but despite the grandiosity of the exterior the period art deco detailing in the shopping arcade on the ground floor is stunning. (The building as a whole is vaguely reminiscent of the University of London's administrative home, Senate House—no surprise as it also was designed by Holden; Senate House replaced 55 as the tallest building in the city when it opened a few years later.) On each side of the building, just above the sixth floor, there is a pediment with prominent sculptures by leading young artists of the day. Linger a bit before Jacob Epstein's "Day" and "Night," two nude male figures that caused a great deal of controversy when they were first revealed. Epstein was forced to cut one and a half inches from the penis of the smaller figure on "Day," which seemed to end the fuss. Transport for London moved to new offices in Stratford in the 2012 Olympic site; 55 is to be transformed into a luxury hotel.

A little further on, north of a small traffic roundabout and veering off to the east, is Queen Anne's Gate (originally named Queen Square), presided over by a statue of the queen herself and boasting a number of pristine early Eighteenth-Century terrace houses. The houses date from around 1705 and are among the earliest examples of the brick row houses that were to become the standard London town house, but they are distinguished from later versions by the very elaborately carved wooden canopies that shade their front doors. There are a few older row houses extant in London, but none more attractive. The statue of Queen Anne that looks benignly on the street named after her was evidently not part of the original plan, but it seems to have been in this spot as early as 1710. Look carefully at the queen's face and you'll see that her nose has been broken off and rather badly repaired.

The right angle where the two parts of the street meet opens into an alleyway leading to St James's Park. The park has a fascinating history: originally marshy land (fed by the Tyburn), it was at first the *de facto* garden of Whitehall Palace. James I used it as a private zoo. Charles II—who introduced the pelicans, descendants of which are still very much in evidence—opened it to the public. There was then a canal stretching the whole of its length, one end of which was later drained to create the Horse Guards Parade. Years afterward, the Prince Regent, later George IV, at the same time that he turned Buckingham House into a royal palace (ever since the principal royal residence in London), retained John Nash (of Regent Street and Regent's Park fame) to landscape the park into its present form, with its elegant lake and at first a—rather, *the*—Marble Arch, which served as the formal entryway to the palace. (The arch, you will recall, was relocated to its present site at the west end of Oxford Street in 1851.)

St James's is for me the most pleasing of all the royal parks in Central London. The canal has been modified with gentle curves that provide a convincing imitation of a natural lake, complete with islands at each end. Make for the bridge in the center, which affords the best views both of Buckingham Palace to the west and to the east what almost looks like a Disney castle but in fact are the roofs of the government buildings of Whitehall, with a bit of Big Ben and the London Eye visible to boot. Charley Dickens remarks that the lake is the safest place in London to ice skate, but rare indeed now is the winter when it freezes over. My own memories of the park center on summer visits when my daughter was quite young and we were staying in friends' borrowed houses in Westminster. We often walked to the park to feed bread to the waterfowl and then rewarded ourselves with an ice cream. As for the palace, it's just as well seen from a distance as close up, so we will exit the bridge and turn right, perhaps stopping for a cup of tea at the busy but capacious park café, and then press onward to Horse Guards Parade.

Cross the open parade ground, and then pass through the archway; if you are lucky, you will see the modest ceremony accompanying the changing of the guard by the mounted troopers of the Household Cavalry. These are the fellows who sit in their saddles for hours facing Whitehall while they and their mounts display impossible restraint when they are prodded and poked by armies of tourists. Almost directly opposite is the only surviving part of the old Whitehall Palace, the Banqueting House, designed by Inigo Jones and completed in 1622, and one of the first neo-classical Palladian buildings in England. (The honor of "first" generally is accorded Jones's Queen's House in Greenwich, begun in 1616 although not completed until 1635.) Its interior is graced by a ceiling painted by Rubens. I have to admit it that impressive as the ceiling is, it leaves me cold: I can't really appreciate art that can only be viewed at the price of a neck ache. (Speaking of necks, it was from Banqueting House that Charles I walked out to his execution by beheading.)

Whitehall itself is a broad street that connects Trafalgar and Parliament Squares and in addition to the Horse Guards is home to many of the cabinet ministries, including Defence, Health, Work and Pensions, and the Treasury, as well as Downing Street itself (on a short spur, now protected by massive security gates). Number 10 is of course the official residence of the Prime Minister. I remember well that on my first visit to London in the early Seventies I was able to stroll casually past Number 10, occupied at the time by Edward Heath. The whole of the street then was not only open to the public but (if I remember aright) the door of No. 10 was guarded by a single helmeted and apparently unarmed bobby. Now, of course, security is a far greater presence, seen and no doubt unseen. The gate at the junction of Downing Street and Whitehall, however, is not related to the current epidemic of terrorist attacks; it was built in 1989 at the height of the IRA bombing campaign in London.

Double back to Horse Guards Road via King Charles Street, which terminates in stairs that pass the entrance of the Cabinet War Rooms, a fascinating warren of underground spaces that sheltered Churchill and his senior staff for a good part of the war. Churchill at some point had realized that the site was not actually bomb proof and so he had it reinforced with a five foot thick concrete slab; even that probably would not have withstood a direct hit from a V1 or V2. There were in the event a few near misses, but fortunately for us all, no serious damage. Catty-corner on the left at the end of the road is Storey's Gate, named after Edward Storey, the Keeper of the King's Birds for Charles II, a short street that is overlooked by the massive Westminster Central Hall, formerly the headquarters of the Methodist Church of Great Britain, and now a conference center (with a very nice basement café that is open to the public). It is a stunning example of over-the-top Edwardian baroque style, and it is also one of the first public buildings in Britain to benefit from a reinforced concrete frame. If you can, do enter the Great Hall, and look up at the vast domed roof supported by that very frame.

We now return to Victoria Street—the best way to approach the entrance to Westminster Abbey. The western aspect presents one of the most recognizable profiles of any medieval building in the world, but its most distinctive features—the two towers—in fact are not medieval at all. They date from early in the Eighteenth Century and were the work of Hawksmoor. The rest of the building dates to around 1245, and though it was part of the larger abbey, it escaped destruction at the time of the Dissolution when Henry VIII renamed it the cathedral of the Diocese of Westminster. It didn't retain cathedral status for very long, and for most of its subsequent history it has been a royal peculiar directly controlled by the Crown.

At most times of the year, the Abbey is packed with tourists. Entry is a rather steep £25, which gives you the run of the place, but it is also possible to attend a service gratis—I'd recommend Evensong at 5 pm on weekdays. It is fully as impressive a building as its reputation suggests, but for me its most interesting features are the memorials. The list of distinguished people buried and/or memorialized here is immense and reads like the *Who's Who* of British history: it includes many of the reigning monarchs along with other royals (including Princess Diana and Mary Queen of Scots) but also many politicians (both Pitts, Gladstone, and Neville Chamberlain), a few scientists (Newton, Darwin, and Hawking among them), and of course the literary luminaries in Poet's Corner (including Burns, Dickens, two Eliots [George and T.S.], Keats, Kipling, Milton, Pope, Tennyson, and Wordsworth). Others include Jenny Lind, the so-called Swedish Nightingale, and a few actors, including my nominee for the greatest male actor of all time, Lawrence Olivier. It is rather enjoyable to peruse the names both for those still famous and for others now largely forgotten (e.g. Nicholas Rowe, a poet laureate and the first editor of Shakespeare). I am always intrigued by monuments to those who were considered irreligious rogues and villains during their life-times (e.g. Byron and Shelley) but who appear to have been forgiven by the church on account of their fame. A few unlucky souls, Oliver Cromwell and some of his associates, were once buried in the Abbey and then later by order of Charles II disinterred, their remains thrown together in a pit in nearby St Margaret's Churchyard.

Just west of the abbey entrance is an arched gateway that is the entrance to Dean's Yard. The yard is home to the Westminster School, which dates back at least to 1179, though its probable origin was closer in time to the founding of the Anglo-Saxon abbey in 960, making it one of the oldest schools in the world. The school buildings are not open to the public, but the yard often is. Walk through the archway to Green (with no article) which is surrounded by mainly Eighteenth Century houses that belong either to the Church or the school. The school managed to survive the dissolution of the monastery and it was granted a charter by Henry VIII; it was also one of the original seven "public" schools recognized by Parliament in the Public Schools Act of 1868. Notable (and infamous) alumni include Ben Jonson, John Locke, Christopher Wren, Edward Gibbon, Jeremy Bentham, A.A. Milne, and Kim Philby. It deservedly enjoys the strongest academic reputation of any of the ancient public schools, and its record in placing students at Oxbridge colleges is unmatched. I had the good fortune once to spend the best part of a summer in a Westminster School faculty flat in Dean's Yard; a good friend was the house master. Dean's Yard was then and is still a remarkably tranquil island in the very center of one of the most crowded spots in all of London. My daughter, then aged about four, loved the flat, especially the turret room at the top of a medieval round stone staircase. One day by chance we bumped into the Queen Mother as she was leaving the Abbey; though we were the only onlookers, she stopped a foot or two away from us, smiled benignly at my daughter, and gave her a little wave. For years, my daughter told anyone who would listen that she had met a real queen, and so she had.

At this point, I'd be remiss not to suggest ending today's long, tiring ramble in the Abbey café, a comfortable place to rest to have a sandwich or a snack. However, after this long walk, it might be appropriate to splurge on the very creditable afternoon tea, every bit as good as the one at the Ritz, though far less expensive.

Chapter 13

Sloane Square

The station at Sloane Square is something of an engineering marvel. Opened by the District Railway in 1868, its engineers devised a radical solution to the problem of the line crossing the Westbourne River—rather than bridge over it or tunnel under it, they encased it in an iron conduit above the eastern end of the platforms so the trains could run unimpeded beneath it. The conduit now lies below an office building that spans the tracks but it is quite visible from the platforms and still eminently functional.

During the Blitz, this was also the site of some of the most serious damage and loss of life among all Underground stations—a direct hit in November 1940 completely destroyed it and killed 37. Not long before the war, the original station building had been replaced by an Art Deco structure that after the war was rebuilt more or less as it had been. That included space on Platform 1 for a pub called The Hole in the Wall, which sadly closed in 1985, the last of about half a dozen pubs located inside Underground stations. (It's now a convenience store.) The station was also damaged by an IRA bomb in 1974.

The station and the square are named after Sir Hans Sloane, who had purchased the manor of Chelsea from the Cheyne family in 1712. (There are still reminders of the original owners in the form of several Cheyne street names nearby.) Sloane came from a relatively modest background but by 1712 he had become one of the wealthiest men in England. After studying medicine both in England and on the Continent, followed by a spell in Jamaica where he collected plants locally including on slave plantations, he married the widow of a sugar planter and acquired her considerable fortune (including enslaved persons), gradually building a medical practice popular among the great and powerful—including George II. He became President of the Royal College of Physicians in 1719 and succeeded Newton as the President of the Royal Society in 1727.

But it was as a collector—of virtually everything—that he is now remembered. Though he never traveled abroad again after returning from the West Indies, he engaged an international network of agents, both paid and volunteer, and with their active assistance, he spent vast sums acquiring books, manu-scripts, fossils, mineral specimens, plants, bones, and indeed anything that struck him as curious or unique. On his death in 1753, he bequeathed it all conditionally to the nation—the condition being that it be purchased on behalf of his estate for what admittedly was the bargain price but still con-siderable sum of £20,000; it was duly purchased, forming (together with the library of George II) the core of the collections of the new British Museum, opened in 1759 in Bloomsbury. (He also left the Chelsea Physic Garden to the Worshipful Company of Apothecaries, who were his tenants there, and whose livery hall we have already visited; we will walk past the garden presently.) In addition to the square that bears his surname, there are also nearby a number of "Hans" street names hereabouts. The entire district was once called Hans Town, a name that for some reason didn't stick.

Emerging from the station onto Sloane Square, with Belgravia just to the North, Chelsea to the South, and the King's Road straight ahead, one can almost smell the ambient money. Since the Sixties, the King's Road has been one of the most fashionable and hippest shopping streets in London, and, to judge from the hordes of fit and well-attired young people one sees here now, it shows no signs of losing its appeal. The term "Sloane Ranger," popu-larized in the late Seventies, denoted wealthy, often aristocratic, teens and twenty-somethings who had been educated at the most elite public schools and "Oxbridge," who were conservative in their politics and values, and who dressed in the latest (and very expensive) designer styles. They were known in the popular press more for fast living than intellectual prowess. (The public school connection to Oxbridge is a little less strong than it used to be as the colleges for the most part now admit on the basis of academic merit rather than family connections.)

But before we depart the square, regard the Royal Court Theatre on the same side of the square as the station entrance. The present building opened in 1888—or rather a building with the same façade did, the interior having been altered and rebuilt more than once. It has had a chequered life, before World War II serving for a time as a cinema and during the war suffering heavy bomb damage. It was reconstructed and reopened in 1952, and reno-vated yet again in 2000. It has a long-standing reputation as the incubator of new theatrical talent, havianag showcased early work by John Osborne, Caryl Churchill, and Sarah Kane, among many others, and also nurtured talented directors, including Tony Richardson and Sam Mendes.

We will walk west along the south side of the square to the Duke of York's Square, built at the turn of the Eighteenth Century and originally home to a school for the children of military widows; over the years it had served a variety of military uses until 2003 when it was sold to the Cadogan Estate for around £100M. The estate turned most of the site into an upscale retail shopping and dining venue. More elegant shops and cafes in such a small space would be difficult to imagine; the patrons seem equally posh.

However, one large building of the complex, off to the south from the open plaza, is now a cultural icon—the permanent home of the Saatchi Gallery, which showcases very contemporary art (controversially, some of it owned by the Saatchis). Entry is free, and the building, sensitively conserved in its conversion to its present use, is well worth a visit. As for the art . . . well, I will say only that it is very cutting edge and you will like it if that's the sort of thing you like. And though it is a public gallery and admission is free, it does pay homage to the prevailing commercial atmosphere of Chelsea—the shop has some interesting and very pricey items for sale, including original artwork. Here, then, is your opportunity to acquire something by the next Damien Hurst. The robust utilitarian geometric Georgian lines of the building itself are best appreciated from the far corners of the playing fields outside. From the far southwest corner one usually can exit; do so and cross the road to Burton's Court, a private park that is part of the grounds of the magnificent Royal Hospital, whose elegant main building lies ahead off in the distance.

Founded in 1682 by King Charles II to house elderly Army veterans, the hospital is largely the work of Wren, and it has fulfilled its original mission ever since it opened in 1692. It is said to have been inspired by Louis XIV's *Hôteldes Invalides* in Paris, but there was also a cost-saving motive—it was cheaper to provide barrack-style housing for those soldiers "broken by war" than to give them all full pensions. The design—three connected quadrangles of red-brick buildings with Portland stone accents—is a marvelous example of how to achieve greatness on a limited budget. The original formal gardens disappeared when the Chelsea Embankment was built in the 1860s, and many of the buildings suffered damage from German bombs in both World War I and the Blitz, as well as from a direct hit by a V2 rocket in 1945, but despite all that a good part of Wren's original structure remains intact. The hospital was for far too long a male preserve, but women have been admitted since 2009. Chelsea pensioners stand out in any crowd by virtue of their instantly recognizable uniforms, blue when on the grounds, and the better known bright scarlet when beyond the gates. Parts of the complex, including a museum, are open to the public; tours led by pensioners are available with advance notice. The café, which appears to be a concession, is open to the public as well, and it serves rather good food at moderate prices; moreover, walking to and from the cafe is a good way to sneak a peek at the off-limits parts of the interior of the complex.

Chelsea Bridge, directly south of the Royal Hospital, is the second crossing built on this site. The first had opened in 1858 named the Victoria Bridge and for a time it levied a very unpopular toll. Almost from the start, however, there were serious concerns about its structural integrity, and within a few years it had been renamed so as to avoid any embarrassment to the royal family should it collapse. Despite these concerns, it lasted until the 1930s, when the present bridge replaced it. It is in appearance a typical cable suspension bridge, but it is worth noting that the cables are self-anchored; in other words, the horizontal structure of the roadway absorbs the tension on the cables. In theory, you could lift it up and plunk it down somewhere else without damaging it in the least—but since it now is Grade II listed it's unlikely one could get planning permission to do so. The bridge project developed in parallel with the creation of Battersea Park on the other side of the river on land purchased in 1846 to create an entirely new green space of some 200 acres, opened in the same year as the bridge.

We won't cross the bridge, but do note atop the bridge lamp posts the coats of arms of the old Boroughs of Chelsea and Battersea, as well as the old L.C.C. Then look to the east across the river and note the imposing profile of the Battersea Power Station. The old generating plant is a monumental structure, in its style very Art Deco with its iconic cream-colored chimneys soaring over a vast red-brick box. Though it looks like it was designed to its present shape, it actually was built in two phases, the first in the 1930s and the second, doubling its size, in the 1950s. So well done was the addition that it is difficult to tell the "old" from the "new." There are, or were, other power plants built in the same style, including the Bankside Power Station, now home to the hugely successful Tate Modern. Giles Gilbert Scott—you'll recall he was grandson of the famous architect of the Albert Memorial and son of another less well known architect Scott—is often credited with the design, but his involvement was late and limited; the buildings are in fact the result of collaborative work by a number of engineers and architects. Battersea ceased generating electricity in 1983 and the building has spent most of the decades since in limbo, slowly deteriorating, as several owners tried and failed to get planning permission to develop the site. The latest owner, a Malaysian firm, bought it relatively cheaply and immediately hired the starchitect Rafael Vinoly to guide their planning. Now, with the blessing of Wandsworth Council, it is about to debut as yet another "exciting and innovative mixed use [neighbourhood] . . . a place for locals, tourists and residents to enjoy a unique blend of restaurants, shops, parks and cultural spaces." (If that blend is unique, then all of the other developers in London making the same claim need to change their PR teams.)

We will not cross the river; but instead we shall double back around to the front of the Royal Hospital and head west, past its long façade, via Royal Hospital Road. This corner of Chelsea, abutting the Thames, and indeed the entire district between the Fulham Road and the river, is very much the epitome of *rus in urbe*, replete with vine-covered cottages, leafy garden squares, and quiet side streets. It also comprises one of the most expensive housing markets in London (which is saying a lot!); even after the recent Brexit- and pandemic-induced fluctuations in property values, you'll spend at least £2000 a square foot for one of these stunning little jewel-box houses. But as long as looking is free, enjoy the views. Don't miss the turning for Swan Walk, a delightful little lane that runs down to the river, named after the venerable Swan Inn, once frequented by Pepys. That inn—or, rather, two ancient inns of the same name—is gone, but there is a newer one (c.1780), confusingly called the Old Swan.

On the same south side of the road as Swann Walk is the Chelsea Physic Garden, first leased by Sloane to the Society of Apothecaries in 1722. This modest walled enclosure—4 acres at the time, and a little smaller now—is the third oldest botanical garden in Great Britain. After its founding, it very quickly developed into one of the richest collections of plants in the world. For the Apothecaries it served for two centuries a working laboratory, providing the plant materials that were compounded into its medical preparations. The Apothecaries retained control of it until 1983, when it was hived off as a separate charity. It is open a few afternoons a week between April and October; do go in if you have the opportunity, and among other rarities, you will see Britain's largest olive tree and what claims to be the northernmost fruiting grapefruit tree in the world. The café serves a lovely hot lunch, as well, and weather permitting one can sit outside on the terrace amidst the greenery.

Royal Hospital Road leads on to Cheyne Place which continues as Cheyne Walk, which runs parallel to the Chelsea Embankment. Cheyne Walk offers a fine row of mostly early Eighteenth-Century houses. Its most famous resident—albeit for only the last three weeks of her life—was George Eliot; her house, number 4, now is owned by former New York mayor Michael Bloomberg. It set him back £17M, or $25M at the exchange rate at the time, a pittance to one of the world's richest men but an impressive price for a very modest London row house. Not far off, on Cheyne Row (which runs north, perpendicular to Cheyne Walk), is Carlyle's House, for many years the home of Thomas and Jane Carlyle, and one of the few writers' houses in London that remains much as it was when it was occupied. It opened to the public in 1895, only fourteen years after Thomas Carlyle's death.

At this point, you will be looking directly at the Albert Bridge that connects Chelsea to the western end of Battersea Park, and a curious bricolage it is. The original bridge was built in 1873 to a cable-stayed design. It was soon found to be structurally unstable, and only about ten years later it was partially rebuilt as a cable suspension bridge by Joseph Bazalgette (of Embankment fame). In 1973 it was altered yet again, with the central section turned into a beam bridge. Despite all the structural mucking about, it looks thoroughly Victorian and it serves as a pretty enough backdrop to this picture-postcard corner of Chelsea.

Also impossible to ignore and opposite the bridge entrance, outside an upscale auto dealer, is an oversize bronze statue of a boy with a dolphin, entitled "Boy with a Dolphin" and the work of David Wynne, dating from 1974. It depicts—you will have guessed—a boy with a dolphin. (It may or may not be alluding to the famous "Putto with Dolphin" attributed to Leonardo's mentor, Verrocchio.) If you are very observant, you will recall having seen at St Katherine's Dock a very similar and slightly earlier work, "Girl with a Dolphin," which depicts . . . well, enough said. Wynne is best known for his bronze "Gorilla," a portrait of Guy the Gorilla, for many years one of the London Zoo's favorite inmates; if you want to see it, you'll have to travel all the way to Crystal Palace in far south London where it resides.

Many more literary associations abound in this little corner of Chelsea, including a connection to Henry James, who lived on Cheyne Walk, and who is memorialized by a plaque in nearby Chelsea Old Church, which stands directly ahead of us now. There has been a church on this site since 1157 and it once also housed a private chapel belonging to Sir Thomas More. Here, in the 1520s, More built his country home, later known as Beaufort House. It was mostly torn down in the Eighteenth Century, and Beaufort Street was built on the site. (The remaining bits of More's City residence, Crosby Hall in Bishopsgate, were taken down in 1910 and rebuilt on Cheyne Walk, where they are now part of a private house.) It was from here in 1534 that More was taken to the Tower and in 1535 executed. The statue of More in front of the church dates from 1969 and must be one of the worst monuments in London—he looks like a garishly colored cartoon version of himself. Another chapel in the church belonged to the lords of the Manor of Chelsea, including Hans Sloane (buried here), who gave the church a number of books that still are there, chained to ensure they are not stolen. (They are now the only chained books in a London church.) The church looks convincingly as if it deserves the adjective "old" in its name—including quite a few ancient tombs—but what you see is an illusion. The church was badly blitzed in 1941 and most of what is there now was lovingly reconstructed in the 1950s.

Across the road is a sunken garden named after More's son-in-law, William Roper (played memorably by Corin Redgrave in *A Man for all Seasons*). The street at the front of the church is called Old Church Street, as well it ought to be, and it leads us northward past more chocolate-box cottages and charming terrace houses back to the King's Road, so named because it was Charles II's private route to Kew Palace. It remained a private royal thoroughfare (though sometimes open to non-royals) until 1830. It stretches to the west for another mile or so, terminating in a neighbourhood named World's End, named after a pub. World's End now mostly is subsumed into a vast housing estate built by the Kensington and Chelsea council in the late Sixties and early Seventies in the then popular "brutalist" style. It includes seven high-rise towers linked by walkways above the street level, much like the coeval Barbican. While like the Barbican complex it features cast concrete construction, it is clad in reddish-brown bricks, which give it a somewhat softer and less severe aspect—the kinder and gentler face of brutalist architecture.

But we will turn eastward, to the right, and walk along the King's Road back toward Sloane Square. The shops we now pass on the King's Road are for the most part suitably expensive outlets for furnishing a Sloane Ranger home and wardrobe, if that should be your goal, but it is at the Sloane Square end of the road that a quite different retail landmark appears—the department store Peter Jones, which despite retaining the name of its Victorian founder long has been part of the John Lewis partnership. Jones was a draper who moved his shop here in 1877 and somehow secured a 999 year lease with the Cadogan Estate. The annual rent was £6000, a tidy sum then but a pittance now, and remarkably the lease is still in force. It probably stands as the best (for the tenant) or worst (for the landlord) real estate deal in London's history. (A small shop in this corner of Chelsea rents today for about £500,000 a year.) The building itself is the epitome of Art Deco, largely unchanged since it opened in 1936. It was one of the first buildings in London to feature a glass curtain wall and with its gently curved corners it still is quite striking. The John Lewis chain (anchored by the main store in Oxford Street) holds a special place in British middle-class hearts and minds as the place where you can buy sensible, stylish (but not modish or faddish) clothing, furniture, household appliances, kitchen supplies, draperies—in fact, just about anything—at reasonable prices, with delivery generally free. Like all of the department store chains, John Lewis is struggling at present, though bearing in mind the bargain ground rent, one suspects that Peter Jones will not be one of the locations closed in the near future.

We are now back at Sloane Square, and just north of the square on Sloane Street is Holy Trinity, the widest church in London—exceeding the width of St Paul's by a full nine inches. It is the work of John Dando Sedding, retained by the 5th Earl Cadogan in 1888 to replace an earlier, smaller Victorian building. ("Smaller" is a relative term—the original church was said to have seated 1600.) The exterior is a mélange of the Gothic and Arts and Crafts styles, or perhaps more accurately an Arts and Crafts reinterpretation of the Gothic. With its alternating bands of brick and stone, and despite (or because of?) its confusion of styles, it is both impressive and attractive. Its grand ambitions were to be fulfilled with an equally imposing interior, but much of what was planned was never begun or if begun never completed. There is, however, a gigantic east window with stained glass designed by Burne-Jones and Morris. The church was badly damaged in the Blitz and then restored in the Sixties.

Perversely, soon after the restoration, it was threatened with demolition, but public outcry saved it and its continued survival now seems secure.

And now we find ourselves again on Sloane Square, not a very pleasantly landscaped public space, but it does have a dignified monument to the dead of the First World War and a central Venus Fountain. Why Venus? Look carefully at the relief at the basin—it features Charles II and his most famous mistress Nell Gwyn. Gwyn never lived in Chelsea, but she is said—on the basis of no evidence whatsoever—to have inspired Charles to found the Royal Hospital. Hence her commemoration here.

And so back into the tube and on to South Kensington.

Chapter 14

South Kensington

The South Kensington Station first opened in 1868, from the very first serving both the Metropolitan and the District Railways and the place where their competing lines first met. The Metropolitan service had been extended southward from Paddington and the District westward from Westminster. Although they shared the station, they co-existed uneasily for decades, maintaining separate tracks and even separate ticket offices. The Victorian station building has vanished, but from the Circle Line platforms one can make out surviving sections of the original platforms and tracks. The present building, with its well-preserved and busy shopping arcade, dates from 1907, when the entrance was rebuilt to serve the new deep underground line built by Great Northern, Piccadilly and Brompton Railway, the ancestor of the Piccadilly Line. (I can remember the ancient lifts still in service in the 1970s, when they finally were replaced by escalators.) The GNP&BR station building on Pelham Street is still there, instantly recognizable by its red terracotta tiled exterior.

South Kensington is defined by and synonymous with its large and enduring institutions; indeed, the neighbourhood came into being as a museum quarter in the wake of the Great Exhibition of 1851 which had taken place on a site inside nearby Hyde Park. The South Kensington institutional establishment now includes museums (the Victoria and Albert, the Science, and the Natural History), educational institutions (Imperial College and the Royal College of Music), and the huge performance space of the Royal Albert Hall.

It is possible to exit the station underground and to access directly the famous South Kensington museums through a dedicated tunnel, almost always crowded with tourists and school groups. The tunnel opened back in 1885, having cost the then astronomical sum of £42,600 (add three zeroes for a rough estimate in today's money). At first, there was a penny toll, but after a few years, it was generally kept shuttered and opened only for special events. In 1890, it was slated to be incorporated into a new cut-and-cover railway line linking South Kensington directly with Paddington Station, but strong opposition to digging up Hyde Park killed the plan and the railway was never built. The tunnel reopened without the toll in 1908 and it has been in use ever since. It is a favorite of buskers, who sound louder here than anywhere else in London. If you are an entertainer whose goal is to annoy innocent passersby, this most definitely is the place to do it.

We shall avoid the tunnel and instead climb the stairs, exiting through the arcade, turning left (south) as we emerge from the station. Straight ahead is Onslow Square, quiet, attractive, and residential on three of its sides, despite its proximity to the tube station and its crowds. Lovely little streets like this remind us why this neighborhood is so popular with foreign visitors. Have a good look round and then return to the station, passing back through the arcade, and as you exit it, turn right onto Thurloe Street, which leads directly to the bottom of Exhibition Road, which we will take northward toward the museums, by so doing avoiding the crowds and the reverberating noise of the tunnel.

Thurloe Street anchors a pleasant little shopping precinct that has gone very up-market in recent years, but there remain a few of the old businesses that seem to have been there at least since I first visited London in the Seventies. There is among them still (as I write) a quirky remainder book shop and a remarkably inexpensive Chinese restaurant, whose decor looks as if it was last renewed in 1970 or thereabouts, but then you can't eat décor. It still is possible to have a good, freshly prepared, and filling meal there for well under £10. I highly recommend the roast pork over rice; I try to lunch there whenever I am in the neighbourhood. (A ships' chandlery whose windows I always enjoyed browsing alas has recently disappeared.)

Just ahead on the south extension of Exhibition Road is the Ismaili Centre, one of the six global religious and cultural centers of the Ismaili Muslims, a Shiite group that recognizes the Aga Khan as their 49th Imam, and whose succession may be traced in a direct line back to the Prophet Muhammad. This site once had been reserved for a new national theatre, but after the Second World War it was correctly judged too small for that purpose. (In the end the theatre was built on its present and much more suitable location on the South Bank.) The property languished undeveloped for thirty years until it was acquired by the Ismailis in the Seventies. The building's design by Sir Hugh Casson attempts not only to be faithful to Islamic architectural traditions but also to blend in with the grand museums surrounding it, and at the very same time to make a bold contemporary architectural statement. When it opened in 1985, with Margaret Thatcher doing the dedicatory honors, it was given a prize as the worst new building in Britain, but over the years it seems to have settled into its site comfortably enough, perhaps because so many worse buildings have been erected in London since.

Across the busy Cromwell Road (don't attempt to cross against the lights, as traffic whips around the corner on a turning signal invisible to pedestrians) is the vast, grand façade of the Victoria and Albert Museum, in effect the reason that South Kensington exists. The museum was a direct offshoot of the tremendously popular Great Exhibition, held in a massive cast iron and glass pavilion (thus the popular name, the Crystal Palace) in Hyde Park from May to October of 1851. Meant to showcase manufactures from all over the world, but mostly Britain, the exhibition was largely the result of the dogged persistence of Prince Albert and Henry Cole, a civil servant who (among many other accomplishments) also had produced the first commercial Christmas card in 1843. The success of the Great Exhibition—it was visited 6,000,000 times, a number equal to nearly one-third of Britain's population at the time— led to the establishment in 1852 of a permanent collection of manufactures and design, initially the Museum of Manufactures. In 1854, as its permanent site then had been selected, it was renamed the South Kensington Museum. (The land, by the by, was purchased with funds from the profits of the Great Exhibition.)

From the start, the museum reflected the vision of Cole, its first director, emphasizing the practical or applied arts and sciences as a means to maintain the supremacy of British manufacturing, and, equally and not unrelated, to promote access to fine designs for the working classes. (Dickens pleads the same case in *Hard Times* [1854]). With that latter goal in mind, in 1857 the museum opened its modestly priced refreshment rooms, the first in any museum, and it pioneered evening hours the following year. Its first building was erected around Brompton Park House, a rambling structure whose core dated from the Seventeenth Century and that once was the home of the famous gardener, Henry Wise; the vast building to the west of the present entrance came later. Queen Victoria laid the foundation stone of that later building in 1899—her last official public appearance—and it was then renamed to honor her and her long-deceased consort.

The collections are incomparable—but first, instead of examining objects and exhibits, let us focus on the building itself. The interior is a cornucopia of Victorian high design, various bits of it the work of well-known designers and artists, including Owen Jones and Frederick Leighton. The northwest corner of the first floor is my favorite section—the staircase, the work of Frank Moody, is entirely covered by ceramic tiles in Renaissance revival style. The café is also a tiled extravaganza. Of the exhibits themselves, nothing can be said that conveys adequately their eclectic variety and phenomenal depth. Despite its initial remit to focus on British manufactures and design, the museum has some of the world's largest and finest collections of East Asian, Islamic, and South Asian art, but also of all periods and types of ceramics, glass, metalwork, fashion, and jewelry from around the world, as well as housing the National Art Library—some 750,000 volumes. One could mention more of its collections, but there is one particular (and my absolute favorite) gallery on the ground floor that is virtually unique and must be seen to be believed.

The Cast Courts are devoted to full-size plaster casts of historically significant sculptures and monuments. There are scores of them, packed together in a dizzying amalgam of historical periods and architectural styles. Among the displays are the lower half of Trajan's column from the Roman forum (the top half wouldn't fit) and all of Michelangelo's "David." The practice of making such casts dates back to the Renaissance, but they were much in vogue in the Nineteenth Century as a means of establishing study collections for the emerging national museums of art and design. The guiding principle seems to have been, what you couldn't own you could at least copy. Indeed, in 1867, fifteen European nations signed the International Convention of Promoting Universally Reproductions of Works of Art to facilitate the sharing of casts across borders. No longer used as a means of art education for the masses, many casts have proven unexpectedly valuable as their originals have suffered from wear and tear, ill-advised restoration, pollution, and of course war. In some instances, the originals have been destroyed altogether and the casts are all that remain.

Also on the ground floor and worth special mention and a visit is the museum shop. Like most of its kind, it sells endless numbers of overpriced post cards and cheap museum logo souvenirs, but it is also a showcase for contemporary craft and design, especially jewelry and ceramics. There almost always is a sale going on and the unique craft objects are quite affordable. I never visit but I succumb to temptation at least once. There is also a (separate) fairly well stocked book shop.

One easily could—and no doubt one should—spend days wandering inside the V&A, and certainly every time I visit I find something new (or, at my age, more likely I rediscover something I once knew but since have forgotten), but let us now leave via the new western entrance, landing us square on Exhibition Road. (Until very recently, this area was named after the Sackler family.) Across the road is the Natural History Museum, the offspring of another venerable institution, the British Museum. As we have seen, the British Museum at its founding in 1756 had become the keeper of the huge and very miscellaneous collection of objects amassed by Sir Hans Sloane. But it was difficult to display so many thousands of items, and in the 1830s it was determined that many animal and vegetable specimens were missing while most that were extant were falling slowly (and in some cases quickly) to pieces. Nevertheless, nothing was done to remedy the situation until 1856, when Richard Owen, by training a paleontologist (it was he who coined the term "dinosaur"), was appointed Superintendent of the natural history departments, the first such appointee to hold relevant professional expertise; not long after, a site for a new, purpose-built science museum was found near the South Kensington Museum. The building finally opened in 1881, though it was not until 1963 that it separated from its parent and it was formally chartered in its own right.

This is another of the great London museums in which one could lose oneself for days on end, but I'll mention only what visitors upon entering the building now will *not* see—the monumental plaster cast of a diplodocus that in 1905 had been a gift from Andrew Carnegie, who had donated the original to a new museum of natural history in Pittsburgh, where it still is on view. Over the years, Dippy (as the plaster reproduction was known in the popular press) became the museum's *de facto* mascot, first displayed in the Reptile Gallery and then in 1979 moved to the cavernous grand entrance hall (now named after Sir Michael and Lady Hintze, who funded its recent restoration). Very recently, it was removed and sent on a tour of other British museums, replaced in Hintze Hall by the equally monumental skeleton of a blue whale. (Dippy's new home is the museum's Reptile Gallery.)

Walking north on Exhibition Road, we soon pass the Science Museum, which began life as overflow galleries from the main complex; it was hived off in 1914 and in the same year construction began for its own impressive building. The museum abuts Imperial College, or to give its proper name, the Imperial College of Science, Technology, and Medicine. It was founded as the Imperial Institute in 1887 to promote science research and scientific education throughout the far-flung empire; its main building was seemingly as extensive as the entity it served, fronting a massive 700-foot façade pierced by a tall central tower. In 1907, the institute and several other scientific schools and colleges (including the Royal School of Mines) were amalgam-ated into the new Imperial College, created as a constituent college of the federal University of London. But, like University College London and Kings College, it recently declared its independence from the federal University, and like them it now grants its own degrees. It is generally considered one of the top-ranked scientific universities in the world.

Still further north, and just to the west, is Kensington Gore, which leads to the Royal Albert Hall, whose site was also purchased with profits from the Great Exhibition. (Theories abound on how many holes it would take to fill said hall; I refer you to the Beatles' album, *Sgt Pepper's Lonely Hearts Club Band,* for further details.) Opened in 1871, it was designed to seat 8,000 (capacity since has been reduced to a mere 5500), but its cavernous interior and its huge glass and cast iron dome together made it an acoustical disaster with a pronounced echo: jokers quipped that the hall was the only place where a British composer was guaranteed to hear his work performed twice. The acoustic challenges were mitigated but unresolved until the late

1960s. It has in modern times hosted all sorts of performances—including some notable rock concerts—as well as special events like circuses and the Eurovision Song Contest. The hall is best known in the U.K. as the venue of the BBC Proms (short for Promenade Concerts), an annual summer music festival that it has hosted since 1942. Don't pass by without carefully inspecting the mosaic frieze that surrounds the top of the outer circular wall. Its sixteen panels together depict "The Triumph of Arts and Sciences."

Across the busy road at the southern border of the park is the Albert Memorial, just within the eastern borders of Kensington Gardens, and at 180' in height it can be seen from almost anywhere in the park. During the prince's lifetime, the City Corporation had proposed erecting a monument to Albert's labours in connection with the Great Exhibition, but he had firmly said no, opining that any money raised would better be given to charity. But after Albert died suddenly in 1861, Queen Victoria was determined that there should be a suitably grand memorial to him somewhere in London. It took years of squabbling between civic authorities and the Palace before a gothic revival design by Gilbert Scott was selected and construction begun. The memorial opened in 1872, but at first absent the statue of Albert, which arrived three years later. The frieze around the base (denominated the Frieze of Parnassus) and the surrounding sculptures together comprise allegorical depictions of the arts, commerce, science, and manufactures, as well as the four continents of the Empire, Africa, America, Asia, and Europe. (Australia was too young to make the cut.) Charley Dickens has nothing much to say about it other than that it cost a staggering £120,000 to build. It was seen at the time as an odd mélange, mixing medieval Christian architecture, classical sculptures, and Byzantine mosaics—aptly characterized by the *Survey of London* as "eerie but stolid incongruities"—and even with the smoothing passage of time it still comes across as nothing so much as a dog's dinner. It is best seen from afar, so that the rich detail doesn't overwhelm the eye, or from very close up, so the details stand proud from the overall design.

The City eventually did get an Albert memorial of its own in 1874, the statue of him on horseback in the middle of Holborn Circus that we saw on our Farringdon walk. The prince, you may recall, is there depicted with his hat held above his head, as if waving hello to commuters, although as near as I can tell, it is completely ignored daily by tens of thousands of passersby. I've rarely to encounter a Londoner who knows it's there.

The Albert Memorial is not far from the Ring, the undulating north-south road that divides Kensington Gardens from Hyde Park. Taken together, the two parks comprise a single vast expanse of 625 acres of green space. (By way of comparison, Central Park in New York is slightly larger at 825 acres.) At its southeastern tip, Hyde Park touches the northwestern corner of Green Park, which itself abuts St. James's Park, so if you were to put your mind to it, you could walk two miles or so through Central London wholly on grass. Again we are reminded that London has been fortunate that so much of the land in the West End now devoted to parks was in royal hands and thus not open for commercial or residential development.

Just north of the memorial is the Serpentine Gallery, founded in 1970, and very soon established as one of London's leading exhibitors of contemporary, cutting-edge (and sometimes decidedly edgy) art. Artists whose work has been highlighted include Man Ray, Andy Warhol, Michel Basquiat, Gerhard Richter, Damien Hurst, Jeff Koons, and Marina Abramovic. The neo-Georgian architecture of the main building, the Serpentine South, seems rather inappropriate for its avant-garde mission, but it was quite appropriate when it began tis life in the 1930s as a traditional tea room. There is now a second gallery, the Serpentine North (formerly the Serpentine Sackler), an older building repurposed to a design by Zaha Hadid; it lies just across the Serpentine Bridge, an elegant structure designed and built by John Rennie in the 1820s. The Serpentine is reputed to be a magnet for suicide by drowning; one of the earliest recorded was that of Harriet Shelley, the poet's abandoned first wife, in 1816. Visitors in the summer will also encounter a temporary pavilion designed each year by a famous (or soon to be famous) architect or artist; invitees in the past have included Hadid, Daniel Libeskind, Frank Gehry, Jean Novel, and Ai Weiwei.

The Serpentine itself was formed by damming the Westbourne, and when it took its present shape in the 1730s, it was one of the first curved artificial lakes in an English landscape garden, reflecting the shift in taste from neo-classical straight lines and geometric shapes to a more "natural" picturesque garden style. (Nowadays the water comes not from the river but from bore-holes into the aquifer below.) The portion of the lake to the west of the bridge in Kensington Gardens has its own name—it is properly called the Long Water. It has hosted a summer swimming lido since 1930, and during the 2012 Summer Olympics it was one of the water sports event venues, one of which I was lucky enough to witness. At its very northern end are the impressive ornate Italian Gardens, a set of formal gardens built around four large rectangular ponds, the gift of Prince Albert to Victoria shortly before he died.

Leaving the park as we entered it, instead of retracing our steps on Exhibition Road we shall walk a short distance to the east, crossing the road and then turning south onto Ennismore Gardens. This will take us past the rather grand Russian Orthodox Cathedral of the Dormition; built in Italian Renaissance revival style, it began its life in 1849 as a Church of England parish church. Wander the adjacent back streets southward toward Holy Trinity, a Church Commissioner's gothic revival building dating from the 1820s, which in turn abuts the rear of the Brompton Oratory.

The Brompton Road and the Oratory are just about all that remains of the old village of Brompton that once was here before it was overtaken by South Kensington. The Oratory is a vast late Nineteenth-Century Renaissance revival building that was to serve London's rapidly growing Roman Catholic communities. The Brompton Road probably is best known nowadays for leading to Harrod's famous department store, a few hundred yards to the east. If you fancy a somewhat over-the-top retail experience, do go inside, but for my money the food hall is the part of the store most worth a visit.

Perhaps you have stepped inside, or not, but in either case, we now will turn to the west, continue past the entrance to the V&A, and then turn back into the Underground to travel on to High Street Kensington.

Chapter 15

High Street Kensington

High Street Kensington Station came into service in October 1868 as the Metropolitan Railway pushed outward from Paddington. (The station name ends with "Kensington" but the street name begins with it.) Later, the station building was shared uneasily with the District, leading to the building of what became known as the "Cromwell Curve." The District was meant to run trains on the Met's tracks between this station and Gloucester Road, but rather than pay for the use of the line, the District built its own set of parallel tracks, creating a curved section of about 800' solely for use by its own trains. There had been no Parliamentary approval for this short line, leading to nearly endless legal disputes, finally settled in 1903 when the District lost the battle and was barred from using this section of track. (The track is long gone, and the land that lay under the curve became the site of the old West London Air Terminal, now a block of flats.)

The present station building at dates from the early Twentieth Century, when the original 1860s structure was rebuilt to create a shopping arcade with streetfront units that could be (and are still) rented out as shops, generating a bit of extra revenue for TfL. The arcade's sky-lit internal octagon today is much as it was when it was first built, and the space it encloses remains filled with shops and eateries, including a wonderful Belgian *chocolatier*; the space is almost always busy with pedestrian traffic. Kensington High Street—its straight course follows the lines of an old Roman road—at the turn of the Twentieth Century was very much devoted to shopping, eventually attracting several department stores catering to the middle classes, among them Pontings, Derry and Toms, and Barkers. Though the large stores disappeared decades ago, even before the era of internet shopping, "High Street Ken" still is very much a shopping mecca.

My first acquaintance with High Street Kensington dates from the early Seventies. The principal attraction then was Biba, Barbara Hulanicki's unique shop. She began successfully selling her distinctively styled and moderately priced women's clothing in the early Sixties; she moved the shop several times to ever larger premises, finally in 1973 taking over the vast Derry and Toms building on the high street; to fill the space, she added lines of clothing for men and children, as well as household goods and furniture, and even groceries. My wife was a great fan of the clothing, and for decades we owned a few tins and jars we'd bought when it first opened, all of which display the curious attractive mix of mod, Art Deco, and Art Nouveau in black and gold that was her signature style. Alas, her last expansion was one too many, and she soon was forced to sell out, but the new owners couldn't make a go of it either and the store closed only a few years later.

The Royal Borough of Kensington and Chelsea, London's smallest, was formed in 1962 by the merger of two even smaller independent boroughs, Chelsea and Kensington, and the two parts still seem quite distinct from one another. Kensington and Chelsea is not only London's smallest borough, but it is also London's richest (by some measures), and London's fourth most densely populated. It is also one of London's most international local authorities: 51.6% of the borough's residents are foreign born. A further 38% self-report as having a non-British primary identity and one-fifth speak a language at home other than English.

Who are these foreign-born residents? The image conjured in the mind's eye by the name Kensington is one of sparkling white stuccoed terrace houses and huge villas occupied by Middle Eastern sheiks and Russian billionaires. Though there are quite a few sheiks and billionaires in residence, there is more to Kensington than meets the casual visitor's eye. Like Tower Hamlets, the borough contains within its borders extraordinary disparities of income and education: the northern and western borders of the borough have several "social" housing estates and the borough struggles with all of the challenges associated with low-income communities. The borough ranks first in income inequality in London, and it is the 12th worst in indices of child poverty. One of those housing estates included the Grenfell Tower, site of the recent tragic disastrous fire. This is the central London visitors never see.

We will begin our tour by walking west from the station. One passes here a number of grand Edwardian brick-and-stone mansion blocks, their commercial ground floors tenanted by all of the usual high street stores—Boots, Tesco, Starbucks, and so on. Indeed, Kensington High Street has been so thoroughly "chained" that it no longer feels like an authentic London neighbourhood—it is more like a middle-market outdoor shopping mall.

Our first stop, just across the road, behind the shops, and parallel to it, is Stafford Terrace. Number 18 is the Linley Sambourne House, once home to this *Punch* illustrator who was for a time designated its "First Cartoonist." Decorated in the late Victorian Aesthetic style, the house has been preserved exactly as it was when Sambourne died in 1910. It was for a time owned and managed by the Greater London Council, and at the time of the demise of the GLC it was passed on to the Borough of Kensington and Chelsea, who operate it as a museum. It is open to the public four days a week; if by chance your visit is during one of those times, it is well worth an hour of your time.

Continue west along the high street on the north side, past the possibly tempting shop windows, and before long we come to the entrance to Holland Park. Holland Park's origins are as a private estate, and despite the intensive development all around it, it remained privately owned well into recent times. At the center of the park is Holland House, portions of which are still in use. It was built in 1605 by Sir Walter Cope and eventually it was home to several generations of the Fox family. In the Nineteenth Century, the third Baron Holland and his wife made the house a center of Whig political circles and literary life; they regularly entertained such luminaries as Byron, Scott, and Dickens, along with grandees of the Whig political establishment. The house was badly damaged in the Blitz and in 1952 it was sold to the London County Council by the last Fox to own it. What remains is essentially a single wing of the old house, occupied now by a youth hostel; the grounds are also home to an opera company. The most impressive feature visually is the loggia, a Victorian addition in period style. There also is a pleasant park cafe, modestly priced and with comfortable seating. On a warm day it is possible to sit at tables outdoors.

Holland Park first passed from the LCC to the Greater London Council, and then when the GLC was terminated, it too was passed on to the Royal Borough of Kensington and Chelsea. The borough does a creditable job maintaining it: while it is clean and everything that ought to be in good condition is, more or less, the park feels a bit less polished than the royal parks, which to my taste is a good thing. One doesn't feel here as if one is committing a crime by walking on the grass, and here and there a few mere weeds are permitted to flourish. And unlike the other Central London green spaces, it is very heavily used by its own community: the sports fields are always full at weekends and the pathways are crowded with dog-walkers.

Among the park's treasures are the formal gardens adjacent to the remains of Holland House, and just to beyond them, two lovely Japanese gardens. The older of the two, the Kyoto Japanese Garden, so named because it was a gift from that Japanese city, is especially charming. Do look for the astonishingly large koi in the central pond. Nearby is the newer Fukushima Garden, a gift from that city in gratitude for the support Londoners provided after the recent nuclear disaster. Both are pleasant places to spend a quiet half hour.

Best of all, the Holland Park has yet to be discovered by tourists; it is by and for Londoners. Correction: there is now one small corner of the park that has been found by visitors. Back at the entry to the park there is a massive and quite striking building in the high modernist style—once the Commonwealth Institute but now the Design Museum. Opened in 1962 to showcase the cultures of the many member states, especially those newly granted independence, the institute foundered in the Nineties, rather like the Commonwealth itself—in part because of the cost of maintaining the building—and its collections were dispersed (with some parts inappropriately sold off). It took more than a decade to unravel its finances and close its books, but finally in 2012 the Design Museum was confirmed as the new occupier and the extensively refurbished galleries were opened in 2016.

The building—designed by Robert Matthew Johnson-Marshall and Partners—has lost none of its visual impact, especially when approached from the southern park entrance—the angular shape and the soaring, gravity-defying roof are impressive still, both as a design and as a marvel of engineering. But the reworked interior is something of a disappointment. The atrium is huge, but it is so vast that it severely limits the space available to display the museum's permanent collection, which one might argue is why in the first place it is a museum. My advice is to savor the building from a bench outside, but do make time to stop by the design shop which has some very beautiful and very expensive things on offer. I've never actually bought anything in the shop but I have spent a few pleasant hours imagining what I would buy if money were no object.

A short detour from the southwest corner of the park leads by way of Ilchester Place to Melbury Road. This is a neighbourhood of large mid- and late Victorian villas, and, just to the west at the next turning, Holland Park Road leads immediately to Leighton House, once the home of and now a museum dedicated to Sir Frederic Leighton. Leighton painted in the late Pre-Raphaelite style, though he was never formally a member of the group; his solid contemporary reputation as an artist's artist was sealed by his long service as President of the Royal Academy, from 1878 to 1896, the year of his death. The house was built by Leighton as both a studio and a residence, and the much of the interior is in the Moorish style. The "Arab Hall" with its fountain and tiled walls is not to be missed and never to be forgotten. Several of Leighton's canvasses and other contemporary art works (and period decorative objects) are on permanent display, and the museum also hosts small special exhibitions focusing on late Victorian art. There are in particular many ceramic pieces by William De Morgan, one of England's first art potters, also all in the Moorish revival style. A recent refurbishment has crated space for a café, and the small garden behind the house is a pleasant spot to sit for a few moments, weather permitting, before continuing on our walk.

Suitably rested, retrace your steps back into Holland Park and walk eastward past the Holland House terrace. At the far eastern edge of the park, turn left or northward along a straight path (watching out for racing cyclists). Further north still, the park ends shortly before Holland Park Avenue (not to be confused with Holland Park Road, which we trod a few minutes ago), which is the western continuation of Notting Hill Gate. Notting Hill Gate itself is undistinguished—though it is home to the famous Gate Cinema, a long-established "art" film showcase—but it is the access point for the Portobello Road antiques market. The film *Notting Hill* and the flea market together have made this a top-tier tourist attraction, and the shops and stalls along the road cater shamelessly to that population. Here and there, one can see flashes of the village-like atmosphere that once made this an attractive place to live, with brightly painted stucco-fronted cottages and leafy squares. Personally, I've never been charmed by Notting Hill—it takes itself a bit too seriously, and now it has become one of those places that tourists visit just because every other tourist visits. If you must visit, then do so, take the selfie, buy a few souvenirs (all made in China), and quickly move on to the next place on the list. Warning: at weekends the tube station gets so mobbed that it may be closed. If it is open, it will be packed with visitors.

Notting Hill is also famous (though once it was infamous) for the Notting Hill Carnival. The carnival began on August Bank Holiday weekend in 1966 as a more or less spontaneous celebration by London's vibrant, rapidly growing West Indian community, but it really took off in the early Seventies. Though by then the carnival boasted steel bands, costumed marchers, and large crowds, there still was no official sanction for the festival, and in the late Seventies, misguided police efforts to control it or close it down altogether led to street riots. Nowadays the tensions have mostly dissipated, the parade is huge and features organized marchers in fantastic costumes, and the weekend draws something on the order of a million visitors. This is London at its best: diverse, fun-loving, proud, and inclusive. Definitely go once—but if not, you can watch the highlights on TV.

One building worth a slight detour north just at the beginning of Kensington Park Road is a humble green shed with a peaked roof in the center of the road. This is one of the 13 remaining cab shelters—there were 61 at one point—built by the Cabmen's Shelter Fund, founded in 1875 and still in existence, though no new shelters have been erected since 1914. The shelters were adjacent to cab stands, and as the drivers could not leave their horses and carriages unattended, they were convenient places where they could water their steeds, rest man and beast, and procure an inexpensive cup of tea or even a hot meal. There was, as with many Victorian charitable ventures, a bit of social engineering in the mix: the Seventh Earl of Shaftesbury was one of the fund's founders, and he very much wanted to provide cabmen a teetotal alternative to the public houses they then frequented—thus these shelters served no alcoholic beverages. A few of the little green huts survive in odd corners scattered across Central London (for example, there was one you may have noticed behind Temple Underground Station, and there's another at Russell Square), and most are still serving food. All are now Grade II protected buildings.

It is time now to cross the road and to start walking south on Kensington Church Street. This pretty lane has long been a center of the high-end antiques trade, and although quite a few of the old antiques shops now have become coffee or wine bars, many remain. Walking down the street is almost like entering a time machine: if Londoners were all wealthy and well-dressed, and if every house were part of an immaculate Georgian terrace, and if all the shops were either French patisseries or upscale clothing boutiques or gorgeous antiques emporia, it would look and feel very like this corner of Kensington. Even the layout of the road itself is charming, with a gentle curve to the southeast about two-thirds of the way down the hill. The only intrusion of mundane reality is the traffic, which is usually bumper-to-bumper at any and all hours of the day and night.

Some distance down the street, past the lovely curve, is a small turning on the left, York House Place. This passes through some of the most expensive and desirable residential real estate in all of London, terminating at Kensington Palace Gardens, immediately behind the Palace of the same name. This street has not one but two nicknames, Embassy Row and Billionaires Row, as it is home to several embassies (among them Israel, Nepal, and Russia) and an impressive number of billionaires (mostly Russian and Saudi). There are security guards and bollards to restrict vehicular traffic at both ends of the street, but (at least at the time of writing) pedestrian access is unfettered and unrestricted. Ignore the security guards glaring at you suspiciously and have a leisurely look at the sort of digs £100,000,000 will buy you these days, and then continue eastward, after a little pedestrian dog leg, on Palace Green toward the back of Kensington Palace.

Kensington Palace is very much a functional residence, for many years home to the Duke and Duchess of Cambridge, who lived in a "grace and favour" apartment once occupied by Princess Margaret. (They now have moved to Windsor.) The royal personage that the palace is most closely associated is the Duke's mother, Princess Diana, who lived there both while she was married to Prince Charles and after their divorce. The palace was originally a modest two-story Jacobean brick building, purchased in 1689 by William and Mary, and then much enlarged for them by Christopher Wren. Wren retained the original structure and added space in the form of two large pavilions, one at each end of the building, giving the resulting structure a graceful symmetry. After the death of George II, the last monarch to live in it, it was for the most part used to house assorted lesser royals, and it still very much in service in that role. The state rooms are open to the public for a twenty pound admission charge. In truth, there's not all that much to see; I'd suggest a wander around the gardens instead.

Kensington Gardens was originally just the western half of Hyde Park, hived off from it in 1728 by Queen Caroline to create a separate landscape garden. A proper Eighteenth-Century English landscape garden then was no small affair—it generally involved moving tons of earth to create hills and valleys, and exploiting nearby water sources to create lakes and ponds. We have already wandered around the Serpentine, but now is a good opportunity to stroll along the northern half of the lake, the Long Water. Kensington Gardens retains a bit of its old character: unlike Hyde Park, which is open to the surrounding streets, it is gated and generally closed after dark. Wander a bit, and you may stumble upon some of the old landscape garden structures still there to be found: Queen Caroline's Temple and Queen Anne's Alcove (designed by Wren and later used as a gardening shed!). There is also a famous statue of Peter Pan, homage to J.M. Barrie who frequented the park, and another monument—a red granite obelisk—memorializes John Hanning Speke, "discoverer" of the source of the Nile (an outflow from the lake that Speke named after Victoria). Walk in a southerly direction and at the very southern edge of the park are the Coalbrookdale Gates, made at the factory of that name in solid cast iron deceitfully painted a bronze color, and originally the entryway to the Great Exhibition.

From the gates walk west and you will find yourself on Kensington Gore which soon enough turns into Kensington High Street. Just ahead where the road meets Kensington Church Street is St Mary Abbots, the church that provides Kensington Church Street its name. There has been a church here since 1262, but as ancient as this one looks, and (at the time of my last visit) as much in need of repair as it is, the present building is Victorian. The first church was built on land that had been given by the de Vere family (later Earls of Oxford) to the Benedictine Abbey of St Mary at Abingdon—hence the church name. Several times rebuilt and enlarged, the present church is by George Gilbert Scott (whose work includes the Albert Memorial and the Midland Grand Hotel above St Pancras Station) and it is one of the most gothic of his Gothic Revival buildings, notable for its cloister and for its oversized spire, at 278' the tallest in London. Several older and very impressive funerary monuments remain inside, and one window commemorates Isaac Newton, possibly after Princess Diana the most famous of its former parishioners.

Newton's physics is built on the principle that time is absolute and invariable throughout the Universe; in this world, however, on a perambulation like the one we have just completed, it passes quickly enough. But this is not simply the end of our walk around Kensington, it is almost the end of our journey around the Circle Line. Accordingly, before we cross the road to enter the tube station, I should think a celebratory drink is in order, and the Goat, at 3A Kensington High Street, is an eminently suitable place to quaff it. The building dates to 1695, when it housed a coffee house that a few years later turned into a public house. Early in its working life, the local parish bought the freehold and used profits from the pub to support a charity school. These days, it is most famous for its connection to the "Acid Bath Murderer," a fellow named John Haigh who murdered a former employer and assumed his identity as a means to secure his fortune. The scheme worked so well that he repeated it twice again, but the third time was his undoing and in 1949 he was caught, tried, and hanged. Hitchcock considered making a film about Haigh, but it never got off the drawing board. (Kensington has had more than one famous murderer: to the north, a bit out of our way, are Bartle Close and Andrews Square, built over what once was once notorious as 10 Rillington Place, the home of the serial killer John Christie; for details see the film, with Christie played by Richard Attenborough and directed by Richard Fleischer.)

Let us celebrate, then, with a pint—or even two—and then it will be time at last to enter the tube station and to continue on to Paddington, which of course is where we began. But not exactly where we began—we will end at the "other," slightly later Paddington Underground Station. All the same, we have traveled 17 miles (or 27 kilometers) by rail, visited fifteen stations, and explored much of contemporary Central London, all the while sampling the two thousand years of history that lie behind it.

I would say you have earned that pint.

Chapter 16

The Circle Squared

We are back at Paddington, though not exactly where we began. This Paddington station, sitting across the road from the main line station on Praed Street, was the second of that name, built to accommodate the southward turn of the emerging central circuit. Circle Line trains here going north and east now terminate at Edgware Road, just one stop away. Trains going south and east begin their journey back through all of the terrain we have traversed on our walks, and then stop at the other Paddington Underground station on their way to the terminus in Hammersmith.

While we wait for a train in whichever direction you intend next to travel, let us take a moment to reflect. I began this circular exercise by asserting that there was no guiding principle or strategy determining or underpinning my reflections on the London we've now traveled. Yet all the same, I reckon some very definite themes have emerged in the course of our perambulations.

Perhaps most obvious is that London is a palimpsest, each layer of the city build upon all of the layers of the past, stretching back to Roman times, and beyond. Indeed, London's history is still very much with us, in many ways literally visible (living on in its place names and at times in its not so deeply buried ruins), and that past still very much shapes both our conception and our experience of the city. The Temple of Mithras lying in the heart of the spanking new Bloomberg complex near Mansion House epitomizes the persistence of the past in the present—the remains of one of London's oldest buildings housed in one of its newest.

Such moments when and places where past and present come together are everywhere in the city. London manages the mix of past and present so well that it seems effortless, but other cities remind us how easy it is to get it all wrong. In New York, the past is almost completely obliterated by successive waves of redevelopment; in Rome, the past is everywhere and dominant. In London, the balance seems just right—past and present both given their proper due.

Moreover, London remains a city of diverse and distinct neighbourhoods. We have seen that even in the very center, despite market forces that encourage increasing uniformity, many of London's former villages—for example, Chelsea, Westminster, Bloomsbury—retain their traditional, distinctive identities, even as they have developed new ones. And often even when districts are in close proximity, their defining characteristics persist: The area around Sloane Square still is replete with leafy squares and quiet mews; next door South Kensington still is the museum quarter; and one tube stop away, Kensington High Street still is a center for shopping. The same generalizations might have been made at any time in the last century, and likely may still be made one hundred years hence.

And even in Central London, we see much to remind us that the city also has always been a nexus of immigration, and it has benefited and continues today to benefit from its ability to draw together millions of the world's most talented, inventive, and interesting people. There are large communities today in London of Polish, French, Somali, Bengali, Jamaican, and Nigerian immigrants and their descendants, and many, many more groups from every quarter of the globe. Each has stamped a part of London with its own image and at the same time each has become a cohort of true Londoners, an identity that complements and transcends local differences. London's people for the most part are tolerant of difference, especially when it takes shape in the multiplicity of ethnic cuisines thriving in thousands of restaurants all across the city.

Finally, there is London's dynamism. A journey around the Circle Line underscores the undeniable reality that the city has for two thousand years been a place of movement, and in the Twenty-First Century it continues to grow, change, and innovate. And—for better or for worse—London provides a model for our increasingly urbanized world. I for one wholeheartedly embrace it.

Appendix

Circling London

It may seem odd to ask this question, but why is there a Circle Line in London? To the best of my knowledge, other major metropolitan underground railways pass through their cities' centres, linking suburbs to the core, often in a hub-and-spoke pattern, but none has a centrally located circular service quite like London's. Why and how did London become the outlier?

The Inner Circuit (as the Circle Line first was called) officially opened on 6 October 1884, but it had been conceived long before at mid-century. The idea for a circular service dates to the opening of the Metropolitan Railway, the very first underground railway in London—indeed, the very first in the world—on 10 January 1863. That first section of the Underground, ultimately incorporated into the Circle Line, was only four miles long but it proved beyond all doubt that underground railways were practicable and, just as important, profitable. Within just a few years, the Met (as it came to be known) had added more miles of track and several other new underground lines had appeared alongside it.

The Underground railway itself was a response to the realization that Victorian London was choking to death on its own traffic—in effect, London was a victim of its demographic success. With 2,500,000 inhabitants in 1850, it was already by far the most populous city in the world, and it was poised to grow even larger. But London's medieval street layout and the lack of any central authority to plan new roads or indeed to sponsor any major public works projects made it increasingly difficult to move people and goods to, through, and around the city centre. Further growth, which was certain as death and taxes—the city was to reach 7,000,000 by the turn of the century—was likely only to make matters worse. So the question arose with some urgency: how could passengers and freight be removed from the streets and yet still be transported quickly and efficiently? The inspired solution was a railway built underground, thereby avoiding the endless delays of street-level traffic.

By modern standards, the original Metropolitan Railway was not much of a line, barely four miles in length. (There are 250 miles of track in the system today.) Plans for an underground railway to cross the Fleet Valley first had been proposed back in the 1840s, the pipedream of a London solicitor and *quondam* Member of Parliament, Charles Pearson. Pearson thought that the trains could be propelled pneumatically, and while nothing came of his first proposal, in 1854 a Parliamentary commission did advise the construction of a line linking the several London railway terminuses located at the northern edge of the city—Paddington, Euston, King's Cross, and Farringdon—all conveniently spaced out along the New Road (now divided into Marylebone, Euston, Pentonville, and City Roads). And so in August of that year, by act of Parliament, the Metropolitan Railway was chartered to build a subterranean line from Paddington to Farringdon, with several additional stations at points between.

The first challenge the "Met" faced was to raise sufficient capital to start construction—rather difficult for a line dependent on technology and engineering that were yet to be invented and equally dependent on what were no more than guesses about potential ridership. The fledgling company might well have failed before a single track was laid, but for a timely intervention and investment by the City of London itself. Pearson persuaded the Corporation to buy shares in the new firm to the value of £200,000; the City then sold a good portion of the rights of way back to the company for £179,000. In effect, the City gave away the necessary rights of way for virtually nothing to ensure that the line would be built. (In the end, it was a good deal for all: the railway was built, the company paid generous dividends, and eventually the shares were sold by the Corporation at a healthy profit.)

Construction began in March 1860. And even though the line ran through some of the most crowded parts of London, the first urban underground passenger railway in the world was completed in a mere three years—all the more impressive in that the excavation was done almost entirely by shovel and barrow. No less impressive was the relative ease with which the construction advanced: the worst setback was the rupture of the Fleet sewer in June 1862, flooding the works, but even that delayed completion by only a few months.

While we know this as the first section of a system that in time became the London Underground, "Underground" was something of a misnomer. The first line and others built soon after were constructed mainly by the "cut-and-cover" method; only one 700 yard section of the original route was a real tunnel, and it was a shallow one at that.

The cut-and-cover construction process was simple: a deep ditch was excavated and the tracks laid down in it; then it was covered by a canopy that supported the roadway above (although in a few places the ditch was left partly open for ventilation). 150-plus years later, a good portion of the original canopy is still in place—testament to the quality of the work of the engineers and builders who designed and constructed it. An interesting side note: much of the excavated "spoil" (as the dug-up earth is called) ended up at Stamford Bridge in Fulham where it now undergirds the Chelsea Football Club stadium. (To see what the original construction process looked like, check out a fascinating series of 56 photographs of the building of some of the early lines and stations, 1866–1870, taken by one Henry Flather, now housed in the Science Museum and available on the museum's web site.)

Cut-and-cover was a fairly cheap construction method, but aside from being cost-effective, there really was no other way the line then could have been built—the locomotives were coal-burning monsters, and they needed both quantities of air for their engines and open space to dissipate the steam, smoke, soot, and noxious particles they spewed. Hence a deep underground service was technologically impossible.

The first locomotives and carriages were borrowed from the Great Western Railway, which ran on wider broad-gauge tracks. This required a three-rail track system to accommodate the distinctive GWR rolling stock alongside standard gauge trains. Before long, the Met had commissioned specially designed locomotives that condensed their own steam. Nevertheless, the ventilation problem was never completely resolved until electrification some forty years later. (The deep "tube" trains in London that relied on electric power were built much later—the first in the 1890s. They were veritable tunneled lines, at least in their central sections.)

The first day of full service in 1863 was an indisputable success. (Pearson, alas, was unable to take part in the ceremonies, as he had gone permanently underground at West Norwood Cemetery the year before.) Technically, however, the first day of operation in fact was the second day—9 January having seen a trial run for some 600 invited guests, the ride terminating at Farringdon, where a ceremonial banquet was laid on, complete (as were most Victorian public dinners) with many rounds of toasts, and attended by various luminaries including Willian Gladstone, then Chancellor of the Exchequer. On the next day, the 10th, when the public opening took place, many thousands of Londoners appeared at the ticket windows, eager to satisfy their curiosity. Ironically, the railway registered a number of other less welcome "firsts" that day, experiencing problems that continue to plague the system to this day. For example there was significant overcrowding, so severe that managers had to close several stations until the backlog of ticketed passengers was cleared—a phenomenon well known to rush hour passengers at Oxford Circus even now.

The system also registered its first serious delays—the *Times* reporting that journeys that were timetabled at 18 minutes took as long as forty. Yet, by the end of the day, despite the challenges, 38,000 passengers had been carried.

No sooner had the Met begun to operate when conversations began about extending the first underground line and adding new ones, and, before long, plans were afoot to link them all together in a ring around Central London. The driver of the project was the location of the main line rail stations, for the most part arranged in a stretched-out circle just at the outer edges of central London. The Metropolitan had been built to link four main line rail stations to the North, but there were others—including Bishopsgate (later Liverpool Street), Fenchurch Street, London Bridge, Cannon Street, Blackfriars, Waterloo, and Victoria—equally busy and still to be connected to the Underground. Since there were essentially no through services across London, passengers who arrived at one terminus and who wished to continue their journey via another were faced with a difficult and slow journey through the seemingly intractable city centre traffic. In fact, for some time, the railways had been forbidden to push lines from the country into the centre of the city—in part because the political will to force the issue clearly was lacking, and also because it had become fabulously expensive to acquire the rights of way and the land for a centrally located terminus. (Of course, this being Victorian London, there were a few exceptions allowed.) Linking the stations by an underground circular service presented itself as the most elegant and at the time the only practical solution to moving long-haul passengers through the city.

Moreover, the immediate success of the first section of the Metropolitan Railway suggested that any such larger project, while inevitably expensive, nevertheless had a reasonable chance of becoming a profitable concern. In its first year, the Metropolitan carried 9.5 million passengers, roughly 30,000 a day. The next year, it was 12 million. If that could be achieved on one section barely four miles long, how much more potentially remunerative would it be to carry traffic on a longer line?

The idea of the Inner Circuit—and much of its route—actually had been anticipated back in 1855 by Joseph Paxton, then newly famous as the designer of the Crystal Palace. He presented to a parliamentary Select Committee on Metropolitan Communications a scheme for a Great Victorian Way—a 72' wide, glass-enclosed development built around an "atmospheric" (pneumatic) railway. Unlike the eventual route of inner circuit, Paxton's line would have crossed the river and thus more fully incorporated the rapidly growing South Bank into central London. (In the event, it took nearly another half century for an underground line to cross the Thames.) Strangely, this scheme rather presciently anticipated the "mixed use" property developments of our time, with plans for both retail and residential spaces adjoining the railway, as was appropriate to the neighbourhoods it passed through. The proposed pneumatic system avoided the nuisance of the smoke and noise of steam-powered engines. The Select Committee, at any rate, was impressed, and authorizing legislation was passed by Parliament, but the costs of acquiring land and rights of way and of the construction itself were astronomical and so the scheme never got off (or rather under) the ground.

Though Paxton's ambitious (and wholly impractical) plan was left on the table, Parliament was convinced that a circular service, however powered, was the ultimate goal. So in 1864, only months after the first Underground line opened, the legislature moved forward in a decision worthy of Dickens's Circumlocution Office by granting the Metropolitan Railway authority to extend its existing line east to Tower Hill, but then chartering a completely new company, with a confusingly similar name, the Metropolitan District Railway, to build the rest of the route (which, in the end, it failed to do). The District (as it soon came to be known) was to be an intimate sibling of the Metropolitan Railway and accordingly it was launched with overlapping board membership. Despite that, the amity did not last long. By 1871, the new line had severed completely its ties to the older one, and it had instituted its own completely separate and independent service, with distinctive green locomotives and carriages (the signature color now serves as the color of the District Line on modern tube maps). The two lines developed different cultures as well: it is to oversimplify only a little to say that the Met generally regarded itself as a main line railway that terminated in London, whereas the District saw itself as a London line that extended out into the suburbs.

Other extensions and sections followed piecemeal, but progress slowed as the two companies, meant to work together, instead became fierce rivals. It didn't help matters that the two companies' long serving chairmen, James Staats Forbes (the District) and Sir Edward Watkin (the Met), were bitter rivals, each hoping to secure a monopoly of underground services. Moreover, the final section also would run through some of the most built-up and densely populated areas of the City. And then, in 1874, as if this were not challenge enough, Parliament authorized yet a third player, the Metropolitan Inner Circle Completion Railway Company, although fortunately before it could do any damage it was bought out by and incorporated into the Metropolitan. The last section to be built, from Tower Hill to Blackfriars was expensive: each mile cost £1,000,000, as much as the entire original line—hardly surprising given the value of land in the heart of the City and the absence of convenient roadways under which the line could be sited without compensation to owners above. (The Corporation was now allowing the railways to build under public streets without payment for the right of way, but private landlords had to be compensated.)

Finally, on that fateful day in October 1884, the Metropolitan and District lines were spliced together, allowing travel all the way round and the circular service more or less as we know it came into being, although to passengers' confusion, trains initially were operated by both companies, one running all its trains clockwise and the other counterclockwise. (There were also soon afterward middle and outer circles, as well, neither of which was terribly successful nor lasted very long; sections of their track, however, are still incorporated into the present-day Overground rail system.)

The inner circle was at last operational, but while the Metropolitan and the District had managed to cooperate long enough to get the line built, the marriage remained one of convenience and it quickly broke down. The arrangements for operating the circular service did not help. Ownership of the track was divided fairly evenly (the Met owned seven miles and the District six, with two miles held jointly), but in the abiding spirit of non-cooperation, each company sold its own tickets which could not be used on the other line. So whenever the two were not cooperating (which was most of the time), each ticket office would steer passengers onto its own service, even if it meant a far longer journey the "wrong" way round.

There were other problems that affected service adversely. To generate additional revenue, both the Met and the District ran freight trains on the same tracks as the passenger trains, and they allowed other companies to run additional passenger and freight trains on them as well. The result was that traffic almost from the first day overwhelmed capacity and the circular service itself was chronically late. Yet, despite all these challenges, in their first full year of service, together the two lines carried 114,500,000 passengers, or an average of over 300,000 a day. An impressive number: by comparison, nowadays, the Circle and the Hammersmith and City lines combined (the relevant unit for which Transport for London publishes its counts) carry about 110,000,000 a year, or did before the pandemic.

Who were these passengers? As we have seen, the line was built to serve passengers of the main line stations, but they attracted other types of rider as well, including an entirely new species of rail traveler—the clerk or the civil servant or the professional making a twice daily journey from home to work and back again. In other words, a commuter, to use a term first employed in this sense in the 1860s. (The word derives from the phrase "commutation" ticket, a fixed number of rides at a reduced rate.) And not all the commuters were in white collar employ. Indeed, as early as 1864, the Met was obliged by Parliament to provide cheap workmen's trains early in the morning and again in the evening, and as these lines pushed out from the centre, new small, relatively cheap houses were built near the Met's stations to accommodate working-class families. On the District and other lines, as they connected to London some of the nearby "better" quality villages like Wimbledon and

Richmond, larger and more expensive housing was built to serve the new armies of middle-class professionals and lower middle-class clerks. All the while, the residential population of the City plummeted rapidly (even in the early 1860s Dickens observed that the City had gone deadly quiet outside work week hours) but as businesses flocked to the City, the daytime working population literally exploded. The new Underground railways were transforming spontaneously into the first commuter lines.

Another new class of railway passenger was comprised of middle-class women, for whom the underground railway was a powerful engine of social change. Its service allowed them to leave the family home by delivering them safely to the new department stores springing up seemingly everywhere in the centre of the city. From the 1870s, there were more and more women shoppers—women domiciled in the rapidly expanding suburbs who were drawn back into town by the new, vast retail emporia, like the Army and Navy Stores in Westminster, Whiteley's in Bayswater, and Harrods in Knightsbridge. It was of considerable importance that these shops provided clean, safe, and private dining and toilet facilities, extending by many hours the time that women could remain outside the home. 1874 also saw the first provision of ladies-only coaches on the Underground. That the Underground was perceived to be a secure space for women traveling alone was crucial to their traveling outside the morning and evening rush hours when the train had excess capacity.

Yet even with the impressive ridership figures and new kinds of passenger, the inner circle was by no means a financial success. The costs of construction of the line had been so high that soon after its completion both companies, but particularly the junior partner, the District, were struggling to pay their shareholders' dividends. What the circular route needed was to connect with something more—which happened in two ways.

First, as we have seen, both the Met and the District began extending their lines out into the surrounding, undeveloped countryside. Even as early as the 1870s the Metropolitan was driving its tracks north and west, whilst the District was pushing south and west. The small towns and rural villages they began to serve at first did not generate much traffic on their own, but the advent of rail service drew out investors who rapidly turned open fields into suburban tract housing. In effect, the railways were creating the housing that generated demand for their own services.

The second factor undermining profitability was the development of new, deeper underground lines, competition that began to appear in the decade before the turn of the century. Construction by the cut-and-cover method had worked well enough in the 1860s and into the1870s, but by the 1880s it had become hugely disruptive (and costly) to dig up the city's ever-busy streets for months at a time. The next wave of underground construction would have to be deeper. Fortunately, London, for the most part, sits atop several hundred feet of clay, which allowed tunneling at relatively deep levels with then existing technology. Deeper lines, however, obviously could not be powered by coal-burning steam locomotives, and while some schemes afoot again had mooted pneumatic propulsion or cable drives (like that powering San Francisco's street cars), ultimately it was the advent of electricity that proved transformative.

The first deep line built was the City and South London, running from King William Street in the City to Stockwell across the river (since incorporated into the Northern Line). It was constructed by tunneling and then fitting together in the excavated space prefabricated tubular sections of cast iron— thus "the tube" as the Underground ever has since been known. Crucially, it was also the first electric line, and from this point in time, it was clear that sooner or later all of the existing underground lines would have to be electrified, too.

Progress was slow, the ongoing rivalry of the Met and the District continuing to present a considerable obstacle to effective collaboration. The managements of both companies were sensible enough to recognize that they must adopt the same system (the viable options were either overhead power lines or a third rail) but stubborn enough to refuse to agree on one. Ultimately, a judge was called in to arbitrate and he decided in favor of the District's proposed three-rail system, which somehow became a four-rail system when it actually was built. (It still is a four-rail system.) It took nearly five years for the work to be completed, and the first electric trains set out on 1 July 1905. Alas, all too predictably, no one had checked to ensure that the equipment on each company's trains was wholly compatible with the other line's tracks; not only were the powering systems wholly incompatible, but when Met trains crossed to District track they were completely disabled. Steam engines had to be called back into service, and it took until September for the all-electric service to operate satisfactorily. (Steam service run by other companies on a few sections of the Circle Line tracks continued into the 1960s.)

The timing of the launch of the inner circuit electric service was not ideal: the fully electrified Central Line already had opened in 1900, and its direct route through the commercial and business heart of the city was not only faster but, at tuppence, cheaper than the Inner Circle. Moreover, the development of each new line by a separate profit-seeking company meant that there was no easy interchange from line to line, as there is now; even where it was possible to change from one line to another within the same station, it was necessary to pay separate fares. And, in another blow to the service, from 1902 motor buses began to take over the streets, rapidly replacing horse-drawn vehicles, and they quickly created new, cheaper, and faster pathways across the city.

What was needed was for the separate Underground lines—and indeed all of the several transport services—to be knitted into a network, allowing passengers to transfer from one to another without needing an additional ticket and without paying an additional fare. This finally came about with the formation of the London Passenger Transport Board in 1933, a multi-service network that included most underground lines, among them the District and the Met, as well as buses and trams. Finally, then, with the Met and the District under the same management, full coordination was at last effected. One of the very first and most enduring achievements of the LPTB was to promote the London Transport brand through its iconic and still very much in evidence circle and bar logo (initially known as the "bull's eye"). And in 1949, it was the LPTB that renamed the inner circle as the "Circle Line." The LPTB since has morphed into today's Transport for London (TfL), via intermediate incarnations as the London Transport Executive and London Regional Transport, but it was the LPTB that pioneered the principle uniting them all—that one quasi-governmental body should be responsible for the entirety of public transport in greater London.

Post Script: The Circle Line is still with us, but a sad indignity befell it in December 2009 when it was incorporated into the Hammersmith and City Line, of which now it is in essence a branch.

Index

About the Author

Fredric Schwarzbach is professor of humanities and formerly the dean of New York University's Liberal Studies Program. He holds the Ph.D. from University College London, where his teaching career began in 1974. He is the author of many scholarly books and articles about the city and literature, including *Dickens and the City*. He has also served as the President of the American Friends of London's Dickens Museum. Schwarzbach has lived and worked in London intermittently for 50 years and like Dickens's character Sam Weller, his knowledge of the city is "extensive and peculiar."